IN VIVO

In Vivo

A Phenomenology of Life-Defining Moments

GABOR CSEPREGI

McGill-Queen's University Press
Montreal & Kingston • London • Chicago

© McGill-Queen's University Press 2019

ISBN 978-0-7735-5662-1 (cloth)
ISBN 978-0-7735-5663-8 (paper)
ISBN 978-0-7735-5772-7 (ePDF)
ISBN 978-0-7735-5773-4 (ePUB)

Legal deposit second quarter 2019
Bibliothèque nationale du Québec

Printed in Canada on acid-free paper that is 100% ancient forest free (100% post-consumer recycled), processed chlorine free

This book has been published with the help of a grant from the Canadian Federation for the Humanities and Social Sciences, through the Awards to Scholarly Publications Program, using funds provided by the Social Sciences and Humanities Research Council of Canada.

We acknowledge the support of the Canada Council for the Arts, which last year invested $153 million to bring the arts to Canadians throughout the country.

Nous remercions le Conseil des arts du Canada de son soutien. L'an dernier, le Conseil a investi 153 millions de dollars pour mettre de l'art dans la vie des Canadiennes et des Canadiens de tout le pays.

Library and Archives Canada Cataloguing in Publication

Title: In vivo : a phenomenology of life-defining moments / Gabor Csepregi.
Names: Csepregi, Gabor, author.
Description: Includes bibliographical references and index.
Identifiers: Canadiana (print) 20189068353 | Canadiana (ebook) 20189068361 | ISBN 9780773556621 (cloth) | ISBN 9780773556638 (paper) | ISBN 9780773557727 (ePDF) | ISBN 9780773557734 (ePUB)
Subjects: LCSH: Life. | LCSH: Life change events.
Classification: LCC BD431.C74 2019 | DDC 128—dc23

This book was typeset in 10.5/13 Sabon.

To Éva

Contents

Acknowledgments   ix

Introduction   3

1   Logic of Exception   13

2   Artisan of My Destiny   35

3   Moments of Real Learning   66

4   Foreigner in a Foreign Land   88

5   How Can Anything Be So Beautiful?   119

6   Actions Like That Make Life Worthwhile   147

Notes   165

Bibliography   181

Index   197

Acknowledgments

I wish to acknowledge here with sincere and warm gratitude the precious help I received from distinguished scholars and friends: Paul D. Morris, for his unflagging support and precious suggestions regarding the final form of the text; Rodney A. Clifton, for his helpful comments after reading the first draft; Alan Walker, for his illuminating thoughts on the subject of music; Pablo Urbanyi for his valuable advice on literary art; and Thomas De Koninck, Jean-François de Raymond, Franck Chignier-Riboulon, Yves Bouchard, and the late Gerd Haeffner, for their sustained encouragement while I was writing the various chapters of the book.

For the attentive help and continuous support I received while submitting the proposal, revising, and preparing this book for publication, I am very much indebted to Khadija Coxon at McGill-Queen's University Press.

IN VIVO

Introduction

Any life, however long and complicated it may be, actually consists of a single moment – the moment when a man knows forever more who he is.

Jorge Luis Borges

Time is an intrinsic factor of human life and it encompasses each passing experience within our lives. We live in a state of becoming, advancing from one moment to another, from one experience to another, and from one stage of life to another. Our personal becoming may, at various times, speed up or slow down; sometimes we have the impression that it has come to a standstill; we then live, for a while, in the timeless present. Lived time is not homogeneous; the duration of a temporal segment is perceived according to the importance or unimportance of the personal experiences that take place in it. As the Bard tells us, "time travels in divers paces with divers persons."[1] While we are engaged in a fascinating conversation, an hour goes by quickly, and in retrospect, it appears fulfilling and long. If, on the other hand, we listen to a boring lecture, the same sixty minutes pass with a painful slowness, and later we recall this period of duration as empty and brief. We experience time with a specific quality: it is rewarding or depressing, beautiful or difficult, growing or vanishing, maturing or diminishing, auspicious or inauspicious.

Some of our activities have to be accomplished at a favourable moment, which may be seen as a culmination of a series of previous experiences and events. We just have to patiently await its arrival. We then experience time as the coming and going of singular moments at our disposal: we can seize them or let them go, use them well or waste them. The qualitative difference of each temporal segment is based, in part, on the cyclical return of experiences, events, and activities in our lives. There are natural cyclic processes arising not only from our bodies and from our physical and cultural environments, but also from the rhythm of our social interactions and the characteristics of our personal accomplishments.[2]

The temporality of our life span is made up of different time segments, of successively changing contexts of experience and action. Each slice out of this trajectory gives us its particular experience of time: as we all well know, the wheel of time turns at a different speed in our childhood than in other parts of our lives. The birth of a child, a marriage, the commencement of a career, severe illness, retirement, or the death of a loved one – all these life-defining experiences change our living circumstances and the ways in which we relate to our past, present, and future. We have some control over these experiences as we try to make good use of the possibilities that each life segment offers. Youth, adulthood, and old age offer unique and irretrievable opportunities and the art of living consists of seizing them before they fade away forever. Important historical events, affecting the lives of a large number of persons – bringing war or peace, prosperity or poverty, tension or ease, advance or decay – also influence the quality of the temporal portions of our personal becoming.

Romano Guardini proposed pertinent reflections on the educational and ethical significance of the various stages of human life; each of them expresses a fundamental mode of being in the world. These stages – childhood, adolescence, majority, maturity, and old age – have their own characteristics, fit into the totality of the human life, and receive their respective meanings from this totality. Even though we like to believe and to tell ourselves that our entire existence follows a regular and predictable course, similar to that of a reliable clock, the transition from one stage to another does not always happen smoothly. We go through periods of more or less intense crisis: the crises of puberty, of experience, of the awareness of our limits, and of detachment. These transitions may occur slowly or speedily, progressively or abruptly. They may be subjected to rites of passage, which are devised and performed in a colourful manner within a particular form of cultural community.[3]

On the road of human becoming, through growing, maturing, and eventually declining, there are a number of key experiences which are part of human life and play a substantial role in it. Whereas the chief dimensions of our humanity – language, society, history, bodily existence, consciousness – are enduring traits, these experiences are

Introduction 5

transitory occurrences. Our capacity for gradual and marvellous adaptation to a unique physical environment – the Arctic region, the Amazon jungle, the Gobi desert, or the Andes mountain range – is certainly one of the central and lasting features of human life. The result of the adaptive process may be a modification of attitude, behaviour, outlook, and purpose, and as well a gradual alteration of the environment. This, in turn, produces other changes. But startling initiatives and unexpected encounters may complement the flexible, adequate, and often necessary accommodation to various living conditions. These moments may bring to human life not only changes, which may be beneficial or unsettling, but also a sense of fulfilment or a feeling of distress.

In this book, I single out six vital experiences that are lived by many men and women: they occur in moments of deciding, of breaking away from actual circumstances, of encountering a model, of immersing in a foreign culture, of listening to a beautiful piece of music, and of experiencing an ethical action. I believe that the disclosure of the nature and import of all of these supreme moments is one of the worthwhile aims of the philosophy of the human person.

Readers may wonder why I focus on these six decisive experiences. There are, after all, other singular moments, which may also be of paramount importance and bring either joy or grief to their lives.[4] I could have reflected on the experience of failure, of forgiveness and of reconciliation, on the peaks of achievement, particularly in sport, on the time when insight breaks into the conscious mind, the "Eureka moment" in the life of a scientist or of a biographer, or on the experience of what one might call Spiritual Presence.

I could also have analyzed the moment lived by all those persons whose normal life comes to a sudden halt as they make the discovery of a life-threatening illness. The world around them undergoes a profound change: for some the surroundings become grim and stale; for others it acquires colour and warmth. Many reassess their values and priorities and feel an urgent impulse to travel or to work or to decide to spend time only with their loved ones. The awareness of their current condition throws a revealing light on their past, their character, family, or jobs, on both their trivial and pivotal experiences. They remember all the joys that their healthy body brought to their lives. By turning away from all inconsequential current events, they want fully understand life while they live it. There are also patients who know that their days are numbered and have lost all hope of healing and yet, while coming to terms with the course of their illness, live with a "fundamental hope" of an indefinite and formless self-realization in the future and of a saving renewal that is not directed to anything tangible.[5] The sudden appearance of incurable cancer and the traumatic moment it creates are lived by thousands of men and women every year. A reflection on the meaning of being-ill and on being threatened by the approaching death would certainly have been appropriate in this book.

Nonetheless, in my choice of themes, I wanted to single out those experiences that we find not only enriching but also invigorating on all levels of our existence, experiences that open up the future for us and offer occasions for steering our lives into a new direction. I wanted to deal as much as possible with the positive side of life and describe those moments, which, notwithstanding the initial tension and distress they may cause, bring us fulfilment and invite us to confidently modify our world or enter into a new world. The themes that I discuss also allow me to formulate observations and ideas on the central problem of education and to highlight the value of those encounters that take place outside the formal and traditional educational context. To be sure, human beings are called upon to rely on their reason when they make decisions freely about their future and when they act in the present. However, the moments that I analyze make clear that feelings and spontaneity also play a central role in their ways of creating fulfilling contacts with other persons, natural landscapes, and works of art and of accomplishing bold, life-altering actions.

Admittedly, as I have said above, there are other exceptional moments that equally contribute to the enhancement of human life, and I hope that my narrative will serve to complement, to clarify, and perhaps to deepen the readers' sense of their own gratifying experiences. There are highly individual moments of bliss, which remain silently alive and seldom yield an explicit communication. According to Roger Scruton, these are moments of revelation, intensely meaningful, even though the meaning that we encounter eludes all attempts to describe it in words. "These moments are precious to us. When they occur it is as though, on the winding ill-lit stairway of our life, we suddenly come across a window, through which we catch sight of another and brighter world – a world to which we belong but which we cannot enter."[6]

The moments that I analyze involve a striking encounter with something or somebody and an individual response to a presence or

Introduction

an initiative. Some interactions are sought consciously, some happen unexpectedly. When making a decision, we are facing possibilities advancing towards us and pressing us to select one of them. We discover models and works of art often by chance, and they invite us to answer to their appeal. Even when, for a long period of time, we have envisaged of breaking free from a familiar environment, the resolution and realization of our departure is quite often a response to a concrete and unplanned opportunity that has been offered to us. Not planning does not mean not being prepared for these unexpected experiences. In order to display receptiveness to these appealing occasions, we have to acquire, and retain possession of, certain abilities and qualities. A person, a beautiful song, or a new possibility may have the capacity to exercise a grip on us if we are more or less adequately prepared for welcoming them and if we have made ourselves accessible to them.

Most often the encounter with the foreign or the sublime creates a surprise or a shock and interrupts the steady and continuous progress of our lives. As focal moments, they may give a new orientation and a new meaning to all our undertakings and thus prompt us to reject a fatalistic view of the temporal unfolding of our life paths. Many of our daily activities – buying and preparing food, taking care of our children and of our home, doing our work, enjoying rest, seeking leisure and entertainment, helping others – need to be integrated into a coherent framework and prioritized by a broader and critical compass of our lives. This overall structure can be influenced and shaped by the insights gained from our unexpected experiences.

One of the implicit contentions that I make in this book can be stated briefly: there is, in every human life, a *possibility* of transformation and of renewal. On all levels of our existence – physical, moral, intellectual, and spiritual – we are dynamic beings, on the move, intrinsically *en route*, even faced with the "necessity for wandering" (Alfred North Whitehead). If we remain open and receptive to the influence of a person or to the appeal of an unforeseen possibility, we may find an impetus for a change even in the seemingly small events of our life journeys. The moments that I examine in this book may alter the direction of our lives and works, subjecting us to further formative and transformative experiences. In this sense, we may become aware, under the pivotal impact of these experiences, of an invitation to shape our destinies and not to merely be the playthings of external forces.

Still, it is also possible to diminish or to refuse the transformative effects of these decisive moments. For some, it is easier to depend on built-in habits and to observe familiar conventions and obligations than to explore something new and unknown and to benefit from a striking experience, an astonishing discovery, or a risky undertaking. Stepping outside of one's normal routine, shaking off the weight of customs, of established codes of behaviour, and ceasing to fit comfortably into an approved general social role can be debilitating and too demanding.

Arthur Koestler held the view that people live on two planes: the trivial and the tragic. Most of the time they walk on the smooth surface of the trivial plane. They go to school, get a job, marry and raise their children, give their children away at weddings, retire from work, and eventually retire from life. But, on some rare occasions, they happen to fall into the stage-trap of the tragic plane. Although they often re-emerge with a changed outlook on their existence, they prefer, once they revert to their daily occupations, to ignore and to rebuff what they have tasted, heard, and seen. "The ordinary mortal in our urban civilization moves virtually all his life on the Trivial Plane; only on a few dramatic occasions – during the storms of puberty, when he is in love or in presence of death – does he fall suddenly through the manhole, and is transferred to the Tragic Plane. Then all at once the pursuits of his daily routines appear as shallow, trifling vanities; but once safely back on the Trivial Plane, he dismisses the realities of the other as the products of overstrung nerves or adolescent effusions."[7]

It is certainly possible to know people, living or dead, upon enquiry into their parents, spouses, and children, as well as about the dates and places of their births, or where they studied and worked and what kind of awards and recognitions they received. This form of information we find in biographical dictionaries. But if we want to get more intimately acquainted with these persons and to capture their full individuality, we would be well advised to learn about the vital moments of their lives: for example, the way in which they behave in unfamiliar surroundings or face the task of making a decision. It is in consideration of these moments that we find out what has occurred above and beyond the trivial plane.

But Koestler's observation cannot be applied to all peoples and to all social conditions. Due to natural catastrophes, ongoing wars, persecutions, deportations, imprisonments, moral corruptions, or

Introduction

violent actions of all sorts, individuals and entire collectivities may find themselves, by necessity and for an extended period of time, on the tragic plane. There is nothing trivial about their experience of adversity, terror, fear, humiliation, hunger, pain, or anxiety. Yet, even under those enduring dreadful, inhuman, and tragic conditions, some moments may stand out and bring into their lives a salutary and unforgettable break.[8]

Stefan Zweig wrote an ambitious and insightful book on ten important episodes in human world history.[9] By using the word *Stern* in the title (*Sternstunde der Menschheit*), Zweig referred to the glowing stars above us; they shine through the "night of transitoriness," the calm and sleepy periods of history. Similarly to the "few rare moments" of creative inspiration in the life of an artist, there are "sublime and unforgettable moments" in the history of humankind. Rare, decisive, and solemn, these particular historical moments determine, over decades and centuries, the lives of smaller and larger societies and even the destiny of all of humankind.

Those exceptional moments are also part of one's personal life history – the moments of deciding between two forms of existence, of participating in a foreign ritual, of listening to a heart-warming choral concert, or of witnessing an act of unexpected generosity. On these occasions, human beings are invited to concentrate on the present, to live in and for the present, which is detached as it were from the past and the future, stirring them deeply and filling them either with a sense of peacefulness or with a feeling of uneasiness. The encounter with the strange or the sublime lifts them from the grooves of their everyday lives; it may attract and inspire them, but it may also fill them with a sense of reserve and of perplexity.[10]

By moment, I don't mean a definite and measurable temporal extension. The moment may last a few seconds or minutes or days or even months or years, as this phrase makes it clear: the years spent in college were a key moment of my life. It could be a luminous occasion, an episode, a crucial phase of our life journeys, or the culmination of a series of external acts or of inner states. A moment is a break in the continuity of temporal flow: it may be induced by the contemplation of the sea, its "deep and calm solemnity" (Søren Kierkegaard) or "infinity" (Karl Jaspers), a touching song or story or play, a word or a glance that makes us fall in love, or a foreign city that we gradually discover. The moment, as I understand it, is not the *Augenblick* that has been variously defined and understood in the works of eminent philosophers, although the moments described in this book involve decisive encounters that compel us to step outside and rise above our everyday homogeneous existence.[11] By moment, I mean a certain duration that, thanks to its deeper importance and transforming effect, stands out with regard to the past and to the future in our personal becoming and may even transports us into a timeless dimension.

In this book, I describe and analyze those "few rare moments" that affect and form our personal existence and make us experience time as "the life of life" (Charles Lamb). I am concerned here to put forward observations, analyses, and reflections rather than proofs. I am mindful to present, in some chapters, both instances and counter-instances that dispel hasty claims of universality. It would be erroneous to allege, for instance, that every individual is eager to break away from his or her living circumstances. However, I can hardly imagine a human life in which no decisions are ever made and no intuitive glimpses of pure generosity are ever offered. The topics that I intend to discuss cannot be treated in a strictly scholarly manner. Therefore, I also draw, occasionally, from personal experiences, either my own or those of other real people. I don't think that relating these experiences weakens the desire for philosophical objectivity and the need for penetrating light. Søren Kierkegaard's account of the demanding teacher in his grammar school makes it easier to understand his central ideas on the subtleties of language in relation to an emotional state, while Maurice Merleau-Ponty's narrative of his first impression of Paris renders his thoughts on the perception of the affective essence of a city more convincing.[12] Thus, my phenomenological description and analysis are completed by concrete illustrations, which are taken, in part, from biographies and literary works. Although some of the examples are drawn from the life narratives of well-known public figures, the points that they make more explicit are relevant to the lives and experiences of ordinary people. Stories, fictional or real, are often the most moving and compelling ways to express profound truths about our nature, abilities, and intrinsic worth, as well as the secret of our hearts, our place in history, and our shared purpose in a civil society. They disclose more vividly and validate more directly, in a language that is natural to all of us, whatever is presented here through abstract concepts. They express it even if, occasionally, what is suggested is more important than what is said. They put us in touch with what we really are

Introduction

and what sorts of motives, encounters, and possibilities move us to transform our lives. They also reveal what preserves our confidence and vitality, and what kind of experience enhances our feeling of uniqueness and enables us to make sense of our lives.

I believe that the phenomenological attitude offers one of the appropriate philosophical approaches for highlighting the essential features of decisive experiences. This attitude is chiefly intuitive and receptive, not disputatious, even when it seeks to rectify a mistaken position. Therefore, my references to various authors and their thoughts on social, ethical, educational, and artistic issues are not intended to offer argumentative discussion of their positions. I call upon them as insightful and inspiring illustrations of the philosophical points and clarifications I intend to make. I welcome sympathetically all propositions and descriptions put forward by philosophers, writers, or artists; their observations help us to reach a better understanding of the various facets of our own experiences of everyday life. And if, occasionally, I bring criticism into play, my comments serve chiefly to question those disappointing generalities and standard opinions that prevent us from noticing those real individuals who live their lives and interact with others in concrete situations. Phenomenology is, in this respect, a critique of the unnuanced application of some abstract categories to human existence.

In light of this philosophical attitude, I share the view of Max Scheler who declares that "the closest and most living contact" with the self-given must precede the distant and critical relation to an object.[13] If, for instance, we intend to write about swimming, we first have to jump into a lake or a river and feel the buoyancy of our bodies or, at least, walk along the pool deck and watch for hours how others do laps and perfect their techniques. Philosophy based on phenomenology is an effort of awakening to the wonder of the world. It looks and marvels at what appears to be the most obvious and self-evident and endeavours to grasp its endless complexity. It prefers the sympathetic and lived participation in concrete and global experiences to the cold and analytical investigation of isolated realities. It is with this kind of philosophical stance that we might undertake the analysis of what is the most familiar to us, what seems to yield only a commonplace of knowledge, and what we most of the time fail to notice and marvel about: for example, our upright posture or the remarkable mobility of our hands. I believe that achieving the clarification and understanding of what seems to be evident yet is, at the same time, a puzzling fact of our human condition is a worthwhile aim of philosophy. It calls for a particular sensitivity, which is, in the words of Thomas Nagel, "the essential capacity to be mystified by the utterly familiar."[14] It is my hope that my book reveals some surprising aspects of the human life as it unfolds in this self-evident world and that it throws additional light on the nature and significance of its unique and life-defining moments.

I

Logic of Exception

Oh, the sins of passion and of the heart, how much nearer to salvation than the sins of reason. ·

Søren Kierkegaard

Perhaps no other writer has emphasized more the gravity and significance of the act of decision than Søren Kierkegaard. Both the breaking up of his engagement with his fiancée, Regina Olsen, and his account of God demanding Abraham to sacrifice Isaac illustrate that a decision forces individuals to consider two possible goods and that, regardless of whichever receives their preference, the outcome remains uncertain and causes inevitable pain. Beyond selecting one of the possibilities over another, people make decisions ultimately about themselves and their lives; essentially they confront themselves in the act of making a decision without any external support in the form of advice or of a moral code accepted and approved by their fellow human beings. Although they may adopt various strategies to escape from the burden of the decision, the obligation to face the task nevertheless remains unavoidable. William Barrett summed up the magnitude and effect of the predicament: "The terror of confronting oneself in such a situation is so great that most people panic and try to take cover under a universal rule that will apply, if only it will save them from the task of choosing themselves."[1]

Sooner or later, we all come to such a fork in the road of our lives, and experience a similar feeling of acute uneasiness. We may recall the daunting task of deciding between staying at home and running a traditional family business or starting an uncertain career abroad. At such moments, we raise questions such as: should I remain in my familiar environment or should I dare to step into an unknown world? Should I stick to the standard of my parental values or should I yield to the voices of adventure and dissent? Or we may remember finding ourselves in an extreme situation in which we were called upon either to act with initiative and to risk our lives or to cling to a well-known living arrangement and the thin comfort of imagined security.

In an interview, the famous violinist Yehudi Menuhin recalled his own quandary: "Choice is one of life's greatest challenges. I had to go through some terrible years when my first marriage was virtually finished: my Talmudic Jewish mind was wedged between the rigors of the Law and the dictates of the heart. There seemed to be no escape from my dilemma. For about three years I couldn't find the determination to decide what I wanted to do."[2] If the task of making a decision is a vital moment in our lives, it is due, in part, to the impossibility of sharing the burden of the task with someone else. To be sure, before making our decision, we eagerly consult others and ask for guidance, but in the moment of decision, we find ourselves in "complete isolation," in absence of any support coming from a tradition, a moral code, or a lesson learned by others. In the terms of Kierkegaard, we have "simply and solely" ourselves and "therein lies the dreadfulness."[3] When, alone and without anyone's recommendation, we are called upon to decide between two appealing or unappealing courses of action, we have to submit ourselves to the painful obligation of giving up one of the two cherished or feared possibilities. If we are appointed to lead a smaller or larger group of people, we most likely have to face and to solve the aching dilemma of deciding between morality and expediency – a dilemma well exposed in the novels and essays of Arthur Koestler. If, for instance, our work consists of running a business operation and of ensuring adequate cost-effectiveness, do we let people go in order to improve our financial prospects or do we keep them in our employment so that they can continue to support their families? If we are social workers in child protection services and see that otherwise loving parents are unable to meet their child's basic needs, what is to be our decision about the child's future? If we were members of the International Olympic Committee, should we vote for or against the continuation of the Olympic Games after a terrorist attack has been carried out against participating athletes and coaches? The task of dispensing with one of the two possibilities presses upon us, and notwithstanding our doubts and hesitations, we cannot escape the agonizing duty of making a decision.

THE SOLITUDE OF MAKING A DECISION

In all of the above-mentioned situations, as we have seen, we are in the presence of two possibilities that we cannot grasp at the same time. The decision is the act by which we select one possibility and discard the other. In fact, in every moment of our lives, we find ourselves in relation to diverse possibilities. As I write these lines, I face the possibility of going on with my writing or of pausing and pondering what I should write, or even of going for a walk. I am tacitly aware of these possibilities as I sit at my desk and project myself into my future. In other words, I am in lived contact with these possibilities even if I do not consciously represent each of them. I experience my lived future by facing and evaluating my approaching possibilities, my lived present by selecting one of these possibilities, and my lived past by consciously surveying or tacitly acknowledging the sum of realized accomplishments. Thus, the temporality of my personal becoming is made up of approaching possibilities, of the factual realization of some possibilities through my actions, and of already realized and thrown away possibilities. Future possibilities, actual realizations, and past accomplishments all determine and create each other: my possibility of swimming in a lake has been opened up by the fact that I have travelled to the lake and my performance of having crossed the lake by swimming is affected by the possibility of meeting a dear friend on the other side. Both my past achievement and my future possibility are functions of the action in the present, leading indeed to the actual realization of swimming and of enjoying a glass of wine with my friend.

The range of both my possibilities and my accomplishments is constantly changing as I pass from one realization to another. I experience these possibilities as extending and shrinking. A general state of well-being opens up the constellation of possibilities; an illness triggers their limitation. The horizon in time is wide open when I am healthy and closed when I am afflicted with an illness. This openness makes me forget my body; it is silently transcended, as I am concerned with the tasks and projects I wish to undertake. The closure of my lived time makes me aware of my body as an object needing care and attention in the present. In my youth, the scope of my accomplishments is obviously smaller than it is at an advanced age. Their significance is also subject to modification; it depends on how and to what extent my actions influence my further possibilities and accomplishments. My actual migration to a new country will exert a different effect on my possibilities and accomplishments than my visit to this country as a tourist.

Through our actions, we grasp possibilities and come to their realizations: I stop writing or reading, go for a walk, or prepare a cup of tea. Most of the time, we act by following habits, customs, codes of conduct, social conventions, rules, or laws. In all these cases, we do not make a decision; we simply do what is expected. When we get into our car and drive to our work, we do not decide to leave on time and to use this form of transport in order to reach our destination. We follow our regular routine, without even thinking about any other alternatives. In this context, sociologists speak of the habitualization of human behaviour. Specialized and reproduced without great effort, habitualized actions provide us with a relief from the burden of consciously making a decision. If, for some unforeseen reasons, we run into an obstacle (a serious delay due to an accident), we reflect on how to reach our destination faster or how to change our upcoming plans. We carefully examine the current situation and, after taking into consideration various courses of action, we may introduce a modification into our usual itinerary. But, here again, we don't make a decision. We simply follow habits or customs without seriously thinking about the choice we are making.

We do however make a decision when we can no longer rely on a habit, a code of conduct, a custom, or a law that clearly and unambiguously tells us what we should do. In these cases, we find ourselves outside the realm of personal or institutional rules. Accepting the dictates of a majority or obediently following the conventions created by an institution or a social tradition is obviously not a decision. "The logic of decision is the logic of exception," remarks Hermann Lübbe.[4] In a situation of decision, the abstract norms, rules, and guidelines that usually define the nature, characteristics, and goals of our actions can no longer be applied. Thus, when we face a concrete instance of deciding between two possibilities, we are thrown back upon ourselves. As I mentioned above, we find the decision a difficult and sometimes even terrifying experience because we are facing the unavoidable obligation of relying on our own resources; we step outside the reliable social boundaries of our existence and find ourselves in a state of solitude. We are unable to lean on someone or something capable of providing us with trustworthy guidance regarding the direction of our conduct or even a clear view into the possible consequences of our action. The term "unavoidable" calls for greater precision. There are situations in which the excluding possibilities leave room for the consideration of other possibilities. If we decide to grasp one of these, we make a decision against a decision.

Of course, our decisions are not made in a purely arbitrary or capricious manner. They are often, but not always, based on motives; we have our reasons for taking the left path and not the right one. (When, for example, we are lost in a forest – or in life's jungle – without a compass, a decision may be taken without recourse to a motive.) A motive serves as a foundation or as a starting point for our decision. When I am asked by someone, or when I ask myself, why I decided to become a musician, I am able to provide an answer that justifies my decision: because I love music, or music allows me to express myself, or I envision making a good living by playing in an orchestra. A motive not only legitimates my decision but also provides an initial thrust for my decision. But this motive does not eliminate other competing motives, which might impel me to take up another profession. We speak of decision when the motives lack obviousness and an unambiguous compelling force and when they fail to dispel once and for all my hesitations. An imminent decision could call for a survey of all of my reasons, a task that, for lack of sufficient time, I am sometimes unable to perform. The final thrust, then, has to come from my inclination and a feeling of confidence in the validity and the justifying force of a reason.

A decision is, therefore, my task; it establishes a contact with myself. Language emphasizes this relation to the self: I make up *my* mind, *je me décide, Ich entscheide mich*. This relation to *my self* is a central element of the decision: I am conscious of being the author of my action and responsible for its consequences. I am also conscious of my process of thinking, which is, in the words of Plato, the mind's "talking to itself, asking questions and answering them, and saying yes and no." And when I reach a decision, which may happen slowly or suddenly, "the two voices affirm the same thing."[5] In a decision, I also define myself as a person in possession of a free will, distinct from everyone else. More than this, I reinforce my freedom and distinctiveness in a concrete manner. By seizing one possibility, I know that I could have grasped the rejected one. By being fully aware of this possibility, I know what it means to be free and to be accountable for the repercussions of my decision.

Freedom is the capacity to make a decision about the accomplishment or omission of a meaningful action. The claim to freedom may be challenged by the supposition that my psychological dispositions and unconscious motives, or ambient external social forces may, in fact, determine my decision – rendering me unable to know the extent and the influence of these factors. Were I to subscribe to that hypothesis, I would be unable to rise above these determining causes and ask the following question: "Taking into account these determining factors, what should I do?" The supposition of the determination of my action and the evaluative assessment of my possibilities would contradict each other: I cannot consider myself determined and simultaneously engage in a free rational inquiry as to how I make up my mind or what makes me decide in favour of one possible action and cast off others. My belief about the determination of my motives and dispositions applies to my evaluative question. And this question is often asked when I am facing the task of making a decision.[6]

When we are called to decide, we do not always see clearly which of the two or more possibilities we should grasp or, alternatively, dismiss. Previously acquired knowledge and the lessons drawn from past experiences do not provide a clear and unambiguous indication. Even a previously made decision does not give us an obvious answer to the question with regard to the right road to take. Indeed, we speak of making a decision when we are unable to predict with certainty the outcome of our action. Our sense of confidence and accuracy may provide us with enough support to grasp one possibility with or without some hesitation. If, however, a disagreeable uncertainty hangs over us, we come to favour one of the possibilities in "fear and trembling." The decision is a human act, accomplished without reassuring certainty about the rightness of an action: it is a courageous leap into the unknown. No one is providing us with a springboard for the performance of this action and no one makes lighter the weight of our responsibility. And in many cases, no one is able to grasp the web of our intimate conjectures, hopes, and feelings. We are alone as we take off from the ground. The leap is not a careless one because, notwithstanding its urgency, a decision still requires an instantaneous or lengthy evaluation of our capacities and of the possible consequences of our action.

Because, in a state of solitude, we have to rely on our own capabilities and to entrust ourselves to unknown reasons and consequences, a decision entails a "sense of power" (Paul Ricoeur), a "form of mastery" (Hermann Lübbe). In the moment of my decision, I define myself as someone who has his own power to take a decisive inner stand and to retain and discard possibilities without the calming and protective approval of a network of rules and habits. The more I make decisions, the more I am able to trust my own strength, to resist external debilitating influences, and to display a confidence in the fortunate outcome of my action. My sense of power is enhanced by my growing confidence in my ability to overcome the threat of ongoing hesitation, fear, and distrust. In this sense, my ability to make decisions alone may bring me prestige and recognition among my peers.

The possibilities I face exclude each other: if I make up my mind in favour of one of the two possibilities, I have to turn my back to the other one. If I decide to immigrate to a new country, I have to give up the possibility of staying in the country of my birth. After a year, I may regret this particular decision and return to my home country. However, I cannot revert to my initial situation, and the return itself will be the result of another decision made at a different stage of my becoming.

Decisions are made within a temporal framework. They are tied to a term located in the future. The presence of this temporal term makes the decision different from the choice. And it is indeed useful and of no small importance to distinguish between the temporal features of a choice and those of a decision. In the case of a choice, we can consider and weigh the possibilities until we have a clear indication about the rightness and wrongness of their realization. We can wait for our purchase of a particular consumer good or our selection of a travel destination. These realities normally remain available as future possibilities. But when it comes to making up our minds about studying for a particular profession or marrying someone, we ought to make a decision within a certain temporal limit. We cannot hold on to these possibilities indefinitely. They have a lifespan of their own. The task of selecting one possibility and not retaining another one presents itself with an expiration date. Decisions are serious affairs: the "either-or" of a decision constitutes a fork in the highway of our lives. Choices, on the other hand, bring no significant changes into the main direction and characteristics of our becoming. As we advance on our life paths, we make a few decisions and many choices. We can undo what we have chosen, but we have to live with our decision. Choices are written with a pencil and can be erased, while decisions are indelible and cannot be effaced. For this reason, perhaps, we forget our choices but remember our decisions. Nonetheless, everyday choices about work or leisure activities may still lead us to situations in which a decision has to be made while, conversely, the decision concerning a job or a marriage could yield a series of choices.

Beyond the presence of two mutually exclusive possibilities, the situation of a decision discloses the pressing obligation of accepting or setting a deadline. In this respect, we rightly speak of the process of the maturation of a decision. In this process, we find both conscious and unconscious mental activities as well as rational and intuitive considerations, all of which influence each other in a reciprocal manner. As we try to look into the future and evaluate the possible consequences of each of the two possible actions, we keep asking ourselves: "Now what should I do?" or "So then, what will be the outcome of this action?" or, ultimately, "What will I make out of my life?" The temporal unfolding of the process of maturation points to, and eventually reaches, a "point of no return," after which, in the absence of a decision, one of the two possibilities fades away and the other one comes to a realization. Hence we feel the urgency of making a decision; the ineluctable task of making a decision appears as a heavy and aching burden that we cannot simply ignore or put aside. All alone, we sense its increasingly forceful and even disquieting presence as the days, hours, or minutes go by and as we move closer to the temporal point of no return.

Here is a telling illustration of the burden and the acute urgency implicit in decision-making. It provides an example of how a decision may become the most memorable moment in someone's life. On 26 September 1983, Stanislav Yevgrafovich Petrov was the commanding officer on duty at the Serpukhove-15 secret air defence bunker near Moscow. The early warning satellite system reported the launch of American intercontinental ballistic missiles potentially with nuclear warheads. In the case of an attack, Petrov was required to notify his superiors who, according to the Soviet strategy then in force, were prepared to immediately launch a tremendous nuclear counter-attack. Let us remember that, at that time, Soviet-American relations had reached their lowest point. Petrov had only a short time to ponder two possibilities: go with his gut feeling and dismiss the warning on the basis of a possible computer error or trust the reliability of Soviet military technology, follow the military protocol,

Logic of Exception 21

and report the incoming attack. During a few painful minutes, in a state of utter uncertainty, he thought over a number of reasons why the alarm might be false. He decided to trust his intuition and not trigger a military alert. Dismissing the warning sign as a false alarm turned out to be the right answer to the painful dilemma.

Uncertainty, urgency, and lack of external support are all constituent elements of a decision and often make the act of preferring one possibility to another an unwelcomed and ʹfraught human experience.[7] When we make one choice after another, we advance in time without experiencing serious disturbances and obstacles and take care of as many tasks and duties as possible. When, however, we are called to make a decision, our unconstrained advance to the future is blocked or slowed down. If, for instance, we have to decide whether to undergo or refuse an important medical intervention, we experience a perturbation of the continuity of our becoming. The call for a decision introduces a break into our regular dealing with persons and things; it creates a *decisive moment* in the course of our lives. The act of decision is, then, lived as a temporary or long-lasting resolution of a crisis that we have experienced.

When we reflect on the progress of our personal lives, it is appropriate to use the image of the path and of movement on this path. The movement has its pace and character, stealthy or bold. The path has its manifold characteristics: it can be narrow, wide, steep, rugged, beaten, or well-paved. On this path, there are "points of culminations" that induce a crisis and call for a decision. Both the form of the advance movements and the quality of the path are determined by the decisions taken at the crossroads.[8]

The Greek word *krinein* refers to a turning point in the process of the evolution of a living being; at this point, a change for the better or the worse takes place. A crisis is a break introduced into the dynamic unfolding of a living and dynamic reality (body, social relation, economic or ecological structure, etc.): due to a disturbance arising in the functioning of this reality, its progress has been slowed down or blocked and its orientation has become uncertain. In a crisis situation, we experience both the failure of the normal functioning of a living thing and the search for its creative regeneration. The period of break and uncertainty can be short or long. Because of its painful character, a crisis has to be faced and, through the active search for solutions, resolved. It is not always clear for us how we will be able to overcome the existing perturbations, what the most appropriate solutions are, and what the possible consequences of each solution may be. All forms of crises – social, political, economic, or personal – require, sooner or later, a decision, thanks to which modifications are introduced and the disturbance is either resolved or, at least, mitigated. An enduring crisis may provoke hesitation, doubt, loss of vigour and insight, and not infrequently, a state of passivity, which, in turn, may aggravate the crisis. In times of a personal crisis, one often considers oneself as one's worst enemy. A decision requires the effort and eventual success of overcoming doubts and hesitations, of shaking off the torpor of vacillation, of putting an end to self-struggle, and of creating effective recovery procedures. Notwithstanding its painful character, a crisis may prove to be highly beneficial in as much as it generates creativity in action: regression opens the way to progression, disorganisation to reorganisation, tension to resolution.[9] The sense of accomplishment felt after making a difficult decision, and emerging from the crisis stronger than before, becomes a momentous and gratifying experience on our life paths.

THE DIFFICULTY OF MAKING A DECISION

To decide, as we have seen, is to come to the realization of a possibility and to accept the disappearance of another possibility. The actualization of the selected possibility will then become the cusp for future events and experiences, and further decisions in our lives. Through our decision, we exert some influence on our lived future: if I decide to live in a particular country, my future possibilities will be shaped by my existence and activities in this new environment. But every decision also means that we have to give up possibilities. By deciding on the musical profession, I renounce a career in business, medicine, or politics. As we move forward in life, from the *not yet* to the *already*, and relate ourselves to both the future and the past in the *now*, the range of our possibilities shrinks and the scope of our accomplishments grows. We may compare our existence to a steadily or suddenly narrowing road: the road shaped, ahead of us, by our ever-diminishing possibilities and, behind us, by our ever-growing accomplishments.[10] But, as Erwin Straus has aptly pointed out, along with our accomplishments, proudly listed in our curriculum vitae, we have to bear in mind our *missed* possibilities. As he puts it, "We are always debtors to the past. Confronted with the past, we are at the bar of justice, and there is nobody who can plead not

Logic of Exception

guilty."[11] But, in our past, besides our *missed* possibilities we also find the range of our consciously and courageously *discarded* possibilities, for which the guilty verdict seldom applies.

We may review with sadness, remorse, and regret both our missed and rejected possibilities. This sterile regret does not allow the complete disappearance of possibilities. It repeatedly returns to them, keeps them alive in memory and says: "If I had not done this or that, I would have had a different sort of life." The productive regret accepts with equanimity the fact that the unused or missed possibilities are irrevocably gone and draws a lesson for both the present and the future. Some individuals, however, display ongoing and outright resistance to the shrinking or fading away of possibilities. For instance, misers attach themselves to something impervious to decay and which keeps its value and durability in time: money. Money, with its primary associations with the future, presents an abundance of persisting possibilities, which, in the life of the miser, is never invested or converted to actual realities. The preserved possibilities, although worthless in themselves, since they are not used for investment or for purchase, offer their holders more satisfaction than the acquired concrete objects or the investment return. In addition to an uncommon feeling of satisfaction, sitting on their money gives these individuals a sense of security in the face of an unforeseeable future. Misers hold on to their possibilities because they are frightened by the uncertain future and, in the absence of the potential power of the money, lack confidence in their capacity to face the world of tomorrow.[12]

Although most people today would vehemently oppose being called a miser, many nevertheless form and display the miser's stubborn bond to the possibilities at their disposal. People undertake their various professional and leisure activities without any sense of passionate commitment. They believe that the trivial expression "keep your options open" should guide them when they undertake a business operation or form a personal relationship. The various public advertisements of contemporary life invite them to retain concurrent possibilities and not to recognize their conflicting and irreconcilable nature. Books, movies, and video games create and entertain the illusion of being able to step outside the state of personal becoming and exert control over all the dimensions of personal time. These products of the entertainment industry satisfy an ingrained desire to overstep the limitations that a decision and its ensuing resignation entail and to recover at will any of the missed opportunities. As a result, many tend to live in the realm of fantasy, where the improbable is attainable and possibilities fail to contradict each other, and not in the world of reality, where decisions have to be made and possibilities converted or abandoned. Those who continuously push away the moment of decision into the future fail to establish contact with reality. Holding onto the possibilities of being a politician and a scholar, without any decisive commitment, precludes being effective as either of the two. To be real, effective, and accountable, the "either-or" is an ineluctable task. There is a deeper cause for adopting such an evading attitude and failing to admit that "life, too, has its demands" (Kierkegaard).[13] When a person does not learn to make a distinction of value between various possible views of the world – but rather considers them equivalent, and thus fails to express a firm attachment to any of them – the ability to make a lasting commitment in favour of a particular life path and purpose becomes atrophied. Therefore, it is important to awaken in children not only the capacity to compare various worldviews and the corresponding attitude of tolerance, but also the ability to attach themselves to one of them through a free decision.[14]

The vivid sense of uncertainty, as we have seen, is another central element of the act of decision. In the moment of deciding, we are unable to assess with clarity or certainty the outcome of our impending action. What appears right and promising in the present may turn out to be mistaken and fallacious in the future. We are exposed to the risk of failing, of losing our job or even our livelihood, of becoming ill or unhappy, of enduring hostility or misunderstanding. No wonder that we are assailed by doubt and fear before making a decision, especially if a previous decision has already yielded a serious disappointment. We are not only uncertain about the fortunate turn of circumstances, but we also lack the confidence in our ability to live with a failure and to endure the pain that loneliness, hardship, and adversity may bring upon us. Overly cautious individuals are preoccupied with the degree of risk they take and the possible negative consequences of their decisions. They harbour a feeling of distrust regarding their own foresight as well as their capacity to accept their eventual downfall. Once again, the concern over possibilities and their future consequences plays a more important role in their lives than the achievements created through decisive actions. In order to "free ourselves of the frustrating tyranny of tomorrow," we have to give up the obsessive and futile search of certainty and to make peace with our ignorance.[15] As Alfred North Whitehead wisely put it, "a man has to ignore much to get on with something."[16] If we were prophetically aware, with full certainty, of all the possible consequences of our actions, we would probably fall into total passivity and cease acting. To avoid this paralyzing effect, we need to rely on our capacities to "live in the provisional" and to relate with confidence and "sympathetic ties" to our world. Erwin W. Straus described this carefree and unconstrained attitude in these terms: "We live 'for the time being,' and we know – more or less clearly – that we live in the *provisional*. However much we strive for conscientiousness, we still put an end to our deliberations. In all action, we give up certainty and entrust ourselves to the future, relying on ourselves, on the circumstances, and on others."[17]

Today children seem to have fewer and fewer opportunities for taking risks and for trustfully relying on a fortunate turn of events. Their parents and teachers are increasingly obsessed with creating a safe and secure environment and, as a result, deprive the overly protected children of the experience of adventure and exploration. Yet recent studies have shown that the absence of excessive protections and of silly prohibitions brings important gains: children learn to trust their own judgment, to make creative and fearless decisions, and to assume responsibility for their actions. Emotional maturity is gradually acquired in an environment in which children are encouraged to take risks while being actively involved in games, sports, or adventurous physical activities.[18]

In a society of fear and of obsession, men and women are constantly warned about the possibility of imminent catastrophes caused by the mistaken decisions of economic experts and political figures. A paralyzing worry about the consequences of human mistakes leaves its mark on the structure and functioning of business and public institutions as well as on the daily lives of individuals. Yet mistakes may be caused by fear just us much as by overconfidence. Fear intensifies the sense of obligation with regard to an unavoidable decision. It risks fostering an inability to determine the auspicious moment of a decision. Fear may also blind someone to an accurate assessment of the plausible consequences of an action.

In a standardized and predictable social environment, in which the number of possible mistakes is reduced to a minimum, mechanical devices play a central role and take away from humans the burden of decision. If they are well designed and serviced, devices – robots and computers, such as the autopilot used on aircrafts – are capable of accomplishing their tasks flawlessly and of minimizing the likelihood of error. Their increasing presence in our lives creates the tendency to compare human accomplishments to the performances of these devices and reduces tolerance for human shortcomings and errors. Unfortunately, our sentimental admiration for, and almost unbounded confidence in, these mechanical devices may also lead us to abandon the use and improvement of our bodily and mental capabilities. We hand these faculties over to the devices. One of our secret wishes is to create a device, which is able to think, to feel, to signal dangers with perfect accuracy, and to completely remove the disquieting feeling of uncertainty. Such a device is not yet at our disposal, but in situations in which we are overcome by doubts and hesitations,we increasingly rely on mechanical aids to assess conditions and changes, formulate judgments and hypotheses, and propose crucial interventions.

It is worth mentioning both the beneficial and stifling roles that social institutions play in human life. Because of the intrinsic plasticity, instability, and incalculability of human behaviour and our susceptibility to the abundance of unexpected possibilities offered by social environments, institutions – with their rules, laws, habits, and behaviour patterns – guarantee the much desired reliability, predictability, and security for our everyday human interactions. More importantly, they offer a relief from the burden of decision-making. The temporary weakening of institutions, as it may occur in times of natural or social catastrophes or during revolutions and the collapse of political systems, brings about disorientation, uncertainty, and a general sense of insecurity. The absence of the structures of law and order fostered by the temporary dissolution or weakening of all those forces, which are established for the defence and protection of citizens and their property, may give rise to unpredictable violence or to unexpected generosity. When, suddenly, individuals are thrown back upon themselves and freed from the binding constraints of laws and regulations, they are called upon to use their own improvisatory abilities and to face, often reluctantly but autonomously, the obligation of making life-altering decisions. On the other hand, the disinclination to face the task of making a decision and the corollary absence of autonomous self-definition become prevalent as soon as individuals are able to count on the dependable guidance and "happy certainty" offered by the surrounding strengthened institutions.[19] As much as the enduring institutions of the social order are indispensable to our human condition, they nonetheless bring with them the powerful temptation to go along; to rely on shared habits of thinking, feeling, and acting; and to avoid situations in which autonomous initiative is required. Curiously enough, there are individuals who are pleased to live under stern political dictatorship simply because the increasing control of almost all aspects of their daily lives closes the range of those conflicting possibilities that could press them to make a decision. In many cultures, family – this basic institution of our social life – often produces the unquestioned acceptance of civil status or career path and stifles the youth's courageous desire to risk deviation from a "tradition that worked so well for the previous generations." Educational institutions with their well-established tenure system and administrative structure also generate a mode of thinking and of living that seem to discourage critical distancing from the obligations of academic conformity. Well-ingrained habits and mentalities are readily adopted by fresh teachers or scholars as well as young administrators, which makes them surrender their willingness and ability to make dissenting decisions. Even those individuals – such as artists and writers, who, in our time, claim to be free from social constraints and professional regulations – rely, for the diffusion of their creations, on a "secondary institutionalization of subjectivity" (Arnold Gehlen). At that stage, they are willing to exchange their creative independence for all the advantages they get from their adherence to the "rule books" written by art dealers, organizers of exhibitions, producers, publishers, and so on. Institutions, despite their indisputable necessity and benefit, exacerbate a "tendency to laziness," about which Friedrich Nietzsche wrote with much conviction and passion.[20] There is, indeed, a kind of laziness, very much present in various social spheres; for fear of making mistakes, individuals possessing this laziness never question the written and unwritten regulations and values of an institution and endorse only those actions and thoughts that are safe from undesirable deviations. There is also a laziness inherent in not risking a protected social status and the comfort provided by being active member of an institution, and in not favouring a courageous inner conviction above the external recognition and fulfilment of material needs.

Another difficulty in making decisions arises with the experience of solitude that people want to alleviate, especially in times of crisis, by seeking the company of friends or family members. There are situations, as we have seen, in which the available traditions, rules, or opinions fail to provide us with a clear indication about the right possibility to seize. In these exceptional situations, we are thrown back on ourselves and envisage our future, its susceptibility to reconfiguration, and the resultant weight of our responsibility without any external support. We are forced to deal with the decision alone, however painful the absence of encouraging advice may be and whatever energy the autonomous stand may consume. But the pain has its reward: we come into a contact with ourselves and strengthen ourselves in the face of others. This moment, Kierkegaard tells us, is more significant, memorable, and ennobling than meeting, and coming under the influence of, world famous individualities: "When around one everything has become silent, solemn as a clear, starlit night, when the soul comes to be alone in the world, then before one there appears, not an extraordinary human being, but the eternal power itself, then the heavens seem to open, and *I* chooses itself or, more correctly, receives itself."[21]

This return of the *I* to itself is today becoming increasingly difficult. We find ourselves in the presence of various social forces that invite or push us to move away from ourselves. Books, lectures, television programs, social media, and self-help courses at universities encourage us to develop a new self, a more successful and a more confident personality. We gladly respond to the call and deploy considerable efforts to exchange our true self for a represented and performing self. We gradually develop a theatrical attitude in our daily contacts with people: we give increasing importance to socially desirable and acquired roles and deny the impulses, moods, and judgments of our irreplaceable and true self, which we are called upon to become. But, sooner or later, after our desperate yet tentative attempt to escape from ourselves and adopt borrowed selves, we are compelled to come back to our true and humble selves and to face, whether we like it or not, the uncomfortable task of making a decision. In this return, notwithstanding our ongoing struggle to flee from ourselves, we come to recognize the impossibility of ridding ourselves of our concrete selves. But what is this concrete self? It is quite often a weak and vacillating self. This is so because we increasingly rely on ready experts who provide their counsel, guarantee success for any of our undertakings, and, by doing so, gradually enfeeble our ability to make decisions,

Logic of Exception

to stick to our commitments, and to assume our responsibilities.[22]

Due to the waning of our confidence in our decision-making faculties, we are unable to resolve the acute conflict between the collectively approved rules and ways of living and our personal convictions and desires. As the above-mentioned dilemma evoked by Yehudi Menuhin made clear, one of the most difficult situations in which we may find ourselves is created by the ineluctable obligation to decide between the prescription of an accepted and internalized convention and the promptings of our heart. How are we going to decide when we are passionate about becoming a musician but our family pressures us to pursue a more "practical" vocation? Or what are we to do in the less stereotypical situation – such as the one in which the young Evelyn Waugh found himself – where family tradition and atmosphere strongly pressured him to become a writer but an inner voice urged him to swim bravely against that tide and pursue another profession?[23] A similar plight may present itself when the decision is made about a spouse or a place of living.

We tend to relate to our feelings with suspicion and fear; we have little confidence in their guidance and counsel. We tend to consider them as blind happenings that must be handled with caution. It is easier to accept and to follow the protective conventions of our milieu than to start a new and different form of life under the suggestion of a more or less vague feeling. There exists, in many of us, an unrelenting temptation to put aside spontaneous feelings and to prefer reasoned reflections. We think, often quite wrongly, that life should be lived chiefly from the head and seldom from the heart. The conflict between the known and the unknown, the discord between seemingly secure and perilous possibilities will persist until we take a decisive stance for or against what our feelings are telling us in a given situation. William Barrett's observation, advanced about E.M. Forster's literary output, seems valid: "The misunderstanding of the emotions – embedded in the popular language and elaborated in the technical works of philosophers and psychologists – is one of the more catastrophic parts of our culture. Passion is blind, we say; yes, but more often than not we will find the blind passion is one contaminated by some fanatical idea. And usually feelings are blind in those who are unused to live by them. On the other hand, would not the perfectly rational person without the appropriate feelings in a certain situation be among the blindest of human beings?"[24] The blind, fanatical idea is often created by a social, religious, or cultural cause that people consider important and worthy of a single-minded and sometimes ruthless fight undertaken for its realization. This idea, as we will see in the next chapter, may also lead someone to break away from an existing living condition and to join a community that promotes subversive and violent actions. The blindness of the fanatical person, so frequent in the history of humankind, is caused by the inability to put the idea into a wider perspective and assess its true value and decisive influence on the life of a wider community. Our feelings may also be blind because the possible road to take lacks clarity and a distinct contour. Will we fail if, facing the possibility of working in a remote part of a country, we decide to silence our reason and all of its warning signals? We look in vain for clear reasons to guide us and simply feel that it is the appropriate and meaningful step to take. Feelings appear to us less convincing though they offer, if not tainted by a fanatical cause, the advantage of embracing complex situations in their totality as well as indicating the unity of experiences we seek in these situations. Eventually, we come to sharpen our sensibilities regarding our feelings just as we develop our other human capabilities: the more we live by them, the more secure and convinced we become about the clarity and the accuracy of their guidance. Concrete life situations offer us numerous opportunities to gain more articulate insights into, and strengthen our confidence in, the message of our heart.

The conflict between the logic of reason and the reason of the heart appears with certain urgency when the decision bears on a profession, a spouse, or a religion. Appearing during the course of a lifetime, when an individual reaches the stage of maturity, it usually involves the clash between fidelity to youth's spontaneity, passion, and creative impulses and the sober and realistic acceptance of social norms and codes of conduct. This tension between the desire to stand by one's convictions and feelings, and the pressure to conform to a social role may be experienced as tormenting and even debilitating; a firm decision and the corresponding awareness of an inner strength may bring relief from it. Another manner of mitigating this distress is to gradually fade into the routine of common days and just forget or silence the poet who lives inside.

LEARNING TO MAKE A DECISION

It would be erroneous to believe that we first acquire maturity and, once a strong sense of identity, resilience, and self-confidence are in place, we then, as it were, try out our decision-making ability at our own leisure and pleasure. In truth, it is only by courageously making decisions – with the associated risks, uncertainties, responsibilities, and feeling of solitude – that we are able to create a strong and mature personality. If the decision-making faculty is not acquired, used, and strengthened, we will be unduly influenced by momentary needs and various social norms, conventions, and customs.[25]

Formal education does not train our decision-making faculty. Concrete life situations make this kind of learning possible. We learn to make decisions the same way as we learn to swim or to ski: our movements are a more or less successful adaptation to the requirements of a situation. Thus, we learn to respond to life's challenges by listening to the advice of our feelings without becoming deaf to the guidance provided by our reason. We learn to consider and resolve, alone and without any external support, the conflicts between desire and duty, originality and convention, expediency and morality. We learn to face, in fear and trembling, the silence of the future, to listen confidently to the voice of our inclinations, and to accept that our actions have a tentative character and inevitably carry the risk of failure.

While deciding, as we have seen, I consider at least two possibilities and give my assent to only one of them: I marry this woman and give up the possibility of remaining single or of marrying another woman. Anyone who wants to make a decision must recognize and accept renunciation, restriction, and limitation. By cultivating our sense of limits and our capacity for renunciation, we come to learn to make a decision. If a decision engages and heightens our sense of power, bringing about the projection and actualization of possibilities, it no less involves and emphasizes our sense of powerlessness, forcing us to release certain possibilities. A decision relies on the right balance between the courage and strength to face the possibilities alone and the humble and realistic admission that we are able to actualize only one of them.

Decisions also require the readiness to give up the search for certainty and absolute control of the outcome of our actions. If we continue searching for certainty, we persist in delaying our action. A decision calls for the willingness to surrender ourselves to the unknown circumstances and to trust to good luck the possibility of bringing about the right turn of uncontrollable events. Giving up the search for certainty and embracing the risk of failure are inevitable conditions for even a seemingly less important decision. This entails not only having faith in our own strength and in the eventual goodwill of our fellow human beings, but also gauging, in spite of the approaching point of no return, the right moment for acting and the degree of risk to take. The act of taking risks does not necessarily call for a heroic attitude. Paul Ricoeur has remarked that, since we have a limited awareness of our world, we have to run a risk even with an unconcerned decision taken under normal conditions. In his words, "There is a simple, calm, extended form of risk, which suits the modesty of a consciousness which has never followed out the alpha and the omega of the world and which apprehends values within the network of a confused corporeal condition and from a limited, partial history."[26] In this personal history, there are times when decisions have to be taken instantaneously. On other occasions, we may enjoy a longer period for weighing possibilities. The resolution of important medical, economic, or political problems sometimes require careful and patient consideration of the possible consequences and implications of the chosen solution. Some of these decisions may seem profound and substantial at first but, in retrospect, they fail to have a serious impact. The converse is also true: seemingly trifling and instantaneous choices may result in devastating results years later and, in fact, prove to be crucial and fateful decisions. Heinrich von Kleist's story *The Beggarwoman of Locarno* illustrates the point. A simple and thoughtless order given to an old woman to rise and move brings about, several years later, a terrible retribution. Unpredictable events and unforeseen occurrences will eventually define and verify the extent, weight, and rightness of both a choice and a decision.

There is a human quality that helps someone to take the right amount of risk and to envisage, with trust and ease, the course of future and partially controllable events: equanimity. The person who makes a decision with equanimity does not rationalize any selected possibility in order to initiate an action. He or she puts an end to the vain search for certainty and perfection and makes the decision by trusting the opportune moment and its eventual consequences. The German philosopher Robert Spaemann defines equanimity (*Gelassenheit*) as "the attitude of someone who regards what he cannot change as a meaningful limit to his ability to act and who accepts this limit."[27] The person who displays this attitude acts decisively and holds on to the hope of changing both the world and the course of his or her life but, at the same time, accepts a certain number of conditions and lets these conditions unfold accordingly. In other words, he or she is able to relate correctly what can be achieved by an action and what has to be accepted as an independent reality. This reality can be changed to a certain extent by the action, but the change itself is possible only if the reality is first accepted with both its changeable and unchangeable features. The same applies to the author of the action. The course of our lives can be changed by the decision to break away from a certain set of circumstances, but we also have to accept that the action does not occur in a void and that its positive or negative consequence becomes an irrevocable aspect of our existence. As we have seen, our decision must also allow for our inability to survey all of our reasons and to anticipate all the consequences. While the purpose of an action is considered valuable and thus worthy of passionate commitment, equanimity is the readiness to accept the objective and subjective limits imposed on our actions, to live with our successes and failures, and to accept the unavoidable dictates of the existing and changed circumstances.

Equanimity involves not only the keenness to make decisions with poise and confidence, and to act in absence of certainty concerning the future, but also the ability to relate to the world, to fellow human beings, and to oneself in a relaxed manner. While acting with confidence in the decisive moment, the person who has equanimity "lets things be and happen." While travelling abroad, he or she lets unpredictable encounters or an event interfere with his or her plan and faces the uncertain future with a sense of adventure. He or she is ready to face a new situation with ingenious improvisation. In a personal or professional relationship, he or she lets the other person undergo changes and thus alter the initial characteristics of collaboration, of friendship, or of love.

Equanimity helps us to see people and things in a relaxed manner, to smile at ourselves, and to laugh wholeheartedly at the absurdity of our desires and actions. The advocacy of any imperfection and exaggeration detected in ourselves is often nurtured by a healthy sense of humour. Hubertus Tellenbach sees in humour the equivalence of equanimity; it is the complete opposite of tension and stiffness. Humour also modifies the ways we see reality. We are aware of our serious duties and tasks without being obsessed with them and we are also able to anticipate future events without being stifled by their gravity. We are able to stand above life and to envisage upcoming changes elegantly and with ease, with an almost irrepressible light-heartedness. Humour cancels out strain and rigidity and sees things in a new light, thus bringing into the fore the open possibilities as well as the inevitable consequences of human actions. Even if it nurtures the adoption of a playful attitude towards what we believe to be our "monumental concerns" and helps to recover, in the presence of people and things, an unreflective and generous spontaneity, humour does not flee from the obligation of making difficult decisions. Far from it, it "liberates the rigid souls and dissipates the obscurity, which makes humans blind to their responsibilities."[28]

The magnitude of the moment of decision is clearly seen in extreme situations. Bruno Bettelheim argued that, under life-threatening conditions, the best chance to survive is to evaluate and accept reality for what it is, but without its oppressive weight. The decision to leave everything behind and to face an uncertain future requires the mature readiness to throw away all material possessions, to face economic insecurity, and to achieve security through emotional attachments to family and friends. Well-integrated persons face their own realities without distorting them and without being pulled down by them, and act appropriately on the basis of their inner strengths, personal convictions, and independence of thought.[29] Here again, we find the ability of not holding onto any external good and of relying on oneself and on the fortunate turn of future events. Raoul Hilberg's study of the psychological profile of Holocaust survivors confirms the conclusions of Bettelheim's analysis. Survivors – those who run away from heavily guarded areas, jump from a train, or dive into icy water to avoid being killed – are realistic about their actual conditions and are able to respond to the opportunities by making decisions instantly, by assessing and accepting the foreseeable risks of their action, and by firmly holding onto an "absolute determination to live."[30]

Fortunately, in the present age, most of us do not need to run or swim for our lives under such extreme conditions. Yet, the capacity of making a sober assessment of our true situations and, at the same time, of being able to rise above them with an attitude of trust and ease, helps us to: achieve autonomy, risk action, and break away from our actual living conditions. This remarkable moment is the topic of the next chapter.

2

Artisan of My Destiny

Let each one test himself to see whether he acknowledges the good
that dwells within him, that moves and fills his heart, the good for which
he lives.

Søren Kierkegaard

In his biography of the writer Joseph Conrad, Zdzislaw Najder
made the following concluding remarks:

> "Man . . . is a product of circumstances and their victim,"
> Conrad wrote in one of his works. He himself was not an excep-
> tion to this rule, but throughout his life he tried hard to break
> away from the power of circumstance. He kept changing his
> decisions and at least five times suddenly altered the course of
> his life: departing from Poland; leaving France; going to Africa;
> beginning to write; and getting married. In each case the escape
> from the pressure of circumstances was both forced upon him
> and made easy. And in each case the escape proved to be only
> illusory because the sense of mastering one's fate may be found
> only in the consistent pursuit of a once-chosen goal.[1]

More recently, Second Lt Lawrence J. Franks Jr focused with
single-mindedness on his once-chosen goal and, with resolute purpose, ultimately reached what he had hoped for. He was destined
to a brilliant military career after graduating from the famous West
Point Military Academy in 2008. He was sent to an army base in
New York State, where, to his great regret, he was confined to a boring desk job. Staying at this military location meant following the
same miserable routine day after day. Yearning for active deployment

into a combat zone, he suffered from severe depression and suicidal thoughts. He wanted to break free from the circumstances that he considered depressing and meaningless, but not from the harsh regime of military life, the discipline, and the duty, to which he felt he was destined and passionately committed. One day he left his base, boarded a plane, landed in Paris, and joined the French Foreign Legion. Under a new identity and in Africa, he felt, once again, that his future had become bright, his life had meaning, and his depression gradually faded away. After serving five years in high spirits in the foreign mercenary forces, he returned to the United States Army to face the consequences of his desertion.[2]

Literature provides us with numerous examples of individuals dissatisfied with their ways of life who seek to create new forms of existence. In *The Red and the Black*, Stendhal painted a famous portrait of the human aspiration for a different life. Julien Sorel, a peasant boy filled with the highest social ambitions, is resolved to do everything he can to move away from his provincial milieu and to achieve fame, wealth, and position. Even though he calculates all of his moves, his tragedy at the end comes not from lacking focus and intelligence, but from the conflict between his persistent desire to insert himself into a new social order and the depth of his true feelings. Pierre Bezukhov, in Tolstoy's *War and Peace*, also decides to break free from his comfortable existence and to participate in the defence of Moscow against the invading the French Army. Witnessing the evils and corruptions of his society, he first joins the freemasons and turns his attention and applies his energies to the eventual realization of his lofty goals and ideals. However, these remain too abstract and remote, failing to touch him and leaving him dissatisfied and restless. Only by joining the army does he satisfy his enduring need to do something concrete and fulfilling.

There are many other well-known or unknown men and women who have achieved similar feats. They sought to leave their actual living conditions, in which they happened to find themselves, and to seek a turn of fortune. Whether they merely followed a socially determined pattern depended on their capacity to oppose their own independently planned endeavour to the externally imposed path. Whether they were successful in this or not depended on their ability to feel fervent about a change, to be eager and courageous to act upon their feelings, and to liberate themselves from the inhibiting forces of their actual circumstances. Poverty and misery are among the chief restraining factors. But, by filling a wealthy person with a sense of security and a sense of permanence and stability, the timorous attachment to a home, to a job, or to a social position can also result in an inability to take initiative and risk an action. It generates an impeding force that transforms "the capacity for action into a means of escape from action" (Kierkegaard).[3]

THE ACT OF BREAKING AWAY

Breaking away consists of taking leave from a form of existence, rooted in a specific social and cultural condition, and adopting a new form of existence. It is an act of decision that brings change to a person's life. The change may consist of a transitory suspension of a social role and the corresponding activities or a definitive rupture from a habitual way of living. It may mean moving away from a particular milieu or staying in the same place but transforming one's attitude towards life. It may lead to the adoption of a new lifestyle, a new profession, or a new web of relationships. Creating, changing, or ending human relations – in the forms of community engagement, marriage, divorce, friendship, or partnership – often leads people to a more or less significant alteration in their lives. Since there are different ways of effecting change, there are also different conditions that cause the break. Some changes demand sustained effort to overcome difficulties and obstacles and some require little exertion. Some may occur instantaneously, following a spontaneous response to a fortuitous invitation; some may happen after a long and careful weighing of possibilities. Before examining the most conspicuous ones, let us first focus on the essential features of breaking free from a particular form of existence.

What is essential is that the life of a person does not follow the same course as before. There is a break in its temporal unfolding. The resolution of declaring "from now on it will be markedly different" or "I take a leave from my profession" or "I walk away from my stifling marital bond" cuts the person's becoming into two periods: before and after. In the moment of decision, as we have already seen, excluding possibilities present themselves. Either one holds onto the habitual form of life or rejects it and turns to starting something new and different. The temporal "point of no return" of the decision depends on the degree of pressure of concrete life circumstances. For those who decide to move away from war or an oppressive political or economic context, there is often an optimal occasion that has to be seized. The possibility of leaving an unpropitious professional or personal situation may be available for a much longer period of time. Although both the past (as I lived before) and the future (as I want to live henceforth) press upon the person with more or less insistence, the present (*now* I introduce the change) is perceived as the most significant temporal dimension. However, in the moment of decision, the past and the future remain implicitly yet influentially present; their respective weights and textures do not fade away. Their worth is appraised in accordance with the present decision and the ensuing action. If the present stands out, it also comprises the complementary yet contrasting assessment of the past and the future, which are viewed in their totalities as antecedent and subsequent possible life-histories.

The new form of existence involves either transforming the person's ways of being and acting in the world or moving into a different world. The world is understood here as a structured environment, in which living and lifeless realities have degrees of significance. The significance is both made and recognized by the acting, responding, questioning, and understanding person. As Robert Spaemann has noted, "the world only discloses itself as that which can do something for us: something becomes meaningful in light of the interest we take in it."[4] In other words, the world is drawn by a set of significances that we ascribe to places, persons, acts, and events. We are interested in having food and rest, but also in finding friendship and love and admiring beautiful things. Our movements and senses first establish an immediate and preconceptual relation with things and persons within a given environment and our reflective and conscious relations are built upon these primary unreflective contacts. The world, encompassing the person within a network of significances, is formed and transformed through actions and responses to actions. It is a dynamic and transforming reality, extended in time and punctuated by enduring and momentary experiences and events. Therefore, for the person, the world comprises a cluster of future possibilities, actual activities, and past accomplishments. For example, the world of a medical student is built from the time of seeking admission to an educational institution until the moment of leaving behind his studies, research, and participation in extracurricular activities. This world includes professors, physicians, administrators, fellow students, and teammates; lectures and examinations;

libraries, laboratories, classrooms, hospitals, institutions, and places for leisure activities; and useful and useless objects. These and various other realities form, in their intricate relationships, a complex network of significant relationships.[5]

Although the world presents some seemingly stable linguistic, social, and cultural features and material constancies, it is, in fact, a mobile and variable reality. Thanks to decisions and choices and the occurrence of experiences and events, the world undergoes transformations. Events are the objective and impersonal alterations of our environment; the city builds a road, a fire destroys a forest, winter sets in. Experiences are radical transformations affecting our personal development: loss of a job or death of a spouse. We may hold an event at bay, but the experiences truly concern us. Of course, an event, such as the forest catching on fire and leading to the destruction of my house, can become an experience and thus it can strongly affect me. Both events and experiences exert lasting or fleeting influences on the worlds in which we act and live.[6]

On the one hand, we live, successively and simultaneously, in several sub-worlds, created and developed around our personal, professional, artistic, or leisure activities and interests. For instance, his active participation in an athletic activity creates a sub-world for our medical student. In order to make the best of these sub-worlds, we have to adapt our speech, attitude, and bodily behaviour to the prevailing requirements and customs. We all have particular and non-interchangeable sub-worlds. Subsequent decisions and life experiences create and transform the relations among these sub-worlds and their relative importance to each other. The totality of our sub-worlds persists in a particular place and time, in which we live and act. It may undergo a more or less radical modification, notwithstanding the apparent stability of our professional and intimate living conditions. We are able to know and to understand another person if we are able to place ourselves in one of her sub-worlds, to carry out actions in it and to appreciate the central role it plays in one of her momentous experiences.

On the other hand, we are able to leave behind the totality of our sub-worlds and, through our initiatives, create an entirely new network of relationships and engage in new activities. We may devote our energies to the healing of the sick in a distant land or to educating and helping poor people in our own countries. We, then, live in a new world and undertake activities and create a network of human relationships according to new principles, values, and aspirations. An evaluative performance precedes the earnest moment of breaking away. The customary world and the corresponding forms of behaviours elicit dissatisfaction and aspiration for living in a different world. The assessment of these two worlds is carried out in light of an explicit or implicit reflection on the meaning of our lives. The question with regard to this meaning is a practical one; it helps us to take a distance from our living situations and evaluate them in light of our past achievements and our future possibilities. We distance ourselves from the present world in which we find ourselves to see how it was formed and how it can be replaced by another world, which is still vague, uncertain, and unreal.

Those persons who have taken the dangerous route of escaping a country governed by a totalitarian regime wanted to leave behind what they had become accustomed to, and what they considered insufficient, avoidable, or unacceptable. They wished to reach for what seemed, for them, preferable and more advantageous. They broke away from a familiar but undesirable world in order to attain what seemed a better one or, if not better, at least a more acceptable one. The "better" and "acceptable" are motivating values, which also constitute a global and inspiring meaning and bring about the resolution to move away from a home, an occupation, or a network of relatives and friends. The values entertained in the present, which prompt a decisive action, not only contribute to a reassessment of the importance of past relations and activities and the corresponding meaning of life, but also define the range of possibilities that may be grasped or left untouched in the future. Whether the desired destination will be reached is still uncertain. And whether those preferable possibilities that are actually seized will eventually yield a satisfactory life is still to be seen. Hence, the individuals experience a feeling of anxiety that both attracts and repels. But, if the possibilities appear sufficiently attractive, they offer a powerful incentive for initiating a courageous resolution to break out from the present situation and to start a new form of existence in a different future personal world.

People may distance themselves from their established ways of life by gradually changing their approach to various activities and relationships. They put less energy into their professional occupations and show a marked reserve towards their neighbours. At the same time, for these persons, the world progressively undergoes a transformation, which, in its turn, sustains and reinforces the break from the old way of life. But, obviously, when people cross a dangerous border and leave behind their debilitating and oppressive conditions, the change is sudden and abrupt. Successful reaching of their destinations brings a feeling of liberation, a sense of inner relief, allowing them to entertain new possibilities and often to anticipate a still unknown future with confidence and renewed energy.

The act of breaking away illustrates the fundamental human desire to be an artisan of one's destiny and not to be constrained by one's fate. Eugène Minkowski perceptively observed that destiny (*destinée*) is the human becoming intimately tied to personal decisions. Fate (*destin*) is a course of life shaped by external influences, relations, and events.[7] Whereas I am actively engaged in the experiences that make up my destiny, I am exposed and subjected to my fate. Destiny is intrinsic to my existence, fate is extrinsic; destiny depends on my engagement, fate befalls me. There are available paths to my destiny, but fate gets me into the river of my life. Destiny brings to the fore an existence which is created, lived, and shaped in the present through actions, difficulties, and emergencies. We notice the presence of a destiny, which is in the process – notwithstanding the delays, crises, and slow progress – of being actively made and is far from being complete. When we talk about fate, we usually refer to something achieved and fixed in the past, even though we still have a part of our lives to live. We seem to have no other option but to acquiesce to our fate, to make peace with it, to accept what it has ordained for us. My immediate and wider environments, as well as some of my decisions and actions, seal my fate. I, as a result, find its inevitableness oppressive and paralyzing. A stroke of fate might even crush me; I am unable to influence the toss of fate's dice; it exists independently of me. But, in spite of the determining influences of my family or of my surroundings, I have some control over my destiny; I am able to form it by making a decision about my own accustomed path, leading it in new directions, and connecting it to new values and principles. Not only can I distance myself from my destiny, but I can also fashion it and become its artisan.

Max Scheler advanced a similar distinction: fate is "something to be confirmed," whilst destiny is a matter of insight and of decision. A human being is able to "deviate to the greatest possible degree from his individual destiny."[8] Destiny is not entirely private in the sense that each person makes a decision alone about his or her own life path. It is possible that another person knows more adequately what is required from me in order to shape my destiny. This person may help by giving me advice, by assisting me in discovering and strengthening my abilities, or by suggesting to me how and when to break free from my present environment. As we shall see in the next chapter, a model is a guide that often helps us to hear the call of our own vocation and our own destiny. Scheler also envisages a common destiny shared by individuals working and living together. They share the common responsibility of helping each other to become authors of their common destinies. The idea of being an artisan of a destiny includes the reciprocal recognition of responsibilities for shaping the future of communities through collectively undertaken actions. In other words, the sense of collective responsibility is just as important for the effort of defining a destiny as the sense of individual responsibility.

WAYS OF BREAKING AWAY

The most obvious way of introducing a turn in one's life is by leaving a geographical location – a village, a city, or a country – in which one makes a living and forms a world. Since immemorial times, whether they set out to a distant location or a nearby place, people have packed up their belongings and travelled to new destinations. Sometimes, in extremes circumstances, when individuals were fleeing from danger or adverse living conditions, they brought with them the bare minimum of their possessions or nothing at all. In recent years, thousands of people have attempted to cross a sea into foreign lands, often in unstable, overcrowded vessels, risking their lives while making the journey. The decision may be taken instantaneously or after months of careful planning. Although it can be overwhelming, in many cases, it calls for resolute determination, the departure from a familiar environment, the undertaking of a new venture, and the overcoming of several serious obstacles.

The change of external circumstances pertaining to lodging, communication, or profession results in the adoption of a new form of existence. People move into a different rural or urban structure, adopt different forms of mobility within this physical space, and adapt their lifestyle to different climatic conditions. A more drastic break occurs when the change requires learning a new foreign language, completely different from a mother tongue. But even a new community where people speak the same language may present itself with different idioms and dialects, forcing newcomers to learn regional expressions and words. In addition, local customs may require the skilful modification of the ways of interacting with fellow human beings and with the natural environments. Giving greetings, expressing inner dispositions, conducting conversations, formulating demands, organizing interior living spaces in relation to the outdoor conditions, tending a landscape, and many other activities call for the fine adjustment of one's actions.

Migration is doubtless an obvious way of moving away from a familiar world. It is also a complex social issue in our time; it is shaped and influenced by a great variety of values, cultural perceptions, motivations, and behaviours. It is impossible to list and analyze all the important aspects of the migratory flow of groups and individuals. Migration is usually defined as a permanent move from a home world to a host world. But there are also return, repeat, or circular migrations: the migrant, after a lengthy residence in the host world, returns to his or her home world or frequently moves between the two worlds. But, in all cases, there is a moment when migrants decide to break away, permanently or intermittently, from their habitual worlds.

There are, as we will see, various motives that prompt migrants to take this decisive step. Millions leave their home by necessity; they face unemployment, poverty, famine, change of climatic condition, or inter-ethnic tension. Persecution, war, political oppression, or other adverse social and economic conditions may also trigger their journeys. Some, as I have said, undertake this journey under perilous circumstances and risk never reaching their destinations. Others, more or less satisfied with their current living conditions, decide to seek better economic, educational, and cultural opportunities. The prospect of improvement in working or housing opportunities may incite people to leave behind their relatives, friends, colleagues, and neighbours. There are those who seek to reach a distant land out of curiosity: they want to taste an entirely different way of living, a new climate and working conditions, and another cultural and social context. Men and women may migrate following a chance meeting with someone or an unforeseen call or appointment or even after receiving mistaken information. How much control do these individuals exert over their actions? Is their migration the result of a conscious resolution? Are they merely forced by current life circumstances to undertake the move or are they deliberately weighing the possibilities of leaving or staying? Will the decision profoundly change their ways of life or will it merely bring a slight change of setting and of context for the adoption of a similar form of existence?

The act of breaking away, as I understand it, is the result of a conscious decision to move into a new world, which gradually gains complexity and extension. The person makes his or her decision freely, without being forced to act by a human order or an external material constraint. Although, for some, the motivation to move is quite complex and not always clear, there are also people who are fully aware of a single reason of their decision to leave. Anthropological studies define migration as "a process in which individuals consciously change their own situation in search of a more rewarding life."[9] In his classic study on migration from the traditional peasant village of Tzintzuntzan, Robert V. Kemper has shown that "migrants are not passive pawns moved by impersonal economic and political forces. They are active agents in shaping their own destinies and, in turn, that of contemporary Mexico."[10] Migrants will travel to a distant and foreign destination and start to live according to new values and social roles, adopting new worldviews and creating a new web of social relations. Or they will make a voluntary decision to leave their homes yet carry out their customary professions and remain attached to their old habits and familiar relations while in new and different social, political, and cultural contexts. In both situations, migrants establish a clear and radical distinction between their life before and their life after the move. They genuinely break free from a number of determining factors in their lives. Although musicians or culinary chefs may find themselves in a distant land in a similar working condition, the decision to join a new orchestra or to work in a new restaurant nonetheless entails a significant change in their professional outlook or in their ways of working. Conversely, they may hold onto their professional outlook, derived from the lengthy practice of their art, but be ready to adapt this outlook to a completely different working condition.

Conversion is another discernible change in convictions and attitudes which deeply affects the person's life orientation in the world, as well as his or her inner self. The emphasis here is not so much on mobility or externally perceptible behaviour, but on the adoption of new principles and values that shape the person's thinking, beliefs, actions, and relations and cause a significant transformation of his or her world. In his essay on the acts of repentance and rebirth, Max Scheler speaks of a change that begins with good resolutions, goes through a "profound

Artisan of My Destiny

alteration of outlook" (*Gesinnungsveränderung*), and ends up in a "genuine transformation of outlook" (*Gesinnungswandel*). The latter is a rebirth, affecting not merely the person's conduct, but his or her whole being. It is the person's "spiritual core," the ultimate root of all moral acts, that undergoes a profound transformation and finds ways to express itself in action.[11]

Scheler works out his theory of repentance and rebirth by first asking whether an evil deed performed in the past can be cancelled out and the corresponding guilt wiped away. Scheler makes a distinction between the objective time, wherein natural events take place, and the *human* time, in which the moments of a personal existence succeed each other. Objective time is a one-dimensional and one-directional continuum; it is like a river, which only flows forward and never allows a return to a previous point. In the stream of objective time, it is obvious, no alteration of the past is possible. But in every moment of our *human* time, the whole of life is present and we are able to make a return to the past. We are not able to change the physical effect of our action, but we are always in the position of altering its meaning and value. Repentance is the act by which we are able to carry out a reappraisal of our past moral deeds, attribute them new significance and worth, and build ourselves anew. At the same time, we are able to remove the guilt of our inner core and, by freeing ourselves from the "determining force of the past," to bring about a radical alteration of our life. Therefore, repentance is more than the knowledge and reappraisal of the past; it is, at the same time, a liberating act, by which we are able to ascend to a higher plane of existence.[12] Scheler's analysis of repentance can be placed in the context of his philosophy of the model person. The salutary repenting self-appraisal can be initiated by the example of a model who invites us to reassess our past and undertake a more complete effort at self-realization. The model puts us in the presence of the difference between our real self and an ideal self, and induces us, through the act of repentance, to rise to the height of the ideal self.[13]

We must distinguish, at the outset, between religious conversion and a conversion touching one's personal life. The former, in the words of Yves Congar, "is a change whose determining principle is our relation with God; it implies therefore an element of positive intellectual conviction regarding God, a certain representation of God and the economy of religion, and, most often, an adherence to the faith and life of a church."[14] The latter is a radical change of the principles and values guiding decisions and actions and affecting the meaning of human relations, of professional achievements, or of personal interests. It may be the consequence of a religious conversion or independent of it.

We may be converted to a political doctrine, a philosophical system, a spiritual movement, or a way of life regardless of any implication of this change on the presence or absence of religious faith. The new orientation may occur following an unexpected illumination or a careful lengthy reflection. A far-reaching and daring decision may be taken by relying on our sense of rightness and without calling upon a very elaborate rational or pragmatic consideration, while we listen to a speech or read a book for instance. Or we may experience a feeling of uneasiness and inadequacy that, after a period of subconscious incubation, perhaps while being ill or during a visit to a foreign destination, comes to the surface of clear consciousness. In this decisive moment, we say: "I no longer want to live this way anymore and here is the new direction for my life." It is a moment of jubilant illumination that makes us realize that we are not entirely defined by our past and that we are able to become the artisan of our own future destiny. And our sudden desire to start a new life finds its satisfaction when we overcome the resistance created by the prevalent values, habits, or life goals, becoming ready to follow the new and unifying principles which bring together all aspects of our existence.

Soldiers and political figures, in times of war or peace, may change their political or military allegiances and, with sincerity, take up the causes and aims of their former enemies. Previously despised or rejected ideals and values become swiftly – or after a long period of questioning and consideration of the alternatives – the very springs of their actions. These newly esteemed ideals make them conscious of what they truly believe and what is really worth living for. There are those who become enlightened by gradually getting to know a culture, chiefly its spiritual and artistic traditions, its religious practices, and its architecture or music. There are also individuals who come under the influence of fanatical leaders and give themselves over to destructive causes and violent acts. They also experience the delighted moment of breaking away from the previously held beliefs and of finding new meaning for their existence. The fanatic is guided by a central idea or doctrine that is tied to an individual or a community and whose realization is supposed to eliminate some kind of deficiency and to bring a desired state of perfection.

He or she entertains an emotional attachment to this idea to such an extent that any questioning or critical thinking about its truth-value is ruled out. The blinded fanatic has concern only for the uncritical postulation of opinions or half-truths. Fanaticism is also akin to bigotry insofar as both forms of mindset lack the sensibility and imagination to comprehend the negative consequences of their beliefs. The difference between the religious or moral conversion and the fanatical adherence to a particular cause lies in the former's orientation to the truth and the latter's blatant disregard of truth and of the monstrous consequences of such a lack of a respect for truth. Holding their beliefs beyond any reasonable doubt and any critical evaluation, fanatical persons are ready to employ verbal or physical violence in order to convert or attack all those who dare to face them with a critical spirit. By doing so, they refuse to trace a moral limit to their actions.

In the various experiences of conversion, whether religious or moral, there is an act of surrender to a power greater than oneself. In religious conversions, this power is a transcendent and invisible God who, with an irresistible force, calls for a reorientation of life. Many converts confirm with utmost certainty that God was indeed the decisive and direct cause of their religious turnabout. In moral conversions, an ideal, a tradition, or a set of moral or aesthetic values exerts a mighty influence on the person.

A conversion may occur in a time of personal crisis or after the resolution of a crisis. A change of milieu and the corresponding sense of rootlessness often provoke an experience of upheaval and destabilization. The passage from one stage of life to another creates profound disturbances and induces some people to revise the guiding principles of their everyday behaviour. Conversion, then, consists of turning away from a socially suggested or imposed behaviour and values and of returning to one's interiority, to what one considers an inner and authentic self. The return to one's inner self and deepest desires is a moment that constitutes the beginning of a new life, which reassesses past achievements and acquisitions and adopts an altogether different lifestyle. This change may represent an uprooting from a particular social milieu and an effort to move into a new spiritual or ethnic community. Or it may consist of giving up all earthly demands and attachments and of turning to ideas, ideals, and spiritual values. This is what, in the *Republic*, Plato famously called *periagoge* – the turning around of the entire soul.[15] The "conversion of the soul" may affect the social and tangible orientation of one's whole life: the way one lives, moves, works, and selects leisure activities in the world. There is another kind of modification in someone's beliefs and convictions, although this rupture is less perceptible in the person's outward behaviour. When people suddenly decide to replace one moral outlook on life with another one, as may happen after recovering from a severe illness, their daily routine of activities remains more or the less the same, but the self that carries them out undergoes a significant transformation. To be sure, the written and unwritten rules of a profession or a community continue to exert an influence on their activities. But the relative freedom from these rules and the different way of seeing the chief purposes of one's whole life create a new atmosphere around these persons, which is felt with more or less acuteness by all those who enter into a closer contact with them.

Migration and conversion offer a chance for taking a radical and definitive departure from a form of life; most migrants and converts make a decisive and irreversible break with their past. There are other forms of rupture that allow individuals to achieve a temporary liberation from their conditions. Art offers a productive and transient form of detachment from adverse circumstances. Artists, living under totalitarian regimes and facing harassment, imprisonment, or a "conspiracy of silence," have been able to keep their passionate attachment to their imaginative activity alive. There have been novelists who not only transcended their cruel or indifferent world, but also depicted characters whose vitality, intelligence, or humour prevailed over their tragic fates and who were able to choose freely the meaning of their inescapable defeat. Their art has also helped their readers to live with their own tragedies. Intelligent writers have also proposed fine surveys of how people react to changed living conditions in new and unfamiliar surroundings.

Often, literary or musical works do not reflect the prevailing conditions in which writers or composers live and create. It happens that when the artist's concrete environment is grim and even threatening, the created work conveys a sense of optimism and inner strength and expresses little about a particularly difficult situation. Afflicted by a terminal illness, Franz Schubert composed heavenly music, such as the String Quintet in C major, during the last weeks of his life. This masterpiece presents no intimation of his approaching death. His creative faculties provided Schubert the elevating power of sparing himself, for a while at least, from his hopeless fate. The composer László Lajtha – considered a danger to the totalitarian regime in Hungary and deprived of all his employments in 1949 after his return from England – wrote to one of his sons: "Just as in the town I have a room that is mine and only mine, so I have in my soul a secret room of my own. It has nothing to do with reality, yet it is more real." Although he was weighed down with concerns about a total lack of income and the anxiety about getting on with living, his fourth Symphony *The Spring*, written in 1951 at the height of the communist terror, is full of *joie de vivre*, charm, and bliss. Composing music was one of the available, freely chosen ways of creating a beneficial distance from his desolate and adverse reality and, at the same time, of reaching out to his audiences and re-engaging himself in the everyday lives of his fellow human beings.[16] One of his collaborators, collecting folk songs with him in distant villages, doubted that Lajtha would have written all of his remarkable symphonies, whose high artistic quality is now being discovered, had he stayed in England instead of returning to his drab and grey home country. This remark seems to apply to many creative artists, although it is always subject to dispute. One might contend that inadequate living conditions, indifference, or harsh criticism sooner or later silence a creative person. But I would suggest that adverse and even inhibiting external circumstances constitute, more often than not, a salutary spur to an inner retreat and a burst of creative activity.

Translations or transcriptions also offer to writers or composers a safe haven when they face neglect or belittling criticism to which they are inevitably exposed. To translate a novel or to transcribe a symphony is to enter into an intimate relation with the work of another author and to maintain an independence from the external world. Those who create or recreate may decide to build an inner world, in which they find and produce order and meaning. This world may constitute a compensation for the lack of social recognition or fulfilling intimate relationships.

Artists, whether they have to endure the pressure of dictatorial and repressive forces or merely take their distance from their predicament, are not the only persons who carry out a retreat to their own inner worlds. People finding themselves in prison or in a harsh labour camp or in a besieged city also need to ease the burden of their captivity through such a retreat. Some wrote diaries during the worst period of the siege of Leningrad in order to overcome their crushing sense of isolation. As one of the siege survivors Lidiia

Ginzburg tersely expressed it, "to write about the circle is to break the circle."[17] Incarceration, requiring inmates to adapt to a monotonous environment and debilitating routines, often brings about deleterious effects. For some, physical resilience is insufficient to withstand the pain and suffering inflicted by isolation, malnutrition, sensory deprivation, and brutal treatment. Alone in their cells, subjected to the worst torment and uncertainty, and deprived of stimuli from the outside world, some prisoners use various techniques to keep their mental faculties alert: they recite or translate poetry, go through musical scores, or build and visit imaginary houses and streets and meet men and women who live there.[18] In the midst of the enormously difficult conditions of a labour camp in northeastern China, Wu Ningkun, professor of English literature, found spiritual strength in Shakespeare's *Hamlet* whenever a blizzard forced him to stay in his cell. Cutting himself off from the back-breaking labour and the threats of corrective education, he was able to overcome his state of helplessness and survive, and, above all, make sense of his suffering and reconfirm his moral stance.[19]

Contrary to Jürgen Moltmann's views on the consequences of removing oneself from larger, pressing social concerns, the turn to an "inner space of freedom" does not necessarily entail the contempt or neglect of the external world or the adoption of an ironic attitude over against the cares and miseries of everyday life.[20] It does not have to lead to an attitude of indifference to the inhumanity of social conditions. True, moving into the suburbs and living in a comfortable and relatively isolated house may lead to the neglect of inner-city living areas. But the strong desire to keep one's distance from the external world and to build up an inner world fosters not only the steadfast determination to rely on one's individual conscience and judgment, but also the capacity to create artistic or scientific works of lasting value, thus enriching the lives of many people.

Freedom is understood here as both the act of distancing oneself from a specific condition and the act of serious commitment, through the realization of worthy tasks, to what one considers the essential good. Retreating into an "inner fortress" is not a form of liberation from desires, wishes, or fears or an effort to assert one's negative freedom by an act of giving up what one cannot have. It is not merely an attempt to find security and serenity by means of self-abnegation. It is an active and intense search for coherence and meaning, promoting contact with the inner depths of one's being and, ultimately, the desired self-understanding. It is an experience of inner freedom, allowing a person to confront – alone – essential ultimate questions and to turn away, for the time being, from inconsequential concerns.

MOTIVES AND CONDITIONS OF BREAKING AWAY

What is it that propels people to leave behind their customary surroundings for a new world? What provokes and sustains their decision to make a total break with their habitual ways of life, uprooting them from their community? What impels individuals to experience an intense moment of reorientation of their whole being towards a different religious belief or a new life-guiding principle?

There are many different incentives and appeals, which prompt people to turn away from the dictates of the past and envisage a new habit of life. It is impossible to mention all of them. One of the chief reasons for persons to make a radical departure from a milieu is the feeling of dissatisfaction. Their actual and unsatisfactory living conditions, educational opportunities, professional perspectives, or intimate relations may provoke their resolution to leave. These may be inadequate, commonplace, corrupt, or tense. They may be stifling due to the various limitations they impose and the uniformity of behaviour they elicit. Obviously, a lack of sufficient food, of adequate housing, or of available job opportunities within a geographical location provides a strong incentive to leave. Or this very same home environment may bring about a monotonous lifestyle, offering no new challenges and no room for initiatives and risk taking. Countless young men and women leave the small community of their birth in the quest for a better job and a more exciting existence. Or let us imagine that someone, day after day, carries out the same activity, around the same schedule and in the same social and working environment. In addition, the activity carried out in a farm or in a factory is too uniform and too mechanical to become the symbol of desires or initiatives. It lacks the thrill of novelty and adventure, which breaks the monotony of daily life and induces strong feelings and fresh, imaginative aspirations. The spirit of someone in such a monotonous situation is progressively crushed and thrown into despair by the absence of new future possibilities.

Kierkegaard brings to the reader the image of a concrete and evocative bodily experience when he analyzes the modalities of despair and its tangible causes. He defines personhood as the synthesis of future possibility and past necessity and compares its continued existence in time to the act of "breathing (*respiration*), which is an inhaling and exhaling." The act of breathing itself takes place in the present when, through actions, particular possibilities become actualities and actualities eventually turn into life's necessities. For the person who suffocates due to lack of air, the appropriate remedy to help him or her to revive is evidently a large amount of oxygen. And possibilities are for the whole person what oxygen is for the body's respiratory system.[21] With this telling image, Kierkegaard draws our attention to a fundamental anthropological truth about the temporality of human existence: deprived of all future possibilities, human life is unbearable. When individuals are no longer able to maintain or to form interpersonal contacts, or when they experience a complete isolation and estrangement from a milieu and die a little each day, the renunciation of a life stripped of all possibilities seems to be, almost in its ghastly inevitability, the ultimate possibility that is still available. But when the physical and psychological makeup of the person and the actual circumstances make it feasible, the desperate act of breaking away from a stifling world remains the last human attempt to recover the cluster of different possibilities. However vague they are, the feebly glimmering fresh possibilities may incite a sufficiently brave person to start a new life, which receives, in the moment of decision, direction and purpose.

A form of despair, boredom brings into focus a singular way of experiencing time. When we are bored, the progress of time seems to slow down or come to a standstill: the future no longer introduces new purposes and the past no longer brings forth accomplishments significant enough to propel us to a stimulating future. For this reason, time – with its barren and closed future, stale and inconsequential past, and dull present – becomes the object of our attention. But this remarked time is not experienced as a genuine becoming, filled with stimulating objectives to attain in a particular world; it appears as a tedious and pointless duration. We become painfully aware of this slowly progressing duration when, for some reason, the objects of our surroundings fail to beguile us and our desire to come across something inspiring is not satisfied. Accordingly, boredom depends to a certain extent on what we encounter in our environment. Travel is boring when the heartless monotony of a landscape or the unruffled sweep of a sea fails to evoke our interest and curiosity. The sameness of the land and the immobility of the water bring us back to a perception of time that we find empty and still. Equally, a particular world, made up of a home environment, a workplace, leisure activities, or social acquaintances, with their goals and challenges, can become colourless and gray. They lack the variety and promise of change and the excitement arising from captivating encounters and events. But, conversely, the thrilling or dull qualities of our personal and social worlds are gauged in relation to our moods and aptitudes. Our inner fullness and well-developed capacities give significance and life to the elements of our world and augur a future full of diversity and change. When, on the other hand, we are assailed with a feeling of apathy, of world-weariness, and sickened with boredom, everything around us looks dreary and dull as if the future were coming to meet us with empty hands.[22]

As a desolate surrounding throws us back to the awareness of the empty time, the unwanted contact with the naked time, in its turn, brings us back to our own disquieting emptiness. But the emptiness we feel in ourselves is also due, in part at least, to the barrenness of our imagination. In the state of boredom, we not only lose experiential contact with the world but also are unable to enrich this world with imaginative possibilities. We perceive it as an unchanging and unchangeable reality. For a while, nothing in this world seems to be subject to an impending transformation and nothing calls a new claim upon our thought and upon our imagination. We are unable to invest them with new significance, to conceive of them in a new light, and to see in them potential development, revision, and growth.

For Blaise Pascal, the experience of boredom (*ennui*) is not merely an intermittent experience of human life. It is chiefly one of its constitutive elements: "*Condition de l'homme: inconstance, ennui, inquiétude.*"[23] A correlate of boredom is the restless desire for change, the search for exciting experiences. Although the desire is often present in all human beings, the satisfaction it finds is different in each individual life. Pascal tells us that boredom inevitably assails us as soon as we are alone, completely at rest, sitting quietly in a room, deprived of stimulating impressions and activities. As we find ourselves in this state of enforced solitude, cut off from the rest of the world, we are necessarily called to think about ourselves. This singular experience of self-encounter forces us to become aware of our fundamental emptiness and nothingness and, in consequence, to feel, in the depth of our heart, *ennui*, sadness, and despair.[24] We do not apprehend our *néant* and our *vide* directly but in the guise of our mortal condition, our potential death. We respond to our dreadful isolation and to our spiritless despondency by initiating some kind of distracting activity, which diverts us from the unwelcome glimpse at our mortality.

What interests us in Pascal's meditations are the observations regarding the corollary of our unhappy and restless condition, or the escape from an "insufferable sadness," which may take different forms: "play, and the society of women, war, and high posts."[25] We may add to these occupations and concerns the great variety of complex distracting activities, which are proposed today by the thriving entertainment and tourist industry. Millions turn to them with the sole objective of escaping their lives, thoughts, preoccupations, and the aching sensation of despair. They are ready to undertake all sorts of dangerous, risky, and boisterous activities in order to take a mental holiday from their everyday lives and avoid the feeling of boredom.

Pascal's remarks are accurate if we consider some of our spontaneous and elementary playful activities. In moments of boredom, as we are no longer involved in the effort to achieve something, elementary playful activities arise spontaneously. We are eager to play with papers, pencils, coins, keys, and many other objects in order to simply "kill time," allay our boredom, and turn our attention away from ourselves. Since these immediately accessible objects trigger our imagination and prompt us to see in them a sort of inviting animation and a cluster of dynamic possibilities, we enter with them into a relation of reciprocity made up of initiative and adaptation. We play with them as much as they play with us. There are more exacting forms of play, consisting of turning to the attractive possibilities generated by our body when it reaches a certain height, depth, or speed. The so-called extreme sports induce in us dizzying vertigo, intoxication, and even the voluptuous panic of a momentary loss of all control over our lives. Masquerades, roller coasters, and fast-spinning carousels help us establish a new kind of relation to things and their surroundings; they offer a temporary detachment from our natural and social worlds and thus bring a salutary relief from boredom.

It seems to me worthwhile to note, however, that not every moment of boredom makes us bemoan the fact that we must die, and not every subsequent attempt at filling time with *divertissement* is an escape from the feelings of emptiness and indifference. Just gazing calmly and unhurriedly out of the window, in order to let the empty time – minutes and even hours – pass peacefully, without any thought in our mind, does not necessarily induce a feeling of despair. And there are many distracting and seemingly futile activities with which we fill our idle moments, which, instead of bringing to our daily life a deceptive joy by averting our thoughts from our unhappy condition, simply contribute happily to our healthy and creative living. To be sure, the acts of conversation, of wine drinking in good company, or of cinema are all necessary and valuable diversions from the drab routine of our everyday lives. As John Berger has shown in a fine essay, a film transports us into an unknown world; it is indeed a form of travelling, it is about leaving.[26] We need occupations that offer complete absorption into an elevating activity and a release from all of the tedious repetition and uniformity imposed by our workplace or home. An artistic activity may create a less transitory and more satisfying detachment from life-quenching and mindless work habits. As we will see, active music-making, alone or in an ensemble, gives us occasion to find playfulness and refreshment in an exhilarating pastime; it involves our intellectual, emotional, and bodily powers. To break free from the monotonous running of the hours and days, art, literature, and music should be considered just as essential as sleep or food or water. What we seek in a novel, a poem, or a sonata is the "fertilization of our soul" (Whitehead) and not necessarily a soothing balm for our sadness about our mortality. True, beyond all of these carefree and fulfilling moments, conversion and other decisive steps open up possibilities whose larger array and diversity, as well as ongoing realization, change the time more substantially as we live it. But the momentary holidays that we take from the dull succession of events and obligations alter no less happily the continuity of our temporal experience.

Pascal was mistaken to affirm that the deep-seated human yearning for consistency, quietness, and rest is muddled and perturbed inside us by a "secret instinct" that craves amusement and inconsistency of thought and of action. Obviously, life is lived and experienced in different ways at different times. Surely, to avert a weekend of boredom, we sometimes need an element of excitement and of uncertainty. But all the periods of rest, of quiet time alone, without a device or a book, that we consciously grant and enjoy are just as necessary for our well-being as are strenuous work and thrilling leisure activities. They are valued for their own sake and, once attained, they do not have to become "insufferable" and be urgently replaced by restless occupations. On the contrary, an existence marked by restlessness, constant unpredictability, and abiding uncertainty – what Friedrich Nietzsche called "a life that would demand perpetual improvisation" – could induce the same acute feeling of dissatisfaction as does the senseless feeling of boredom. The unprejudiced observer finds that the more everyday life-situations seem a series of whirligigs, the greater is the need for routine, habitual, and even tedious practices. The aspiration for constancy and sameness may appear in the lives of those who, for years, have engaged in some forms of criminal behaviour and who have turned to alcohol or drugs in order to find a temporary escape from an erratic lifestyle. They seek some kind of relief, as they inextricably become victims of their own actions. The desire for some kind of stability does not come merely from the awareness of perilous and unpredictable living conditions, but from the comparison between identities formed by drug use or criminal behaviour and identities created by the avoidance of these activities. Here one sees the disadvantages of a life of crime (the imminent dangers of arrest, loss of a permanent home, family breakdown, deteriorating health, or violent death) and envisages the advantages of a conventional life (strong and lasting family relationships, steady job, reassuring routine, healthy lifestyle). Doing something useful and long lasting in a workplace quickens the sense of urgency for a permanent change. The awareness of the discrepancy between actual and possible future identities, as well as between the actual and possible worlds corresponding to these identities, generates the motivation for desistance. The discontent is gradually eliminated by the realization of a conventional self and the concrete avoidance of a criminal self. The change in identity is further motivated by the transformation of the network of social relations and the formation of new sub-worlds.[27]

I have already mentioned that many converts experience a divine initiative and respond to it with an act of faith. Another motive for conversion, a motive greater than oneself, is the strong appeal of a religious community and the possibility of a spiritual renewal and the warm acceptance it offers. A chance encounter with an adherent of a faith or a theological treatise may also bring someone into a devout community and into an ensuing religious commitment. But the adhesion to a welcoming community also occurs in the absence of religious faith. To consider a famous example, Paul Gauguin's turn to painting and his travel to Tahiti were prompted by his insecurity, his isolation, and his subsequent idolization of a new society, which, in his eyes, provided him with freedom, self-expression, and stability. The question of whether the expected fulfilment of the receiving community was real or imagined did not affect his desire to abandon his stifling bourgeois lifestyle and milieu. The attraction of the exotic in Tahiti was nonetheless powerful enough to make him leave France and, to a certain extent, the Impressionist painting style.[28]

People join all sorts of religious, scholarly, artistic, or political communities, and open or secret societies. The appeal of these communities can be just as strong as the call felt by Gauguin to leave everything behind in France. The question arising from such a devoted adhesion to smaller or larger human communities is whether the regulations and conventions in place leave enough independence of thought and action to the newcomer and whether the objectives entertained and propagated by the members are morally justifiable. Not infrequent is the realization that the true beliefs, values, and goals of a community are not fully grasped in the moment of taking the radical step.

The sheer unwillingness to continue living any longer under the prevailing social, economic, and political conditions is strong enough motivation for many prominent and ordinary citizens to leave their homes in search of new living environments. Instead of finding peace, joy, and inspiration in an inner world, or comfort and meaning in a community, they may leave their physical home world without having a clue about where they are heading. Their resolute refusal to settle for their existing living conditions is the only motivating factor for breaking free. Their decisive act is sustained by their keen sense of coherence between a pattern of life and a steadfast attachment to a self-determining freedom. To be sure, before making their decision, they live and act like everyone else, according to the prevailing norms, roles, and "worldview" of their social environment. These provide them with guidance and relative security while they take care of tasks and pay attention to the details of their everyday needs. At the same time, however, they are able to envision their own future possibilities and, independently of the necessities and habits of life suggested or imposed by a social and economic context, decide in favour of one of them. They take a critical and evaluative distance from their seemingly unchangeable ways of life and venture out into what is, for them, a still uncharted world.

In a somewhat similar spirit, opposition or even revolt against a parental figure may prompt someone to question his or her "life as usual" and to leave home. But here the future is more clearly defined and seen. Children would like to explore what their fathers or mothers missed in their lives or did not dare to pursue – perhaps a less lucrative but more rewarding path in the arts or sciences or a life of passionate dedication to an uncommon purpose in a distant land. William Barrett claims, I think quite rightly, that there is invariably a price to be paid for not following an inherited or transmitted course of life:

> Some children repeat the lives of their parents, even down to omitting all those things the parents themselves avoided. So the continuity and stability of the race are assured. Other children, and they are fewer, seem driven to search out and experience the unlived life of their parents. These are voyages of discovery that broaden the mind and enrich the spirit of the race. But even when successful – and most of them are not – they are always paid for in suffering, as if the children must make atonement for the sins of the parents, and perhaps most of all for their sins of omission.[29]

By following their own routes, which may take them into highly competitive and adversarial milieus or into strange and unreceptive cultures, these children may become consumed by loneliness, misunderstanding, and self-doubt. In return, however, they may be able to foster their capacity for invention and, by undertaking some creative activity, to find compensation for their lack of satisfying integration into their new environment.

In this context, the theme of the unhappy voyages of children's discovery leads me to touch briefly on one of the central aims of education. It is the human ability to imagine new ways of living that education – carried out chiefly at home, outside the formal school setting, under the principles of freedom, discipline, and adventure – should develop and nurture. This education should grant children ample leisure time so that they can imagine a different world and all the avenues this world may open up to them. They need to pursue their learning in a quiet environment where they can gaze into space, daydream about their current and future lives, conceive of imaginary worlds, and, by doing this, develop their own inner lives. As the result, they will eventually have the courage and strength to rise above their current circumstances and to make a resolution to change their life paths. Unfortunately, today, due to a lack of sufficient leisure time, many youth are distracted from such self-contact. Bruno Bettelheim is surely right to lament the hectic and demanding conditions children encounter at home and in their schools. They are deprived of those long hours of leisure, which allow them to toy with thoughts and images and thus to develop their creative faculties. As Bettelheim explains, "The biographies of creative people of the past are full of accounts of long hours spent sitting by a river as teenagers, thinking their own thoughts, roaming through the woods with their faithful dogs, or dreaming their own dreams. But who today has the leisure and the opportunities for this?"[30] I suspect that many children's passivity and indifference come from their inability to develop, quietly and alone and without the addictive use of communication devices, a rich inner life. What they need, above all, is a peaceful environment, where silent, unhurried introversion and the exercise of creative idleness can be taken up. Likewise, young men and women attending institutions of higher learning should be encouraged to learn to recognize those moments when should they remain alone with their own thoughts and feelings and when they should liberate themselves from the grooves and binding forces of particular traditions. I don't mean rejecting a tradition; I mean seeing it from a distance and, by doing so, cultivating the free and bold formulation of possibilities and the passionate realization of one of them.

Following the views of Eric Hoffer, we may contend that discontent alone with respect to existing social and cultural conditions or family traditions does not create a desire for change. People will more naturally oppose themselves to their surrounding gravitational forces if they possess or develop a kind of inner power and if this power succeeds in sustaining their faith in the future.[31] In my view, in many cases, this power comes from their *passion* – a passion for a profession, an art, a social cause, or a new sort of life.

Passion reveals the orientation and meaning of our destiny. Thanks to our passion, we can free ourselves from dispersing occupations, concentrate ourselves on the attainment of a single purpose, and bring into a coherent whole all of the potentialities of our being. Passion is a capacity and a disposition to act according to an inner impulse, which may be independent of external approval. In the words of Louis Lavelle, "It is perfect receptivity and consent to the inner impulse, and total imperviousness to any voice coming from without which would seduce it out of its course."[32] It allows us to persevere and concentrate, with all of our abilities, on the attainment of specific goals. If we are passionately engaged in an activity, we are able to endure hardships and privations to finish the task that we had set for ourselves. Passion manifests itself in a realistic appreciation of tasks, in a self-forgetful, energetic, and even subordinate devotion to a unique and dominant purpose. It is "a heightened form of devotion," according to Helmuth Plessner.[33] To be sure, passion limits freedom, bringing with it the constraint of a higher and almost overpowering intent to attain objectives. The intense "suffering of passion" (*das Leiden der Leidenschaft*) entails some powerlessness, occasionally genuine hardship.[34] Yet, due to its appeal, the object of passion offers, at the same time, the "joy of fascination" and the promise of future achievement.[35] Paradoxically, passion brings a certain obligation of restraint in our quest for self-realization, but it also offers fulfilment through steadfast dedication to a purpose.

Receptivity, attention, focus, contentment, and respect are all integral elements of passion. The source of contentment and respect is not merely our purpose and our achievement with regard to this purpose, but also, and above all, the inner impulse itself, the affective disposition that the person feels within. There is a difference between the pianist's attachment to the art of music and the gambler's addiction to the roulette table. The latter lacks the awareness of satisfaction and fulfilment in presence of the feeling that motivates and fuels his or her actions. Although true passion tends to be exclusive and isolating, its single-mindedness comes from the intensity and quality of the person's affective resonance with an object or an action. While being seized and dominated by an inner impulse, a person filled with passion enjoys assurance and comfort in his or her devotion to a science, an art, a social cause, or an athletic activity. In Lavelle's words, "Far from rending our soul and abandoning it to all the evils coming from distress and impotence, passion brings us, on the contrary, inner certitude, equilibrium, tranquillity, and peace."[36]

There are persons who, by placing excessive emphasis upon security and prudence, avoid taking risks and the adventures that come with risks. They "remain for ever spectators on the side-line, for ever holding back and refusing to join the game."[37] Diffident, conventional, and self-protective, they often close the door to every sort of change and defend their conventional attitudes by self-righteously attacking the assertiveness and blindness of passion. Yet passion is blind and reckless only in the lives of those who are not accustomed to act in accordance with its suggestions. They have neither the strength nor the ardour to follow a requirement of creation or a call for a thorough transformation of their lives. Entering into the game means, in this context, facing risks of an all-absorbing commitment through which one works out a particular destiny and accepts the fact that the outcome of one's decision may be unknown or partially known. We come here to another aspect of passion: the ability to put an end to hesitation, doubt, cautious deliberation, and the tendency to try to predict and control the outcome of an action. Because of their confidence in their inner strength, passionate people are able to face a provisional and uncertain future and to act in accordance with the call of the present. The question they raise is not how they will safely direct the course of their lives in ever-changing future worlds, but how they will leave behind the routines of a tradition and a culture and how they will know when to take their decisive action.

In a religious conversion, as we have seen, the transformation or experience of new birth is provoked by a divine initiative. An important element of this abrupt change is the adoption of an attitude of surrender: God cannot act upon the soul in the absence of a complete receptivity. There are also some external factors that facilitate the adoption of the right frame of mind and an openness towards the divine influence. Grief, illness, or isolation is often necessary for the reassessment of one's life and the readiness for the person to adopt a new belief. But, as Victor Monod has shown in his excellent and long-forgotten study, travel and uprooting frequently constitute the determining catalysts of a religious conversion.[38] It is during a journey abroad, while finding oneself in a state of complete liberation from roots and traditions, that the conversions of a number of famous people occurred, including those of Saul, Augustine, Luther, John Wesley, and others. This kind of incentive is also strongly felt outside the religious sphere. Away from home, some individuals are more inclined to turn their backs on the obsolete requirements of social conformity, long-held beliefs, and binding habits. A journey minimizes the "weight of the past" and fosters a return to the inner self. It is an interesting fact that the absorbing interest in extraneous realities produces, at the same time, a discovery of a deeper life within. As we will see in a later chapter, the perception of foreign realities may set in motion the questioning self-awareness and the subsequent revision of one's ingrained points of view. Those who travel feel rejuvenated – free to remake their personalities and to adopt new values – as well as strong and courageous enough to overcome fear and doubt with regard to an unfathomable future. Uprooted and disengaged, they admit that their personality is not yet settled and complete and they remain receptive to a divine intervention or to the purely secular suggestion of starting a new form of existence.[39]

It is not unusual to see someone rising above his or her current living condition following a chance encounter or an unforeseen event. Odo Marquard is perhaps right in saying that, as we make our way through life, we create our own paths more through accidents than decisions.[40] All those who, while making a journey or studying abroad, have received an unintended incentive to change their professional career path or spiritual allegiance would probably share his views. The historian Arnold Toynbee has confirmed the prevalence of random encounters in one's life: "When one contemplates in old age the chain of accidents that has decided one's fate, one is disconcerted."[41] The writer, art historian, and sinologist Simon Leys expressed the same opinion when he was asked why he moved to Australia: "I don't know if it is a recurring feature of my personal existence or a more general and universal phenomenon – but it seems that the most decisive turns of life, the most important encounters, the most felicitous initiatives occur by accident."[42] Many people quit their comfortable but unremarkable situation not on the basis of their desire to fulfil a well-conceived plan, but thanks to an encouraging word or a benevolent call to action that unexpectedly befalls on them in a particular moment. There were Hungarians who, in 1956, left their country after the crushing of the insurrection merely because there were seats available on one of trucks heading towards the West. They overcame their momentary fear and, without any previously formulated goal or any certitude about their future, made what appeared to them, in an unexpected situation, the appropriate decision.

The human responses to what Odo Marquard calls "arbitrarily accidentals" are neither impulsive nor instinctive. They are spontaneous acts and, as such, may include some of those characteristics that we find in a creative process: inspiration, sudden springing up of ideas, and promptitude. There are situations where we tend to neglect arguments, justifications, or even hesitations, and, drawing on the dynamism of life within us, we act spontaneously and unexpectedly. Our actions provide a direct and personal, though not infallible, answer to the opportunity arising in an actual situation.

The situation itself, an accidental event or a chance encounter, leads us, sometimes much to our surprise, to overstep a dilemma, which, at least for a while, did not seem amenable to happy resolution.

FAILING TO MAKE A RESOLUTION
FOR A NEW BEGINNING

In his book entitled *Persons*, Robert Spaemann speaks of those acts, through which we take the whole of our lives into our hands and, by doing so, make our lives truly our own. We enter into the sphere of self-realization as persons. These acts create a caesura in the continuum of our lives and, when they bring about a change of direction in the course of life or a conversion (*Umkehr*), they present the characteristics of a beginning, a fresh start. According to Spaemann, "Conversion implies abiding by the moral decision one has made, perpetuating the new beginning, which continues to be 'new' in relation to the stream of nature."[43]

In one of his *Upbuilding Discourses* dealing with the nature of resolution, Søren Kierkegaard advances similar views on the meaning of such a decision and the subsequent change introduced into the continuum of a human life. It is through a resolution that individuals come to a radical departure from a way of life and engage in a new form of existence, in which they are joined with the eternal in devotion and in trust. "Resolution is a waking up to the eternal," says Kierkegaard, and it "brings the eternal into time for [the individual], jars him out of the drowsiness of uniformity, breaks the spell of habit, cuts off the tedious bickering of troublesome thoughts, and pronounces a benediction upon even the weakest beginning, when it is indeed a beginning."[44] Resolution is not made in exceptional situations, but in the circumstances of everyday life: one no longer wants to be "trapped in everydayness and habit."[45] Everydayness is understood here as an existence that lapses into a thoughtless routine and lacks deeper and transforming impressions and experiences. Resolution is not merely a punctual act, but the continuous renewal of the initial act. Therefore, it is deceptive to say that everything is decided on the day of resolution. Kierkegaard contrasts a good beginning with the act of coming into stride at the beginning. It is not the image of a bold dive into the sea that offers a proper illustration of resolution, but the act of walking: the steps are weak, carried out with vacillating gait, and at times go backwards instead of forwards.[46] Resolution calls for constant effort and wholehearted, unambiguous dedication to the chosen path; it is not merely a single heroic leap, which is followed by the lukewarm acceptance of the consequences of one's action. The constancy of resolution gives continuity and coherence to all aspects of life, both to one's most important and central endeavours and to various less significant concerns. As Kierkegaard puts it, "Resolution has a winsome faculty of concerning itself with little things, so that one neither disregards them nor is lost in them; so that life goes forward in the resolution, strengthened, refreshed, and invigorated by the resolution."[47]

In this subtle analysis, applicable to both religious renewal and the human effort of transformation, Kierkegaard highlights one of the factors that prevent individuals from making a resolution and breaking free from their circumstances. Resolution is undertaken in the face of a task (moving to a distant land) and by virtue of a capability or talent (being able to leave familiar surroundings and to adjust oneself to the requirements of the new milieu). If the capability is exceptional and the task seems too easy, individuals never reach the point of truly acting. They first say that the task is not worthy of serious consideration. They also anticipate that the task may turn out to be much more demanding than it appears at first sight. By not acting, they are saved from admitting their errors and weaknesses. Or, conversely, if their capabilities are slight, they may say that it is not worth thinking about such far-off tasks and facing the humiliating consequences of failure. Pride motivates both attitudes: an individual is too proud to consider his or her possible action in relation to his or her capability. But, as Kierkegaard aptly points out, pride depends on a powerful feeling: cowardice. Cowards do not want to take on an easy task that may become difficult or to admit their insufficient means to tackle a demanding task. They fear that a trifling task may turn out to be enormous or that their weak initial disposition will not be enough to renew the commitment necessary for a resolution. They are concerned no less with the anticipated change in the unfolding task than with the lack of change in their own potential development. They distrust both their own abilities and the nature of the task requiring a resolution.

Cowardice rarely appears in its original expression. Endowed with a fine psychological sensitivity, Kierkegaard compares it to a vapour of stagnant water that buries itself deep in the soul, from which "deceptive phantoms rise."[48] It is the most flexible, the most adaptable, even the most pleasant of all the feelings. It may even take the appearance of power, love, discipline, and self-control. It envisages important and exceptional deeds, even the continued striving towards far-off goals.

A great ally of cowardice is the passage of time. Neither cowardice nor time wants to hurry. Time will not say "now is the moment to act"; it does not single out a specific day or, for that matter, any day. Cowardice wants to delay everything, and time helps since it just flows and does not stop for a decision to be made. The running away from decisive action can take a variety of forms: being too busy or staring constantly into the clouds or considering many high and unattainable goals.

Obviously, resolution is strengthened by the opposite of proud cowardice: the humble and silent courage in the face of weaknesses and uncertainties. But the basic attitude of trust also fortifies the resolution of breaking away from common circumstances. Resolute individuals place their trust in what we earlier called a power greater than oneself, whether it is a transcendent power or not; this power offers a final meaning to their lives. Trustful and passionate devotion to an ultimate principle helps them not only surmount difficulties, but also deal with failures. Facing hardship, indifference, or discrimination in the new world constitutes a possible outcome of the resolution. But without the risk of failure, life may easily become stale and the profound satisfaction and peace of mind coming from having risen above everyday self-preservation to the level of genuine self-realization is absent. Many courageously achieve a breaking away from their circumstances and fail to find what they hoped for: love, friendship, a fulfilling occupation, wealth, or recognition. But, if they are not completely crushed by adversity or by their own irretrievable bitterness, they can say with serenity: *At least I tried!*

3

Moments of Real Learning

To become fully educated, the whole person should, at least once, come under the influence of an all-round and genuine, free and noble-minded model.

Max Scheler

We meet countless people, through an intricate range of contacts and relationships, in our lives. The characteristics of these experiences range from intense intimacy to a complete impersonal detachment. Some last for just a few fleeting seconds, some are repeated and endure for many years – even for a lifetime. Some happen every day and some take place at irregular intervals, without any predictable rhythm. Some are desired and expected and some happen by chance, without any warning. Some entail a bodily presence, a face-to-face conversation, and some are formed at a distance in space and time, by means of letters, books, or technological devices. We bring into this experience – of finding ourselves in the presence of another person – the role that we assume within a social and cultural context and the behaviour that we consider appropriate. Our interests, objectives, cultures, and moods shape the ways that we create, leave, and recreate this role throughout our lives.

There are meetings in the public sphere that, immediately or after a lapse of time, we relegate into oblivion, and there are others that we value either by keeping them in our memories or seeking to repeat them. Meeting eminent public figures face to face leaves us with a lasting impression. We like to tell others that we were able to exchange a few words with Nelson Mandela or a member of the British Royalty, to shake the hand of a well-known musician or a celebrated actor. As we grow older, our repeated encounters with our teachers or our older colleagues may be cherished because, with time, we may come to realize what these wise persons added to our existence: they made us more passionate, more skilful, and more cultured. We consider their influence pivotal and enduring. They are men and women who strongly affect the way we think, act, feel, and relate to our fellow human beings; we consider them our models.[1]

Here is an example of such an intense and lasting attachment to a uniquely gifted person. In his magisterial biography of Franz Liszt, Alan Walker recounts that "whenever Liszt was asked as a boy what he wanted to be when he grew up, he pointed to the wall where a portrait of Beethoven was hanging. 'Ein solcher,' he used to reply. 'Like him.'"[2] Franz Liszt's high regard for Beethoven shaped, to some extent, many of his interests and activities: it found concrete expression in his recitals, his teaching activities, his editorial work on the master's piano sonatas, his conducting of the orchestral works, his charity recitals in aid of the erection of a monument in Bonn, and, most importantly perhaps, his piano transcriptions of the nine symphonies. Beethoven remained for Liszt a lifelong model to be admired and followed in many of his musical endeavours.

Biographies reveal the degree of encouragement and inspiration artists, writers, or political figures received from eminent teachers or mentors. Many other less famous persons would also be able to identify real or fictional characters whose personality and advice have become, for them, an incentive to choose a particular life path. Models do not have to be people with outstanding abilities and achievements. The source of their magnetic influence is sometimes recognized only in retrospect. They nevertheless energize and inspire those who come into contact with them; they deeply affect their protégés' thoughts, beliefs, and life-determining decisions; without their express intent or awareness, they infuse values and principles, and even forms of behaviour, into other people's lives.

WHO IS A MODEL?

A model is a man or woman who, due to his or her perceived qualities, values, and achievements, exerts a profound and transformative influence on another person. A profession, a lifelong interest, or a form of existence may be adopted following contact with a model. A person's identity, social role, and way of life are strongly affected under the influence of a model. The model's impact can become effective in various ways: it may lead to a sudden change or to a gradual metamorphosis of one's actions and thinking. It may offer both guidance and a framework for making the right decision. It may help to specify the person's moral outlook and insight into what is good and what is evil and what it means to live a good life.

When we encounter and follow a model, we do it with our whole beings; our ways of thinking, feeling, and acting are influenced and formed in harmony with the chosen model. To follow means developing in us the traits and qualities of the person we take as a model. If we are musicians, we tend to play an instrument in our model's manner of performing; if we are novelists or poets or playwrights, we cherish the model's style and choice of themes; if we are an athlete, we wish to run, swim, or skate as well and as fast as our model.

Still relevant today, Max Scheler's phenomenological description of the model and his reflection on the functions of various models was prompted by his moral philosophy.[3] One of the greatest moral philosophers and an original phenomenologist of modern times, Scheler describes the object of his interest by comparing it to another object and paying special attention to the differences between the two phenomena. This approach allows him to highlight the uniqueness of the specific object and grasp its finer and less conspicuous elements. He first tells us that our models are not constituted in an arbitrary fashion; they are rooted in a system of hierarchical values and determined by this absolute and eternally valid realm of values. Models make manifest a discernible value or a selective set of values; they are the incarnation of values in a specific historical epoch and a particular social environment. It is not the abstract norms or the universally accepted moral principles of obligation that fashion, in a decisive manner, someone's behaviour. Although tied to values, norms and rules are too impersonal, too disembodied, and too remote from concrete situations and the requirements of these situations and thus fail to inspire people to actualize them. The effective realization of a good action calls for repeated contacts with a good example exhibiting the values in question. To become realized in living persons and concrete deeds, the objective value of justice and the derivative norm of treating communities or persons with equity require the contact with concrete models. According to Scheler, "Nothing on earth allows a person to become good so originally and immediately and necessarily as the evidential and adequate intuition of a good person *in* his goodness."[4] Models help us to understand and concretely exhibit the possible transformative power of norms and values. The value of health and the corresponding norm of moderation are widely known, but we still fail to translate this knowledge into concrete action by not exceeding the appropriate amount of eating and drinking. Our physician's advice about leading a healthy lifestyle will probably make us act sooner if we come into contact with a person who, by his or her example, encourages us to take up regular walking or swimming, and shows us how we should eat and drink with moderation. The same can be said about moral values: seeing someone displaying charity towards a stranger creates a stronger binding effect than hearing someone merely upholding this value in words.[5]

There is, in every child, a predisposition to know the difference between good and bad, just and unjust, fair and unfair. It is easy to see this predisposition in the ways children play: they most often distribute the roles with fairness and imagination and establish rules by relying on their natural sense of what is good and proper. But this natural human inclination for fairness and harmonious collaboration develops and becomes effective beyond the realm of play only if children are able to see the embodiment of values in things and in actions, and if they learn to make a conscious distinction between good and evil, important and trivial, beautiful and ugly. Then, they gradually develop an organ for the perception of objective qualities. "But this happens," writes Robert Spaemann, "in the first place through the encounter with beauty, through involvement with the beautiful, and through learning to do whatever one does in a beautiful manner."[6] The "beautiful manner" appears to them, above all, in the behaviour of their parents and teachers, those persons who are immediately present in their lives. If children repeatedly find themselves in situations where cheating, lying, and using force are ways of achieving an objective, their delicate sense of goodness, justice, and fairness will be distorted. Children listen to verbally expressed values and norms, but they come to internalize these values and norms only if they become manifest in the actions of their models, chiefly their parents and teachers.[7]

Scheler brings out the basic characteristics of a model (*Vorbild*) by comparing them to those of a leader (*Führer*). Leaders are conscious of their roles and their ability to affect the lives of others. Models do not have that self-awareness and do not always desire to wield an influence. To guide and motivate individuals, a leader must be real and accessible. To touch the lives of men and women, a model does not need to be physically present; a historical figure, Socrates for instance, who lived in the distant past, or a fictional character such as Duchess Sanseverina may become a model. Leaders are indispensable and constituent elements of all sorts of human community (family, clan, tribe, gang, nation, etc.) having a more or less stable structure. They do not necessarily display a moral excellence; they can be wise guides or unscrupulous criminals. Unless they are viewed as negative figures, suggesting to us that we do the opposite of what they say and do, models are held in esteem and followed because they embody desirable levels of excellence and express, in their words and deeds, positive values and qualities. "Leaders demand actions, achievements, conducts. Models are concerned with our being, with the character of our soul," Scheler asserts.[8] The influence of a model extends beyond our capacity for action; it pervades our entire existence, it provokes the entire transformation of our habits and our mentalities. In contrast, "To lead means acting, pointing ways, initiating good or bad directions of life."[9] It also means creating respect, distance, and even fear. We keep our distance from our leaders, but we seek the company of our models. Models neither issue explicit commands nor expect obedient attachment to their values. They discreetly extend an invitation to make a good use of our abilities and, if they spur us into action, to set concrete objectives in harmony with a certain life plan. Our whole being is directed towards their values and achievements and this steadfast orientation leaves its mark on our actions and feelings. Leaders do not affect our adoption of models; but our models, along with other considerations and factors, determine our choice of leaders.

What is it that brings about this "growth of the being of the person and growth of the moral tenor according to the traits of the model, growth encompassed by an attitude of devotion to the exemplary model?"[10] We evaluate and measure, secretly or openly, the worth of our plans and decisions according to what we see in our models, those we have freely preferred and would like to emulate. This act of appraisal does not merely affect our thinking and deciding. Like children who acquire, consciously or unconsciously, both the mentality and behaviour of their parents, we tend to fashion the attitudes and actions of our body according to the stirring contacts we have with our models.

ENCOUNTERING A MODEL

We encounter our models in an array of ways: at home, in classrooms, during a concert or a lecture, while being engaged in a conversation, carrying out physical works, or travelling abroad. We may also come upon them while reading a novel, a biography, or a historical account.

These encounters are unforgettable moments: whether the model is a distant historical figure or someone we come face to face with, we detect, in this person, qualities powerful enough to exert influence on our subsequent interests and preferences as well as the way we create our world, accomplish our tasks in this world, and indeed shape our whole destiny. The qualities that we perceive may stand in relation to some socially censured attitudes or professionally discouraged behaviour. We may, then, look at both the virtues and flaws with selective eyes; we ignore the latter and focus only on the former. In my high school years in Budapest, if I may draw from a personal experience, it was my good fortune to come under the inspiring influence of a music teacher, József G. Horváth. In order to support his large family, he had two full-time jobs and three part-time occupations: he taught in two schools, gave private piano lessons, conducted a choir of teachers, and, two or three times a week, he played the piano in a bar until two o'clock in the morning. At that time, I was unaware of his multiple work obligations. Sometimes he arrived to the early morning class dead tired. He then told us: "Children, be quiet, I have to think." He put down his head on the desk and slept for twenty minutes or more. We respected his wish and remained silent. (If the act of *awakening* students' interest or talent is central to teaching, a teacher sound asleep seemed to be a comical figure.) But when he woke up and taught us *solfeggio* and singing, he proved to be a phenomenal teacher. Never again have I seen so much energy, passion, knowledge, and pedagogical skill united in one person. No one could remain indifferent to his powerful educational and artistic abilities; he inspired hundreds of students to love and play music and a few talented ones to become professional musicians. We learned how to read musical scores, how to sing in tune with clear articulation – in unison, in parts, and in canon – and how to recognize and appreciate the beauty of a folk song, of a Bach choral, or a motet by Orlande de Lassus. He became a model for me and, much later, as I decided to work in the field of education and tried to perfect my pedagogical abilities, I realized, with fond gratitude, the debt I owed to him.

Why are we inclined to take a teacher or an athlete and, later in life, perhaps a writer or a scientist as our model? Why are we ready to disregard their weaknesses and consider only their merits? We do not choose them randomly even though the significant encounter with them can happen by chance. According to Nicolai Hartmann, a model corresponds to some specific requirements or standards that we already possess: "The satisfaction which the model gives ... consists in its agreement with standards which we consciously or unconsciously apply."[11] We recognize a physical or intellectual excellence – musical skill or creativity – in a person on the basis of an intuitive knowledge of values, and the recognition that that form of excellence corresponds to our values fills us with contentment. Similarly, we rejoice about the perceived equivalence between our most esteemed moral values and their concrete expression in the actions of our model. But, as Henri Bergson pointed out, we may have a model who, following a conversation or after reading a book, is born within us and finds its expression through us. In this case, the desire for resemblance is already a sort of resemblance: we long to become what we, to a certain extent, already are.[12]

But when someone asks us why we are attracted to certain persons and why we would like to follow their example, we are not always able to articulate the reasons for our attachment. It can happen that we are pulled towards a person not by the clear perception of isolated acts or achievements but by a fine feeling for the overall value of a form of life. Scheler compares this feeling of rightness to the intuition painters or sculptors have when creating a work and applying the rules and principles of their art: "A painter has no awareness of aesthetic laws; their validity becomes conspicuous only, and firstly, during experiences of deviations from them while the artist may be painting or chiselling; or they become conspicuous when they are in evidential agreement with the artistic structure created."[13] Similarly, we are seldom explicitly aware of all the qualities of our models. The more powerful the model's mysterious influence, the less we are able to form a "positive idea" of the model's physical, psychological, and moral attributes.

In fact, we do not opt for our models the same way that we choose a physician or a financial advisor. When we actively turn to professionals, we know exactly what we demand and expect

Moments of Real Learning

from them. We are drawn to models by a sort of "seduction and secret invitation," without demanding the accomplishment of specific deeds.[14] Their appeal is never a forceful constraint; we detect it with a more or less clear "consciousness of ought-to-be and being-right."[15] Consequently, the response to their invitation is neither a submissive imitation of specific actions nor a blind obedience to orders and directives, but a "free devotion" to suggestions. We try to understand and follow what they tell and advise us. We neither try to copy their actions with precision nor seek to duplicate their living circumstances. We act *as* he or she acts rather than do *what* he or she does. What matters, instead, is to think and act in their manner of their thinking and acting. Under the model's unobtrusive influence, we may decide about a profession, adopt a style of leadership or of artistic expression, privilege certain fields of research, or form human relationships according to specific moral values (nobility or uprightness).

We do not respond to the model's actual or imaginary presence merely on the basis of a rational assessment of qualities. The "seduction and secret invitation" coming from a model is part of an overall atmospheric impression. Just as much as we apprehend, without any mediation, the specific atmospheric quality of a city, building, street, or apartment, we grasp, sometimes with great accuracy, the atmospheric radiation of people we encounter. We grasp their distinctive emotional quality; we find this quality attractive, pleasing, repulsive, or indifferent even if most of the time we do not become conscious of our impression.

Indeed, a particular atmospheric nimbus permeates human beings and endows their gestures and words with a certain tonality. This personal atmosphere reminds us of the phenomenon of expression: a glance, vibrations of the voice, or a nod of the head disclose a breath or a fine cloud, which constitutes the "spiritual aspect of a personality" (Eugène Minkowski). We sense a particular presence or aura and, with it, a certain tonality – joy, vitality, sincerity, sadness – which, like perfume, gradually infiltrates its surroundings. A particular atmospheric quality prompts an affective reaction in us; we respond to it either with approval and attachment or with disapproval and rejection. The animosity or sympathy or even indifference that we immediately, at the first encounter, feel in the presence of certain persons often comes from this exposure to their atmospheric qualities.

74 In Vivo

Children are keenly responsive to the atmosphere created, consciously or unconsciously, by their parents. The parental atmospheric radiation is a "kind of spiritual food" that children need for their healthy growth.[16] The atmosphere they "breathe in" at home considerably shapes their personality and interests. For the same reasons, students may resent or enjoy their learning experience with a particular teacher. In addition to their presented ideas, theories, and puzzles, a teacher's movements, voice modulations, and facial expressions are apt to hang an atmosphere of staleness or of effervescence over the classroom. In general, an atmosphere permeates every sector of our life-world – home, workplace, and leisure and educational environments – and affects, to a greater or lesser degree, the characteristics and outcomes of all human activities.

Among the countless atmospheric impressions, to which we are exposed every day, we single out those that touch the core of our being. Being in love for the first time is one such decisive atmospheric experience. The attraction is so strong that, unless we choose to consider ridicule an all-absorbing passion, any suggestion of merely finding ourselves in a transitory state is strongly and cheerfully brushed aside: being in love, we like to believe, is to love the other person forever.

Encountering strong personalities can equally be a vital and crucial experience, but the enduring character of the person's magnetism is often far from being an illusion. While they do not necessarily possess striking physical traits, these persons are able to exert a distinctively vivid and ineradicable impression on us: they radiate energy, depth, and conviction. Their moral qualities (such as kindness or humility) or particular gifts (such as ingenuity or sound judgment) correspond to our values and we perceive and appreciate them through their bodily and verbal expressions, including their smiles, tone of voice, lectures, conversations, or artistic performances.

The presence of these persons, their appeal and personality, is perceived when we encounter them face to face and we become fully absorbed in the present. The object of our attention is valued for its own sake as both the future and the past become less relevant. This presence is not identical to the dimensions and visible characteristics of their bodies; yet, it cannot be separated from them. As an irreducible and fundamental fact, it comes forth in the space between ourselves and the encountered person. The person gives himself or herself to us in such a manner that we become fully attentive only to their magnetic presence. Through their presence we come across a spiritual quality – inner strength, authenticity, or vivacity; we perceive it even when their bodies are weak, fragile, or sick. There are men and women who withdraw themselves into their bodies, as it happens in old age, and nonetheless have a remarkably strong presence. Their convincing personality becomes manifest in the movements of their hands, in the tone of their voices, and, above all, in the look of their eyes. What radiates in the eyes or is brought forth through the hands is not merely what a person has achieved, possessed, or learned but, essentially, what that person actually is. The movements of the hands reveal moods, dispositions, desires, and attitudes. Each hand has a life of its own and, unless it is under strict control, gives away what the person thinks and feels. The voice of a person, reciting a poem or relating a personal experience, is also an intimation of inner disposition: it may express quietness or tension or dissonance – active creative forces that often still resonate, many years later, in the listeners.

The philosopher Karl Jaspers emphasized the importance of finding oneself in the actual presence of a great person, such as Max Weber. Yet, Weber's "wonderful source of energy" became effective not only when Jaspers was face to face with him, "thinking with him," but also when he was no longer with him, "thinking of him."[17] While Weber was still alive, the intensity of his aura provoked an enriching conversation between the two men and never a docile listening by the younger thinker. And after Weber's death, his words were heard through an enlightening imaginative communication.[18] This imaginative presence of models can surely be reinforced if we visit their former homes or final resting places, or simply surround ourselves with what they left behind: books, paintings, scores, or recordings of their works. Whether it hangs on the wall of our room or sits on a desk in front of us, a portrait makes a model more vividly present insofar as we animate his or her image through our knowledge and our affectionate attachment. The portrait, like the one that the young Liszt revered, becomes not just the symbol of the model's values and achievements, but also the manifestation of a real presence inviting the viewer to express these values and emulate these achievements through an active engagement in his or her world.

It has been said before that we might encounter our models by chance and these encounters are made possible and fashioned by the cultural and social milieus in which we find ourselves and by the types of activities that we have decided to pursue at different stages of our lives. They may be sudden, unexpected, and surprising; they instantaneously convey a strong urge to pay attention to the persons who encounter us with their irradiating presence and, if we are so inclined, consciously or unconsciously adopt their values and incorporate them into our personal lives. Because of the inspiration, confidence, and perspective of future achievement objectives we receive from our models, we often consider these encounters as founding moments in our lives.

Where and how do these encounters take place? Let us consider two obvious situations: reading a fictional work and encountering an influential teacher. While reading a novel or a short story, we engage in an imaginative communication with the characters – lifelike figures and fantastical creatures – and are thus able to take part in their lives. We sense their subtle or extreme emotions; we learn about their beliefs, habits, foibles, and ways of life; we breathe in the atmosphere they create around themselves. What we think and feel is constantly shaped and reshaped by these encounters with imaginary characters. And some of them cast a spell on us and suggest acts to accomplish and paths to follow. Then we may complete the Latin aphorism, *habent sua fata libelli*,[19] with another saying: books reveal our destiny.

We all have our favourite authors, ones who give a clear expression of what we already know and feel. While diving into a novel or an essay, we sense, after a few pages, the convergence of their views and beliefs with our views and beliefs, and we rejoice about this discovery of kinship. Memoirs, letters, or journals bring a creative person even closer to us. We are then eager to deepen this new acquaintance and to search for their other works. If we happen to be philosophers, scientists, or literary artists, we draw stimulation and intellectual guidance from their ideas and styles of writing.

Some will likely agree with Graham Greene who contended that the strongest and deepest influence we receive from a book happens in our childhood.[20] If reading is part of a child's daily life, works of fiction play a central role in the making of his or her world. Walter Benjamin made a similar observation, which, I think, is worth quoting because of the vivid image it provides of the formation of the child's world and of the transformation produced by the passionate immersion in reading:

The child seeks his way along the half-hidden paths. Reading, he covers his ears; the book is on a table that is far too high, and one hand is always on the page. To him, the hero's adventures can still be read in the swirling letters like figures and messages in drifting snowflakes. His breath is part of the air of the events narrated, and all the participants breathe it. He mingles with the character far more closely than grown-ups do. He is unspeakably touched by the deeds, the words that are exchanged; and, when he gets up, he is covered over and over by the snow of his reading.[21]

From this kind of experience, which cannot be forced upon children, comes the imaginative encounter with Anne of Green Gables, the Hardy Boys, or the Paul Street Boys, whose adventures, sparked by fearless confidence, generosity, and earnestness, enthral young readers and leave on them a lasting impact. The charming Nausicaa and the steadfast Odysseus enter later into their lives. Pierre Ryckmans, who is better known under his pen name Simon Leys, stressed the prominent role that fictional characters play in the formation of our interests, thoughts, and fantasies in this way:

Looking back into your own past, among the landmarks of your life, you will find that great readings occupy a place no less significant than actual happenings – for instance, a long and adventurous journey through strange lands, which you undertook in a certain year, may in retrospect appear no less memorable than your first exploration of À la recherche du temps perdu; or again, you might realize that your encounter with Anna Karenina, or with Julien Sorel proved more momentous than meeting most of your past acquaintances. Who is to assess the relative significance, the specific weight that should be ascribed to these diverse experiences in the shaping of your personality?[22]

Indeed, models discovered while reading novels and stories can be a powerful means of moulding a personality. But how do young readers know which models they should consciously and wholeheartedly follow? Should someone advise them or let them make the distinction among all the available models? Any explicit advice would yield limited results since, as we have seen, children do not choose a model; rather, they are captivated by it when they read mythical, historical, or fictional stories. As I already have pointed out, relying on the views of Nicolai Hartmann, they notice with satisfaction an agreement between models they encounter and the standard of values they already have. But how do they acquire and develop this standard or hierarchy of values? This hierarchy comes into being when they gradually learn to objectively differentiate among the values inherent in a reality (music, landscape, school, etc.) on the basis of the degree of joy felt in presence of the reality. The joy arises when they are able to see a reality not only in relation to themselves, but also in itself – that is, when they cease to take it as a means to an end, but as an end.[23] However, I suggest that even when they seek to appreciate the value content of a reality as objectively as possible, they cannot completely silence their subjective preferences. The adopted values of justice and of health make them receptive to the influence of a model and, as I have pointed out, the model, in turn, illuminates the understanding of these values and reinforces the concrete and active attachment to them.

I have already mentioned the inspiring encounter students might have with a teacher. Of course, their relation with their teachers can take many forms and only a few of them touch their lives significantly. The literary critic and philosopher George Steiner wrote a long and well-crafted essay on the relation between a master and a disciple.[24] Although he carefully analyzed the nature of their complex interactions, ranging from exploitation to love, from betrayal to admiration, and from adversity to friendship, he has not explicitly examined the act of teaching, which takes place when a student encounters a model. Yet, in a school or a university, students may become attracted and attached to persons whom they consider worthy of their esteem. Or, later in their lives, once they have taken up a paid occupation, they may meet a mentor from whom they gain inspiration and wisdom. The effect of good teaching can be considerable and long lasting, especially when it consists of letting the students discover what they already know.[25] Unfortunately, the converse is also true: a bad teacher can make them hate a domain of knowledge or of expertise. While teaching can be a reciprocal activity, inspiring someone is invariably a one-sided affair. Teachers seek to elicit an interest and provoke the students' questioning curiosity for a subject. If all goes well, students, in turn, respond to the teachers' effort and learn: they enlarge the scope of their knowledge, use it, and, above all, think, explore, and do research for themselves. Models do not ask for such explicit attention or active collaboration; they merely become examples open for emulation. Students turn actively to their teachers in order to receive guidance and tasks to perform and entertain with them a relation of mutuality. Models come to them, sometimes unexpectedly, and create an attraction by stirring their affection and sense of values. Although the relation between a model and a student is a genuine encounter, since it is not established on command, it fails to display the characteristics of reciprocity.

To paraphrase Bertrand Russell, there are three kinds of teachers: there are figures of amusement, there are those who are competent but uninteresting, and there is a small class of men and women whom students admire "wholeheartedly and enthusiastically."[26] The later ones create an atmosphere of excitement and even fun, evoke their students' inquisitiveness, and demonstrate ways of acquiring and imaginatively applying knowledge. They may become their models and also provoke their admiration. Of course, an admired teacher does not necessarily become a model and, conversely, a model teacher does not always elicit outright admiration. But when students admire a teacher, they feel uplifted by a superior quality that they are able to identify in this person. They are attracted to this quality and try to integrate it into their lives.[27]

The expression "being uplifted by a superior quality" makes us think of another compelling appeal that provokes the act of breaking free from actual living circumstances. The perception of a form of existence generated by the superior quality is a sufficient reason for abandoning an unsatisfactory condition. An admiring person is not merely pleased or carried away, as when he or she listens to a piece of music, but is *lifted up* to a height, which makes a critical appraisal of his or her life circumstances possible. To be sure, admiration awakens a desire to imitate. But, as I have already pointed out, this sort of imitation is never thoughtless and slavish. It is respectful and inventive. It allows students to use their abilities and develop their personal interests. There is an element of disinterested and aesthetic satisfaction in all admiration: students find a harmony and a balance of qualities in their models, such as generosity, integrity, equanimity, and modesty – qualities that they would like to possess. But, contrary to fanatical devotion, which is held with blindness and rigidity, their admiring eyes see and select what is appropriate for their own benefit. They rejoice in being drawn to a person of great learning and moral rectitude, but they also rely on their ability to discern among the perceived qualities.

Students, recent and long-time graduates, may be inclined to explain their attractions by the authenticity of their models. We speak, for instance, of the authenticity of a work of art when the formal elements express truly and genuinely what we consider essential in a novel or a composition. The authenticity of a symphony or a painting has to do with an inner fullness, depth, vigour, and life and these qualities are given in a direct, unbroken manner. They penetrate us, find an echo in us, and take hold of us. In a similar fashion, persons are authentic when their words and deeds communicate directly and without simulation, distortion, and pretence what they think, feel, and want. Their inward state is expressed unmistakably by their presence, conveying to all those who are in contact with them something enriching and stimulating. The authentic is not merely what is genuine and unaffected, but, more importantly, what is essential, solid, vivacious, and durable in the person, and, above all, the wealth of feelings and thoughts and their truthful expression.

But we may find the inspiring influence of this value where we expect it least. Unproductive and inefficient organizations often remain alive and fulfil their function thanks to the presence and deeds of authentic individuals. In early 1932, Arthur Koestler travelled to the USSR and, after visiting industrial sites, kolkhozes, shops, and offices and witnessing everywhere chaotic, stifling, and apathetic conditions, he asked the question: why did the Soviet state not collapse? It was impossible to hold this immense machinery together by terror alone. The state-run propaganda could not give industry and economy an acceptable coherence. So what allowed it to function?

Koestler met a number of remarkable but anonymous men and women who kept the state running. They had varied occupations; they were not marked by rank or office. But they were able to create islands of order, dignity, and efficiency, as well as showing an astonishing resistance against the state's crushing of the human spirit. The result of their resourcefulness was considerable and wide-ranging. Much later in life, Koestler described their civic virtues in these words:

They are motivated by a grave sense of responsibility in a country where everybody fears and evades responsibility; they exercise initiative and independent judgment where blind obedience is the norm; they are loyal and devoted to their fellow-beings in a world where loyalty is only expected towards one's superiors and devotion only towards the State. They have personal honour and an unconscious dignity of comportment, where these words are objects of ridicule ... These upright, devoted, energetic and fearless men were and are the backbone of a régime that denies all the values for which they stand. As a Communist I took their existence for granted, for I believed that they were the product of revolutionary education, that 'new type of men' whose coming Marx has predicted. To-day I realise that their existence is very nearly a miracle, that they became what they are not because, but in spite of that education – a triumph of the indestructible human substance over a de-humanising environment.[28]

This "human substance" made these men and women truly authentic and, ultimately, kept the state economy alive and operating. Their names are not noted in the history books. If, however, their impact was so powerful and so efficient, they must have been inspiring living models for their colleagues. I also happened to encounter a few of these noteworthy persons years after Koestler wrote his book. They made, in different totalitarian states, amidst all-pervading fear and suspicion, the living conditions of thousands of other people more acceptable and their daily toiling more stimulating. They were paragons that never, even to this day, received credit for their uncommon gifts and achievements.

THE INFLUENCE OF A MODEL

In addition to the concrete appreciation of values and qualities, and according to the determination to lead a good life, what kind of influence do models have on our actions and thoughts? In his essay on the forms of knowledge and culture, Scheler stressed the educational importance of models: if we want to be truly educated, we have to let ourselves be absorbed into the values of our models. They enable us to see, with more clarity, our objectives and to better know and use our abilities to reach these objectives. They function as stepping stones and trailblazers. As Scheler puts it, "They explain and clarify our own purpose. By their example we can measure our skills and strive to attain our spiritual selves. They teach us to know our true powers and how to use them."[29] They show us what we are made for, what our place in this world is, and how we can make the best of our abilities. As opposed to laws and norms, telling us what not do to, our models show us what we should undertake and what we can become. Their callings are fundamentally positive and inspiring, seldom negative and restrictive. Models leave us free to pursue our own specific vocations and to fully develop and exercise our own powers. But by their luminous presence, models also remind us that we cannot strive for the realization of all of our desires. We then respond only to those callings that we identify under the stirring influence of our models – models that, for some reason, speak to us.

It is now fashionable to define the formal education offered in schools, colleges, and universities as a process of providing transformative experiences for the human person. I don't deny that such experiences are the ideal we espouse as being fundamental to education. True, educational institutions create and offer the structure and means for the enhancement of students' cognitive competence, technical skills, moral and aesthetic sensitivity, and learning potential. Good lectures not only stimulate the ability to ask questions, advance comments, and formulate judgments, but also trigger the imagination to envisage new problems and explore new areas of research. For many students, the hours spent in the classroom are like an "oasis in the fabric of their daily lives" (Jacqueline de Romilly). If they happen to listen to an invigorating and pleasant teacher, they can easily be captivated by the demonstration of a mathematical theorem or by the beauty and depth of a poem. Two lines of a poem by Racine, recited by a teacher with a taste for the theatre, can exert a lifelong influence on a student.[30] But I claim that a deep and enduring metamorphosis is also, if not more, the result of a realization of human potential that happens outside the context of formal educational settings. Reflecting on the act of teaching, Robert Spaemann remarked that "education is not a process we undertake in order to achieve a set goal. There is no special activity that we can identify as 'educating.' Education is rather a side effect, which comes about while someone is doing all kinds of other things."[31] G.K. Chesterton captured the same idea in this dictum: "Education is implication."[32] Perhaps the most important "other thing" is a direct encounter with an older and wise person who has built up a rich world of memories and insights and has a hidden influence or a noticed transformative effect on the younger person's beliefs and purposes. Alexander Farkas made this point after conversing with a music educator and composer who spoke to him with intense energy and passionate

Moments of Real Learning

convictions. This was a conversation, which allowed him to fully live in the present and, at the same time, to relive the transformative experiences of the other person's past:

> More and more, as I think back over the years of my education, it seems that the more important moments of real learning never happened during the course of a formal lesson. Sometimes a great deal is learned in a very few moments; sometimes it is not even possible to say what it is we have understood for the first time. All we know is that we have been changed in some way; we are now different than we were before those significant moments. The event, however brief, has been the meeting with one person, usually older than ourselves, someone who carries within him some very important history. If we are receptive, we begin to sense the lineage, almost imagining that we too were present at that more distant time, a time when something new and very different was taking place.[33]

But what makes the change possible? Our interests, activities, abilities, relations, values, and worlds are modifiable to a greater or lesser extent. Of course, the change is neither easy nor always possible. Becoming a successful actor or an outstanding athlete is for many people extremely difficult, if not impossible. But if I am a teacher, I can become a veterinarian and if I am a farmer I can decide to become a nurse or a scholar. Such transformations often demand striking encounters. A person can have a direct or indirect influence on me if he or she can find a "leverage point" in my being; this is something that may happen if I take a distance from myself and become receptive to new ideas and values.

The truly influential encounter with another person creates a surprise as it interrupts the ordinary and necessary course of our activities and experiences. It snatches us from the continuity of our everyday life and gives our existence a new and unexpected orientation. Since our future is suddenly filled with attainable possibilities, the decisive encounter prevents the course of our lives from following a predictable or determined direction.

In the above example, we may also speak, once again, of the presence of an older person that touches an existence more deeply and more permanently. This presence is experienced as an act of generous self-giving that offers not merely ideas and values but, above all, wisdom and inspiration. It easily becomes an absence if the person is seen merely as an example of a social role and if the encounter is prepared in advance according to a well-prepared script. Finding oneself in the real presence of another person always remains a contingent and fragile experience and, for this reason, it can hardly be created at will in an educational context or in any other professional environment.[34]

Thanks to a fortunate encounter with an authentic man or woman, who may display only an unreflective wisdom and common sense, we may, then, select activities that arrest our interest and for which we are ready to devote our lives, all our energies, and our abilities. A focal interest – art, religion, science, natural environment, or history – can provide us with income, but it only becomes our true and life-fulfilling profession and leads to the production of original works when we decide to put it at the centre of our lives, regardless of the financial benefit we draw from it. Models may help us with this decision. Following the ideas of the philosopher Harry G. Frankfurt, I would characterize the engagement undertaken under the influence of a model with the notion of care. Caring about something means this: we are deeply and passionately concerned with an activity or an endeavour; we consider it important, we are ready to devote our abilities to its realization, and we are ready to make sacrifices for our own development and success; we relate to it with attention and respect. Frankfurt characterizes the phenomenon in these terms:

> A person who cares about something is, as it were, invested in it. He *identifies* himself with what he cares about in the sense that he makes himself vulnerable to losses and susceptible to benefits depending upon whether what he cares about is diminished or enhanced. Thus he concerns himself with what concerns it, giving particular attention to such things and directing his behavior accordingly. Insofar as the person's life is in whole or in part *devoted* to anything, rather than being merely a sequence of events whose themes and structures he makes no effort to fashion, it is devoted to this.[35]

It may be helpful, in this context, to emphasize the notion of service as well. The idea of service implies not only the functionality or expediency of a specific action, but also the dedication and attachment to a reality that transcends the person. When we offer a service to a person, we aim at a value or a principle that appears in another person but is not identical with him or her. In truth, we serve someone when we see in the person the living embodiment of a value. Such a vision is possible only if we relate to the person in fraternity and generosity and not merely in legal equality and obligation. While serving, we devote ourselves to a reality and, by doing so, we recognize with greater clarity what is important for us and what we are able to do for others.

In addition to inspiring and heuristic suggestions, models also show us obligations and determinations that we acknowledge and respect. In a different context, Frankfurt reminds us that the attachment to an ideal entails the awareness of limitations as well as opportunities.[36] The positive influence of a model, inasmuch as he or she incarnates and promotes an ideal, allows us to value and follow this ideal; the ideal of self-determining freedom, for example, consists of the recognition of duties and restrictions. An ideal, then, turns our eyes to the persons and objects whose existence, legitimacy, and requirement, at least to us, need to be recognized. In its absence, our will fails to meet a positive authority; it risks becoming a plaything of momentary inclinations and impulses. Our behaviour, then, follows the dictates of external circumstances and not what our individual conscience tells us. Without ideals, our lives are amorphous and passive; our desires, wishes, and ideas fail to carry over to a particular course of action.

The common experience of going into a store to purchase a shirt or a blazer and finding ourselves with a large number of choices while lacking any guiding preferences is a case in point: we frequently leave without buying anything. With limitless available possibilities, our will is paralyzed: if everything were possible, nothing would be done. Just like our senses give us a relief from all the possible impressions, likewise our models and their ideals set limits, narrow down our options, and provide us with incentives to act and even embark on an enterprise with both perseverance and creativity.

Ultimately, models offer stable and durable anchoring points for people, allowing them to take care of their tasks with confidence and self-esteem. They bring to their lives clearly defined and well-thought-out objectives and also the necessary limitations for reaching those objectives. Reflecting on the consequences of not having models, Margarete Mitscherlich warns us: "We all need ideals, models, goals, by which we orient ourselves and we can strive for their achievement."[37] She is right by suggesting that human beings need a lasting commitment to a system of values. As we have seen, by embodying values, models can play an essential role in the moral education of the child. There is also a fundamental human impulse for self-realization, which can hardly be satisfied in the absence of the guidance and inspiration of models. As Karl Jaspers noted, a good education fills children with "ideals durable enough to last a lifetime."[38] Alfred N. Whitehead also held that ideals should inspire an education that steers "the individual towards a comprehension of the art of life" – chief among them is the ideal of active wisdom, which is the free mastery and imaginative application of knowledge.[39] In respect of the natural craving for self-development, we may refer to the eagerness of young people to idolize pop culture icons or leaders of gangs and to imitate some of their bodily or verbal expressions. If their keen desire for a positive model is not satisfied and their mimetic energy does not find any outlet, children will turn to easily available individuals whose behaviour and objectives may be morally doubtful. A positive model is someone whose influence is beneficial for a smaller or larger community and satisfies more than individual interests. Following such a model requires the acceptance of enjoying long-term and collectively shared rewards.

To sum up: thanks to our models, we are able to identify what is truly important for us, what deserves our respect and admiration, and what energizes us to plan and undertake activities in our private, professional, and social lives. Suppose we are working as a manager in a business or as a teacher in a school. Our leadership style will be fashioned, consciously or unconsciously, by the values and actions of our model. We might relate to our fellow workers or students with strict severity or indulgent kindness, or we may make a decision quickly or after lengthy consideration of our possibilities. More importantly perhaps, in the face of difficulties, we will find in ourselves the necessary resources and energy to persist and to come up with appropriate ways of achieving results that contribute to the happiness of people around us.

We have seen that making decisions requires halting a course of action, stepping outside the flow of events, and evaluating the nature of our possibilities and their foreseeable consequences. In the pressing moments of a decision, we might, in our imaginations, consult one of our models and ask: if you were facing my task, what would you do now? And, quite often, we find the answer we were looking for and, by making the ineluctable decision, follow our own path with greater confidence and determination.

4

Foreigner in a Foreign Land

Far from our own people, our own language, stripped of all our props, deprived of our masks (one doesn't know the fare on the streetcars, or anything else), we are completely on the surface of ourselves. But also, soul-sick, we restore to every being and every object its miraculous value.

Albert Camus

In one of his short stories, Jorge Luis Borges recounts the encounter of his English grandmother with another Englishwoman who was born in Yorkshire and had immigrated as a child with her family to Buenos Aires. This woman, after being captured by the natives of her adopted land and losing her parents, had completely assimilated into the culture of her captors. Borges's grandmother tries to persuade her to return to her original form of life. The request is made in vain. But the crux of the story is not merely the metamorphosis of a young girl. It is the inevitability of the transformation that happens when an adult woman comes into a contact with a foreign culture. Following this moment of unusual encounter, the author's grandmother came to realize, not without some fear, that she unavoidably will share the same fate: by heeding to a "secret impulse, an impulse more profound than reason," she will, sooner or later, become "transformed by the implacable continent."[1]

Pierre Ryckmans questions the truth-value of the claim that an extended stay in a foreign country changes one's outlook on life and even physical appearance. He refers to a remark of the theologian and philosopher Teilhard de Chardin who, having gone to fetch a friend at the railway station in Peking, suddenly realized that a prolonged journey anywhere in Central Asia would not necessarily affect all those who descended from the train. Ryckmans also sought to discover to what extent years of adventurous travel in different parts of Asia touched this man. He quotes a remark by the writer Somerset Maugham who, after meeting a traveller in China, observed that "the civilised world irked him and he had a passion to get away from the beaten trail. The oddities of life amused him. He had an insatiable curiosity. But I think his experiences were merely of the body and were never translated into experiences of the soul. Perhaps that is why, at bottom, you felt he was a commonplace. The insignificance of his mien was the true index to the insignificance of his soul. Behind the blank wall was blankness."[2] Hence Ryckman's lapidary judgment: travelling to a distant place and living there for an extended period of time does not necessarily transform someone.

ENCOUNTER WITH A FOREIGN CULTURE

These contrasting observations lead me to cautiously advance a distinction between two kinds of experience of a foreign people, place, or culture.

There are people indeed who, as they arrive in a foreign country, thrillingly come into contact with the language, system of values, conventions, and ways of living of its inhabitants. They also notice and carefully study the disposition of the streets, squares, parks, and buildings. While taking their first steps in this new milieu, they apprehend the distinct atmosphere of the place. They are curious to know about its history and social, political, and religious structure. They are ready to alter the organization of their daily life or even make an attempt to adopt some of the culinary and vestimentary habits of the people they meet. They may eat their meals at different hours and, if possible, in the company of local people. They take the train, in a third class carriage, go into shops, visit the market, and participate in some festivals in order to acquire a better sense of the hustle and bustle of an urban or a rural community. They also visit churches, pagodas, and monasteries, and hike rugged mountains or spend relaxing days in the company of peasants living in remote villages. Contrary to expectation, however, all these more or less significant experiences leave no lasting imprint on them; their deep insularity prevails. Their personality remains impermeable to any suggestion of transformation and closed off of to any possibility of enrichment. They remain fixed in their own conditions, views, and prejudices and go as far as confirming their previously formed ideas and preferences. They travel not to broaden and enrich their lives, but in order to select what fits into their well-established worldviews.

There are others, however, who not only eagerly taste a foreign culture, but they also consciously immerse themselves in it: they seek to perceive whatever is new and different, to understand it in its depth, and to react to it in particular ways. For instance, they are not only attentive to the atmosphere of the place, but they also perceive the influence of strangeness on them and their response to it. They notice how people communicate with each other and gradually make some of the bodily and even verbal aspects of these conversations their own. They find out how people feel and think in some decisive moments of their lives (in the presence of birth or death or while expressing love or grief) and absorb these different emotional and spiritual reactions and what holds the disparate aspects of their lives together. The explicit awareness of the separation and contrast between the foreign and the familiar, the new and the old, the unknown and the known, and the willingness to make place for the former in their lives, elicit in them a transformation, which can be slight and short-lived or substantial and long-lasting. They might become aware of an "impulse" towards complete integration – one that Borges wrote about in his story – which allows them to be carried away.

"The foreigner," Eugen Fink tells us, "is someone with whom I am not in a direct community of shared experience. His possibilities for experience are not necessarily mine; initially I am not in connection with him."[3] Fink believes that we are able to perceive, understand, and integrate both the past and current experiences of the foreign. Although the integration takes place in the future after a month or several years, it is present for us as a real possibility. The foreignness of a person, together with the particular quality of his or her milieu – openness, reservation, sadness, warmth, industriousness, serenity – is first felt, in absence of a verbal communication, as an overall atmosphere.[4] This quality presents itself not only when, for instance, we welcome a visitor from a distant land, but also when someone enters into a space, which is, for him or her, not a familiar one. Let us imagine a politician joining a meeting by mistake, to which he was not invited at all, or a technician, called in to fix the heating system, walking through the dining room while members of the family share a meal. The atmosphere is suddenly tainted with the quality of "not one of us," of "not belonging here." The physical closeness with this "uninvited" or "tolerated" person creates the feeling of distance, formality, and contingency because the foreigner does not share "the unique ingredients and particular tendencies of the group."[5] The very same feeling may arise between lovers who, after entering into an intimate and, for them, unique relationship, suddenly experience a moment of estrangement. They find each other foreigners, as if they were meeting by chance at a public space; the common atmosphere they create receives the features of unfriendliness, distrust, but also curiosity.

The encounter with the foreign highlights the primacy of an atmospheric participation upon which elementary and complex human togetherness is founded. If, after the first contact, we share a meal with foreigners or take part in their feast or ritual dance, a more intimate atmosphere is established. We come to know them better and perhaps feel inclined to make our own the particular aspects of their foreignness. The foreign is not merely what is exterior, outside of our world and, as such, not our own, but also what is different, unfamiliar, even peculiar and strange: it becomes concretely manifest in ways of eating, drinking, dressing, worshipping, giving recognition, and showing hospitality, as well as ways of accomplishing the homely tasks of sawing or sewing, along with other activities of the everyday art of civilization. According to the English writer Rudyard Kipling, who lived for a while in the United States, the only way to know a foreign country is to be a householder, to mingle with local people and experience things and chores from the inside. The foreign has to become a living and subjective reality and not merely a distant and objective appearance. In his words, "Tourists may carry away impressions, but it is the seasonal detail of small things and doings (such as putting up fly-screens and stove-pipes, buying yeast-cakes and being lectured by your neighbours) that bite in the lines of mental pictures."[6] In order to actively feel and understand and, after an extended acquaintance, integrate the foreign, we have to enter into a more personal communication with individuals and their worlds, to find a common ground of interest in deeds and not merely in words. We have to make the effort of bringing together two contrasting realms of experience in order to get a full perspective on both of them and, instead of showing scorn or expressing rejection, we have to give ourselves "the means to tame the strangeness and to make it familiar."[7]

It is obvious enough that verbal communications with foreigners happen not without some difficulties, especially when we want to converse with them in their languages. We have to learn not only a range of words and expressions and the most important grammatical rules, but also the appropriate pronunciation and understanding of those words. Even if we may have attained an adequate fluency in speech, we are unable to control how the other person speaks. The tendency to elision and unfinished sentence construction or the lack of clear articulation and appropriate speed of utterance makes the understanding arduous and tiresome. In his often-quoted paper, Alfred Schutz discusses a certain number of factors that supervene between speakers who are strangers to each other.[8] Their words and expressions have emotional values and secondary connotations derived from a specific social context. Even if two people speak the same language, the emotional undertone of words and sentences is different for the two. What is intimately known for one person will be foreign for the other. The foreign addressee is prone to use a dialect and an array of jargons and acronyms that are understandable only after several encounters. Symbolic and metaphoric nuances presuppose the participation in some common past experiences or the appropriation of elements of a cultural tradition. These features illustrate precisely what Fink called the absence of "a direct community of shared experience." Beyond seeking occasions to speak to a variety of foreigners about a variety of subjects, these difficulties can partly be alleviated if the visiting person tries to establish a warm and friendly atmosphere and to adopt a deferential and courteous attitude towards the inhabitants of the foreign world. He or she has to be attentive to clues that dispel ambiguities and convey clarity in the communication. In my view, Anthony Burgess's statement applies not only to visitors of a foreign land, but also to natives of the place: "Speaking a foreign language is acting: the mouth and body are both involved."[9] In some verbal exchanges, bodily movements prove to be essential; it is only through the observation of the partner's hand or face that the meaning of sentences can be accurately understood.

In this sense, the moments of encounter with foreign people and their cultures, starting with an atmospheric experience and later taking the forms of conversation, collaboration, or celebration, may eventually result in a genuine attempt to understand and to change. The individuals in question then gradually, over a long period of time, adapt to forms of conduct, skills, languages, and a system of norms and values in such a way that the addition does not cancel out all the elements of their original identities and cultures. They acquire, as it were, a dual citizenship: they bring together and display what seems to them the best and the most pertinent of both worlds. This integration may create in them a sense of complementarities and harmony or an acute feeling of dissonance and of tension. Whatever may be the case – accord or discord of perspectives – the adaptive process is felt as fulfilling and rewarding. Their point of view is multiplied; their spiritual being is enlarged.

The inner richness, whose absence is noted by Maugham, comes from the ability to place foreign cultural elements into a wider perspective provided by the familiar. When we create or welcome moments of encounter with what appears to be a foreign cultural behaviour (ways of greeting, courting, negotiating, preparing and sharing a meal, furnishing a home, playing games, or conducting meetings), elements of our own culture remain present as a horizon in the background against which we perceive, compare, and evaluate whatever we identify in the foreground.[10] This comparison and evaluation are possible since there is always a grain of similarity in what we find foreign. What is so dissimilar as to be beyond comparison cannot be taken as foreign. As a consequence, what has so far been familiar and conventional with regard to the economic, artistic, or domestic aspects of our lives gains, under new light, a heightened understandability and precision; and what has been encountered and possibly integrated into our lives as something foreign becomes gradually more apprehensible and acceptable. Essentially, it is the contrasting relation that makes the foreign more comprehensible and serves as a motivating springboard for productive action. To my mind, it is the presence, acceptance, and expression of simultaneously contrasting points of view, modes of existence, and cultures that create, in the person, an inner richness and a sense of self-worth.

In his book on the dynamics of creativity, Anthony Storr discusses in depth some of the characteristics of creative people.[11] They develop the capacity for self-transformation according to their inner standard of values and the ability to tolerate within themselves the discomfort of dissonances, the clash of conflicting opposites. They are both "inner-directed" and sensitive to what is radically different, new, and foreign in their environment. Their drive to create springs from their awareness of opposites and unresolved inner tensions, as well as from their abilities to remain open to foreign knowledge, to assimilate the significance of new experiences coming from outside, and, if possible, to learn and change accordingly. The greater the opposition within, the keener the desire to bring the opposite poles into a unity, into an orderly whole. Storr is probably right to conjecture that the creative drive has little to do with the material comfort and security that many seek to obtain in academic circles. In fact, the disappearance of any concern about one's future well-being tends to stifle numerous talented persons' originality and creativity. These require, for their possession and expression, acceptance of an inner disharmony and wealth of ideas and feelings that individuals bear within themselves. They also call for a readiness to remain receptive, without any calming thoughts about the future, to both the new envisaged in the present and the old inherited from the past. In addition, creative persons must also face and accept the resistance and struggle that their new theories and unusual works may generate.

Self-transformation is achieved if, beyond the effort of taking distance from the self and actively considering it in a different manner, the person becomes attuned to the foreign and integrates some of its elements into his or her life. Extreme, rigid opinions and thoughtless, familiar paradigms are discarded and inspiring alternatives are entertained. This integration, I would argue, is only possible if the foreign is understood. But this understanding, in turn, is only realizable if the foreign is somehow actively and directly integrated. We may express this formative circularity by applying to our theme the oft-quoted words of Viktor von Weizsäcker: "To understand (a foreign) life, one has to participate in it. But to participate in (a foreign) life, one has to understand it."[12] By *understanding*, I mean essentially this: knowing a reality, including its purpose, function, utilization, significance, and constitutive elements, the ways these elements relate to each other and form a unity, and its capacity for affecting the relation of other realities. An understanding can be both useful and useless. But a useless understanding also has its particular usefulness. The apparently useless activities – walking beside a river, telling humorous stories, drinking wine during a summer evening, learning a song by heart – are useful insofar as they create a more intimate contact with something or somebody and, as we have seen before, change the quality of the enveloping atmosphere and the ensuing verbal communication. Thus we understand an object of everyday use, a bodily expression, a ritual, a convention, a social skill, a language, a work of art, the meaning of a feast, a way of life, a stream of events, a train of thought, and the bliss or sorrow of a fellow human being.

Schutz mentions two considerable obstacles that strangers have to face when participating in the activities of new social surroundings.

In the first place, they find themselves to be outsiders, without any definite social status, and, secondly, they cannot assume that their interpretation of a cultural pattern, as well as their action within a social situation, coincides with the understanding and ways of behaving of the members of the foreign group. They have to "reckon with fundamental discrepancies in seeing things and handling situations."[13] As we will see, the discomfort of being at the periphery of a social environment can sharpen people's vision, nurturing their ability to survey a situation with less prejudice and establish more freely an adequate plan of orientation. And the possible discord of interpretations could prompt them to see a particular cultural reality (the mores and customs within families or the functioning of a legal system) from a distance, bereft of the power of habit and convention, with an inquisitive and critical eye.

But let us return to the claim that we are unable to come to understand and to actively integrate what is distinct from ourselves. It has been strongly defended by Victor Segalen, an enigmatic French writer who broke free from his provincial and petty-bourgeois milieu and travelled to French Polynesia and whose work reached a wide audience only years after his death in 1919. In his posthumous *Essay on Exotism*, Segalen maintained that contact with foreign cultures yields incomprehension and inadaptation rather than understanding and integration. He put it in these terms: "Let us not pretend that we can assimilate customs, races, nations – the others; on the contrary, let us rejoice in our inability ever to achieve such assimilation; this inability allows us to enjoy diversity forever."[14] Exotic knowledge is the sense of diversity, the perception and acceptance of radical differences. This knowledge carries with it a benefit: a heightened awareness of the limits and possibilities of the self. The encounter with a definite and irreducible otherness throws us back onto ourselves; we then may gain a better knowledge of ourselves and the inner springs of our growth within our own familiar culture. What could stifle the awareness of this growth is not the incomprehensibility of a foreign culture but the elimination or degradation of diversity, the increasing uniformity experienced in our modern world – a drab uniformity sustained, in part at least, by instantaneous tourism, which is the perversion of extended travel or sojourn. Tourists fail to come across the radical otherness, which could throw them back onto themselves; they value bland homogeneity and flee from the occasions of self-encounter.

96   In Vivo

Uniformity begets prejudice, intolerance, passivity, and, above all, escape from the self; it numbs the sensibilities for the spirit of one's own place and age; it destroys the fecundity provided by the exotic power, the power of being distinct, of coming face to face with oneself and eliminating ignorance and self-deception. Let us add to this harsh but accurate observation that the degradation and disappearance of diversity also rules out any possibility of salutary transformation.

Segalen projected a study on the exoticism of the sexes: the otherness of men for women and of women for men. He believed that there is no genuine love between a man and a woman without an experience of shock and occasional discord making manifest the irreducible otherness of the partner. In the absence of this dissension, the other risks merely becoming the flattering reflection of one's fantasy. Yet, it is often this otherness that attracts a man and a woman to each other, creates in them the awareness of the uniqueness of their partner and their feelings for each other, and also makes possible their mutual enrichment and transformation.[15]

The idea of the impenetrability of societies – and the distinctive creed and mentality of the people living in them – could be questioned if we were to carefully examine some of the characteristics of culture itself. From an anthropological perspective, *culture* is the sum of our acquired ideas and behaviour, as well as their manifold results, as opposed to the abilities, creations, and possibilities of our innate constitutions, which we share with all other human beings. This unity of productive practices and objects may include arts, laws, values, institutions, habits, beliefs, knowledge, customs, styles of living, tools, artistic works, and many other elements. Culture is what people (living in smaller or larger social entities) think, imagine, conserve, articulate, and make of their worlds. A particular culture is seldom immune to decisive influences coming from other cultures. Thus the American culture is, voluntarily and involuntarily, also African, Irish, or Spanish, and, likewise, a specific African culture contains considerable French, English, and Portuguese elements. To a lesser or greater extent, each culture is, in fact, a "culture of cultures."[16] In addition, there is the possibility of consciously appropriating the artistic expressions, religious beliefs, social customs, and dominant mentalities of other cultures and, by doing so, of arriving at the recognition of their positive value in the shaping of both individual existence and communal life. A rich culture is, then, the result of a long and voluntary process of cross-fertilization between cultures. The opposite is also true: a society and a group of individuals may resist, filter, or fight off, tacitly or openly, certain foreign influences. However, hermetic closure from outside influences in the creation of complete cultural homogeneity leads to decadence and eventually to the paralysis of a particular culture.

A society tolerates within itself what is different and foreign to itself but is, to a certain extent, familiar for an outsider; it is this familiar otherness that can set in motion the adaptive and transformative contact with its particular culture. What is true for societies equally applies to individuals. Thus, the exhilarating discovery of other cultures, as well as the appropriative understanding of some of their elements, is made possible, in part, by the doors and bridges created by the presence of what is foreign in a culture and what could be, at the same time, familiar to the foreign individual coming from abroad. If we are able to detect similarities and commonalities between two cultures, then the adoption of additional foreign elements into our lives becomes easier. As Erich Heller puts it, "Every kind of understanding depends on our ability to relate a given phenomenon to a wider field of intellectual or imaginative familiarity."[17] The key idea here is the act of relating: in order to apprehend the foreign, we have to relate it to the familiar and, conversely, in order to better understand the familiar, we have to relate it to the foreign. George Santayana also referred to this act of relating when he advised the traveller to resist the *impulse* to seek complete integration and instead to keep a distance from a foreign culture by remaining a stranger, "so that his definite character and moral traditions may supply an organ and a point of comparison for his observations." Then the travelling person will be able to see his own personal world differently. He should be "an artist recomposing what he sees; then he can carry away the picture and add it to a transmissible fund of wisdom, not as further miscellaneous experience but as corrected view of truth."[18]

SEEING WITH DIFFERENT EYES

Let us explore two important questions: how do we come to the vitally influential moment of understanding and, consequently, what makes the beneficial transformation of our thinking and acting possible? Helmuth Plessner asks these questions in his essay on the way of perceiving human affairs. It is a well-known fact that in the ordinary round of our daily lives in our familiar environs – as we come into a contact with people, respond to their demands, and take care of our business – our vision is very selective, focusing on some specific areas and wandering aimlessly and thoughtlessly over many others. We tend to see them through the lens of conventions, habits, objectives, and familiar verbal expressions. And, as a consequence, we tend to be blind to what appears immediate and self-evident but what plays no practical role in our daily affairs. As Ludwig Wittgenstein noted, "The aspects of things that are most important for us are hidden because of their simplicity and familiarity."[19]

In order to become aware of all these everyday realities, their richness and complexities, we have to perceive them "through other eyes." When we establish between them and ourselves a distance and become exiles in our own familiar milieus, then we begin to see objects and people in their density and fullness; and we might even come to see them as unfamiliar, unusual, and strange realities. We have to gradually turn away from the old and develop our capacity for the apprehension of novelty. "True awareness is wakened in us only by what is unfamiliar," writes Plessner. "To be able to look at something, we need distance."[20]

Odo Marquard is of the opinion, however, that, in an age of "tachogenic unworldliness," in which everything changes with ever increasing speed and the unceasing change makes the surrounding world alien, people need to develop "an appreciation of the usual," and to welcome the sense of familiarity that usage offers. In order to cope with the ongoing transformation of the surrounding world and the loss of continuity it creates, they need to cultivate usual practices, customs, habits, and traditions and to fully appreciate their lasting familiarities. Marquard claims that the sense of familiarity provided by these continuities has now become indispensable.[21] We need, of course, to value our sense of familiarity with the world, and the reassuring constancy it offers, in order to endure the ongoing and sometimes disconcerting changes that we are compelled to face day after day. But, in order to truly appreciate all aspects of the familiar, and its compensatory value and beneficial influence in the midst of an "orientation crisis," we also need to recognize these aspects from the viewpoint of the new, the unusual, and the foreign. The greater need for the continuity of the familiar can be fully satisfied by the intermittent discontinuity brought about by the captivating encounter with the unfamiliar.

Our sense of unfamiliarity needs to be triggered, sharpened, and enlarged by seeing things "through other eyes." Because we become too easily accustomed to our own too familiar world and, consequently, lose the power to perceive its richness and wholeness, Saint Augustine advises us to show it to a guest – and, at the same time, to become a foreign guest with him or her – in order to perceive it anew. He asks, "Is it not a common experience that when we are showing certain lovely scenes about a town or in the country to those who have never seen them, their pleasure in the new experience makes us see the scene with a new delight even though we passed it day after day without seeing it because it was too familiar for us?"[22] We do not need to take any chemical substance to induce this kind of heightened perception. We merely need to become a foreign guest on the territory of familiar realities and to experience a "new delight." To gain a keen and fulfilling perception, the familiar has to become unfamiliar; we have to see the town as if we were visitors discovering foreign realities. In other words, when we are able to free ourselves from certain habits and preoccupations, we become receptive to forms and actions that we typically fail to notice.

We usually consider guests those persons who go to places that are not their permanent homes. Being a guest is either a privilege, for which they are deeply thankful, or a right, for which they pay the proper amount of money. In both cases, in a friend's house or in a hotel, they are called upon to treat people and objects with respect and consideration and to observe some rules. Genuine guests treat any milieu they visit with a sensibility; they adapt to the requirement of a concrete situation and are able to maintain a certain restraint and an appropriate reserve. Although a guest does not relate to a host with a sense of intimacy, he or she enters into the host's living space and community with a sense of "being at home." In this space, the feelings of alienation and disorientation are absent, but not the awareness of distance and unfamiliarity and the need to act with due deference.

When, on the other hand, we visit unknown foreign places without being welcomed as a guest, we often find ourselves disorientated and estranged. The streets, houses, shops, windows, and doors meet us without any familiar and inviting significance. People and their actions often evoke in us the physiognomic characters of unfriendliness, of haste, and of gloom. In one of his essays, Gabriel Marcel wrote about "the distress felt by a child during a trip or change of residence, the nameless sadness we have all experienced in certain hotel rooms where we had the feeling of not being in *anybody's home*."[23] Because of a similar acute uneasiness we feel and seek to temper, we tend to look only for things that appear familiar, perhaps a place of worship, a restaurant, or a park, and, as we start to apply our own points of reference, we tend to become less sensitive to the disquieting features of the foreign. For Albert Camus, who was spending some time in Palma de Mallorca, the cafés and the French newspapers offered the secure points of familiarity: "A paper printed in our own language, a place to rub shoulders with others in the evenings enable us to imitate the familiar gestures of the man we were at home, who, seen from a distance, seems so much a stranger."[24] The identified familiar realities allowed him to feel more at ease, mitigated his sense of unsettlement, and, to a certain extent, alleviated his sense of alienation from the surrounding people and their milieu. Thus we filter the perceptual field either by focusing only on familiar objects or by applying our own abstract conceptions and moral interpretations to the events and social interactions that rise moment after moment. It is with a similar kind of filter that we make our first purchases in an unknown store or read a book from an unfamiliar scholar. We remark on the shelves only the food we like or absorb from the pages only the ideas we know and value. An exotic fruit or an unusual observation remains unnoticed. When we do this, we unconsciously return to our past cultural environment and evaluate objects and people around us in light of our familiar culture, in which we live with a sense of security and confidence. On his return to Germany from North America aboard a ship, the philosopher Josef Pieper met passengers who had spent considerable time in the United States because they wanted to see the New World with their own eyes. "*With their own eyes*: in this lies the difficulty," notes Pieper after returning to his cabin. "During the various conversations on deck and at the dinner table, I am always amazed at hearing almost without exception rather generalized statements and pronouncements that are plainly the common fare of travel guides."[25] Indeed, these individuals lacked even the elementary condition for reaching an understanding of the foreign culture with which they wanted to make first-hand contact.

We often need, as I have said earlier, the stepping stone of the familiar in order to see and accept the foreign reality. Conversely, without any distracting or soothing help, we dare to look directly and unwaveringly for the foreign and welcome it in its foreignness.

But why and how should we cultivate, without any detour, the attunement to the foreign? Konrad Lorenz relates a story about Chulalongkorn, the king of Siam, who, as the guest of Emperor Francis Joseph, was taken to the Vienna Opera. Following the performance of an opera, officials of the imperial court, wanting so much to please, asked the monarch which part of the musical performance pleased him the most. He answered: the short piece played at the beginning of the evening. Further questioning made clear that the visitor meant the unsynchronized practice of the members of the orchestra before the performance, and not the overture of the opera. The king showed his outright preference for what appeared to him familiar and, obviously, strange to the Viennese listeners.[26]

This story tells us that the king and the hosts had their own structural understanding of music, art, and other human realities, an understanding that was the result of the education they had received in a particular cultural environment. It also illustrates their difficulty in correctly perceiving foreign forms. To succeed, they need not only establish repeated contacts with these forms, but also to adopt the appropriate attitude of receptivity to what is radically different. They cannot adopt this attitude in the absence of a firm grasp of what they had learned within their own culture. They are able to develop the desired receptivity if they place into the background their acquired cultural stock (concepts, ideas, theories, conducts, attitudes) and if they adopt a standpoint that seeks and establishes contrasts. In so doing, they are able to perceive the new and strange in its novelty and strangeness with an unprejudiced and unbiased mind. This distanced and contrasting awareness of the foreign also requires the uneasy willingness to combine learning with unlearning, attachment to our cultural roots with detachment from those roots.

But the story is also meaningful for another reason. Through their distancing contact with different realities, people become better able to compare the familiar and the foreign – in this case, the "melodic" music and the "chaotic" sounds – and gain a heightened awareness of what has been, for so long, familiar to them and of what now appears, to a certain extent, foreign. They come to perceive the familiar sounds "through other ears." In order to comprehend and courageously reconsider their own culture and their own conception of all its elements, as well as the tradition from which these elements emerged and the decisive influence they have on future endeavours and creations, they are required to distance themselves from their own familiar perceptions and ingrained points of view and to evaluate their relevance from another perspective, one opened up for them by the foreign.

Following this example, we now better see the extraordinary relevancy of foreign realities and points of view and of the disconcerting and sometimes even distressing, but highly rewarding, moments of direct contact we have with them. The foreign, through which we come back to ourselves, see ourselves afresh, acquire a better knowledge about ourselves, and eventually change ourselves, can be not only a distant land or persons living and working in this land, but also the work of a philosopher, an artist or, a novelist. Their "estranged vision," the way they perceive, describe, and encounter things and people, suddenly opens our eyes and promotes a heightened understanding of the formation and evolution of a whole range of human realities – religious beliefs, educational practices, or forms of human association – which exist in great variety and which are also subject to reassessment and change. Equally, the foreign can be a great variety of realities that we meet outside our immediate cultural environment: a restaurant, a cemetery, a city, a religious community, a school, a leisure activity, ways of entertaining guests, or ritual practices. Here again, we may welcome their entrancing appeal in order to move away from the obvious and to recognize and reap the benefit of the gained distance and enrichment.

There is a particular sphere of human relations in which the susceptibility to the foreign is indispensable and must be consciously nurtured. The successful work in diplomacy requires the ability to decentre from one's usual point of view and to see various situations and matters as the other sees them. After having been posted to various lands, trained diplomats are able to consider with sympathy, and even approval, the ideas and recommendations of their respective partners. In addition to the beneficial modification of their views, they also gain an elevated vision, as if they were looking at the negotiated topics from an altitude. This deportment of aloofness towards problems and solutions prevents them from forgetting the interests of their own countries, a risk created by an extended stay in a foreign land and the ensuing readiness to share the historical rootedness and particular mentalities of the local people. Therefore, their regular return to their own countries and the "wisdom of being transferred to a new posting" foster a vigilant and unfailing attachment to their own concerns without eliminating the ability to see a particular issue as others see it.[27] The responsive sensitivity to mentalities different from one's own is doubtless the most important quality to have in the art of diplomacy. This sensitivity makes possible the enrichment of the personality of the diplomat posted abroad by the elements of a foreign culture. This is the view of the Hungarian diplomat Miklós Bánffy who believed that it was his experience of writing plays, novels, and short stories that helped him, over the years, to acquire and develop this essential asset, since the art of writing requires, above all, the ability to put oneself into the cast of mind of fictional or real figures.[28]

WHAT IS IT THAT HELPS US TO SEE?

Let us now see what other experiences are able to liberate our vision from our own familiar cultural contexts, creating the needed transformative distance from those things and people that we seem to see so well but still fail to know. And, perhaps more importantly, what can help us see a foreign reality in its particular foreignness, to consider it with open minds and open hearts and, by reaching an understanding, to introduce some of its elements into our lives?

We come to distance ourselves from our own situation and face a foreign reality with an unprejudiced mind when we are willing to stop, reflect, and ask questions, and, after receiving the answers and reflecting upon them, we are willing to revise our already acquired stock of knowledge and beliefs. We frequently fail to see others as distinct and unique beings and display toward them the correct form of behaviour because we are unable to detach ourselves from our built-in prejudices and from our habitual manner of dealing with them. We tend to place the people facing us into a set of abstract categories. Seeing others in their individualities and understanding them requires distance and the ability to adapt our words and deeds to their concrete circumstances and actions. By asking a question, we introduce a break into the regular flow of our physical or mental activities and achieve the desired distance from ourselves and from the persons we would like to know better. Not only thinking, but also imagining and seeing, demands distance from our concrete situations and from ourselves.[29] As we immerse ourselves progressively deeper in a foreign culture, we might stop and ask questions about the character, motives, interests, and desires of the people around us. We gradually and tactfully try to go beyond the general and impersonal traits to reach to that which constitutes the uniqueness of a culture and the persons living in this culture. Why does this young woman smile when a tragic event occurs? Why does my neighbour never seem to say openly and directly what he has on his mind? What does my Japanese colleague think and want to say when he uses unusual metaphors? In all cases, in order for understanding to occur, the foreign also has to speak to us; a gesture, an attitude, a sentence, or an event has to be apprehended as a meaningful reality. The meaning is initially provided in the act of our reflective inquisitiveness; it carries a meaning, however vague or ambiguous it may be.

The question might be part of the comprehensive human act of wondering. We start to wonder when we carefully and questioningly peruse a scene in a foreign city and realize that its chief parts, perhaps a shop, all the colourful merchandises, and the venerable merchant before us, cease to appear in their banal and indifferent obviousness; they suddenly and directly come into our view with their at once strange and familiar presence. We wonder when we realize that something which we first consider a habitual act – taking a meal or purchasing food – suddenly presents itself with its peculiar character and requires a considerable effort. First it is the *being* of a thing (a shop) and of an act (taking a meal) that appears astonishing, the fact that a thing and an act *are* and offer themselves to all our senses. As we wonder about the extraordinary presence of the things and actions of the daily texture of life, we might also ask ourselves why and how we are able to notice all those forms and movements that surround us. We then see that we are beings that enter into sensory contact with all sorts of living and lifeless realities. We see that, through our senses, we continually and effortlessly enter into a "partnership" with an opulent and vibrant world.[30] And this primary sensory contact brings us to a magical realm of colours, sounds, odours, heat, and chill that, for the time being, we do not want to translate into symbols and numbers or to capture by a smart phone or a more sophisticated optical device. In that moment, we are not only able to better observe, trust, and know the things and actions encountered in this everyday life-world but, after a while, we also arrive at the point of integrating them into our lives and feeling replenished and enriched by them. Then, the wonder about the fact that we are able to realize life as we live it is completed by the wonder about the fact that we are able intensify our experience of life. We intensify it by noticing and enjoying what can and must happen for the first time. And we intensify it by transcending the boundaries of our familiar world and starting to feel at home in another foreign world.

In the moment of wondering, we stand still, introduce the distance of questioning, pay close attention to something or somebody that is no longer obvious, seek to reach beyond what is apparent and taken for granted or beyond what is opaque and obscure, and start to inquire about some hidden and still unknown elements, facts, or causes. We do this because we become genuinely interested in the peculiar characteristics of the object, we are captivated by its attractive presence, and we seek to perceive it with a benevolent eye. We may be attracted to an unusual relation between two objects, an unexpected occurrence, an odd form, or a paradoxical behaviour. As we come to a stop and wonder about these strange realities, we might admit that our knowledge is partial or completely inadequate and thus insufficient to provide us with the information and orientation we want or feel we need. Conversely, the absence of the sense of wonder comes, in part, from our unwillingness to stop, to tarry, to pay attention to our surroundings, to ask questions, and to place ourselves in a situation in which things, by displaying their pragmatic relevance or enigmatic poetry, can modify or enlarge our knowledge of the world.

But wonder is not merely the result of our voluntary readiness to stop, pay attention, and face what seems unfamiliar and extraordinary. Rather, we are being stopped and our attention is intensely affected by something. Wonder implies that we are seized by something and stirred deeply by the novelty and strangeness of what usually appears common and self-evident. Hence wonder is an experience, which involves and excites our intellect, imagination, and feeling. When we open ourselves to the gift of wondering, we experience a variety of feelings: confusion, suspicion, surprise, attraction, humility, zest, sadness, or joy. These emotional states, in their sequence, regulate the speed with which our eyes travel over things and our mind seeks their understanding.

It is often a feeling of confusion or curiosity that prompts us to ask questions. The question can be addressed to a person with ready tongue whom we happen to meet in a foreign country and whom we would like to better know. Obviously, we need to speak a common language in order ask questions and understand the answers. The initiated conversation helps us see how a human or material reality appears to this person and how his or her views and beliefs are formed within a social and geographic context. We do not merely inquire about observable facts that would be noticed by any disinterested and rigorous observer. We ask questions about realities that are important and even vital for the person and we would like to find out more about the world as it appears to him or her. By becoming acquainted with a particular world, we come to better know the person as well. As J.H. van den Berg correctly pointed out, "We get an impression of a person's character, of his subjectivity, of his nature and his condition when we ask him to describe the objects which he calls his own; in other words, when we inquire about his world. Not the world as it appears to be 'on second thought,' but the world as he sees it in his direct, day-to-day observation."[31]

There is, in the beginning of a conversation, as two persons face each other, an elusive and volatile moment, during which the chief characteristics of the encounter are established. This moment is decisive for breaking the ice between strangers and thus creating an atmosphere of openness and confidence that helps make the conversation a mutually fulfilling experience. The stiffness or casualness of bodily posture, the motion of the eyes and mouth are indispensable elements of this first encounter. It presupposes, obviously, the tacit recognition of the other person as a serious, empathic, and trustful partner who might teach us something or demand us to revise some of our views. While we are engaged in a conversation with empathy and genuine receptivity, we are able to see the world with the eyes of our interlocutor and to foster a receptive disposition in presence of what is different, illuminating, and even disturbing. Therefore, as Jonathan Sacks advises us, "We must learn the art of conversation, from which truth emerges not, as in Socratic dialogues, by the refutation of falsehood but from the quite different process of letting our world be enlarged by the presence of others who think, act, and interpret reality in ways radically different from our own."[32]

But what is the art of conversation when we meet someone in that person's home, which is a foreign place to us? To be sure, keeping alive the unfolding of questions and answers, and getting from this person fresh thoughts, observations, and points of view is a skill. The questions that we ask must be followed by a willingness to listen to the answers and by a sincere readiness to examine things from his or her point of view. But listening is far from being a passive behaviour. There are several ways of signalling that we are paying close attention. We might repeat some words from the answer in order to highlight what appears to be important in the comments or simply express our interest and attentive presence with an open facial expression. We might, quite unconsciously, adjust our speech to the rhythm, melodicity, and tonality of our interlocutor's speech. The successful imitation of idiomatic and sound configurations can result in more engaging communications. We tend to forget that a conversation involves much more than just the verbal exchange of questions and answers. As I have already pointed out, we find ourselves facing another living body; we breathe in an atmosphere that envelops two persons; we are sensitive to the distance between ourselves and our partner; we see the adopted posture, watch the movements of the hands, and remain attentive to facial expressions. The subtle and small-scale movements of the forehead, eyes, and mouth can have remarkable expressive effects; they can enrich words with nuances and all sorts of additional meaning. Aldous Huxley notes that "faces are very important to us, since it is by observing their changes of expression that we acquire much of our most valuable information about the thoughts, feelings, and dispositions of those with whom we come in contact."[33] We hear the words and understand their meanings. Yet the non-verbal sensory and atmospheric impressions that we also receive from a person add an indispensable complement to our attentive listening.

There is another virtue that, I think, is worth mentioning in relation to the art of conversation: the virtue of humour. I have already pointed out that humour modifies the ways we relate to our milieu. Through humour we are able to achieve a certain detachment from our circumstances and see human actions and achievements with impartiality, in a more relaxed and more critical manner. In a study worth reading in its entirety, the Dutch scholar Jan Linschoten highlights the paradoxical characteristics of humour, stating: "On the one hand, humour calls for a distance and a perspective; on the other hand, it creates an intimate relation to the human, an awareness of one's own humanity and the other humans as they are: although absurd, it is also good and beautiful."[34] More important perhaps, this interest in different forms of human life is complemented by an affectionate and unruffled understanding of the total of human experiences and inadequacies, as these often become manifest in jokes or puns. And this feeling of sympathy leaves its mark on the process of conversation and creates an atmosphere of conviviality, confidence, and perhaps even compassion. A smile brought on someone's face by an urbane humorous remark or the laughter produced by a perceptive joke creates an immediate effect; it instantaneously helps to overcome the barriers of separateness and to foster a more relaxed and trustful relationship.

Beyond a conversation with a foreigner who holds different views from ours, difficult external circumstances can help us to stop and to see "through other eyes." In a distant land, as I have already said, we find ourselves *dépaysés,* to use a rather apt French word. Moving around and meeting people without the secure points of reference on which we normally rely in our familiar environments can be deeply unsettling and cause stress or anxiety. But the early moments of discomfort can result in considerable benefit and wisdom. Just as much as in times of trouble, disturbance, and danger we see our own lives – with their main stages, achievements, and shortcomings – under a new light, equally, we gain unsuspected insights into a foreign culture when we live through unforeseen distress. As Plessner observed, "Pain is the eye of the spirit. It awakens us to new consciousness, liberates the vision and makes it resistant to the refractions and the opacities of prejudice."[35] In a foreign land, as we experience loneliness and desperation, we come to see the strange in all its details as well as that which previously seemed obvious and taken for granted. Strain makes our alert mind also attentive to all sorts of real obstacles and possible challenges that arise in our lived present; it makes it feel the sting of reality. More concretely, attempts to create satisfying and even enriching contacts with foreign communities may arise from the feeling of isolation and alienation, from lack of food or water, from being exposed to cold or heat. Distress, spiritual, moral, or physical, can awaken not only a better understanding of foreign cultures but also foster the effort to consciously assimilate mores and habits; the honest desire to belong. And the experience of being helped and of being accepted by strangers and of finding through them a relief from discomfort or hardship, as well as reasons to learn, adapt, and change, remains for many, in their life histories, exceptional and memorable.[36]

In his celebrated Nobel Lecture, Alexander Solzhenitsyn asked the fundamental question about the possibility of understanding another person's lifelong experience: "Who has the skill to make a narrow, obstinate human being aware of others' far-off grief and joy, to make him understand dimensions and delusions he himself never lived through?"[37] It is literature that has this skill. Writers and poets can provide us with the necessary distance and pause for our understanding; through reading or listening to their works, we come to a better perception of what has been taken as familiar and simple and what is, in fact, full of subtleties and mysteries, opening out to the whole of life people living far away from us in both space and time. Literature raises us above our everyday thinking and living; it exposes under new light the common and the habitual; it gives radiance to what often seems to us lustreless and meaningless; it also presses upon us the exotically foreign in various guises. In another Nobel Lecture, Patrick Modiano voiced the same view as did Solzhenitsyn forty-four years before:

> I have always thought that poets and novelists are able to impart mystery to individuals who are seemingly overwhelmed by day-to-day life, and to things, which are ostensibly banal – and the reason they can do this is that they have observed them time and again with sustained attention, almost hypnotically. Under their gaze, everyday life ends up being enshrouded in mystery and taking on a kind of glow-in-the-dark quality which it did not have at first sight but which was hidden deep down. It is the role of the poet and the novelist, and also the painter, to reveal the mystery and the glow-in-the-dark quality, which exist in the depths of every individual.[38]

Oddly enough, and sometimes quite sadly, there are men and women who are unable to accept and absorb the reality of something, familiar or foreign, just because they bump into it in their daily interactions. In order to truly understand, for example, the grief, loneliness, or anxiety of another person, they have to first read about it and thus gain access to it through their imagination. Once their imagination has conceived it, then the phenomenon becomes real, stirs their emotions, and evokes their wonder.

In a brilliant analysis of the works of Joseph Conrad, V.S. Naipaul implores novelists not to ignore the chief function of the novel: to offer an imaginative view and meditation on all the subtleties and miracles of our world. He says, "The novelist, like the painter, no longer recognizes his interpretive function; he seeks to go beyond it; and his audience diminishes. And so the world we inhabit, which is always new, goes by unexamined, made ordinary by the camera, unmediated on; and there is no one to awaken the sense of true wonder. That is perhaps a fair definition of the novelist's purpose, in all ages."[39] One might object that the story about the "world we inhabit" gives us some understanding of a particular individual – the writer – and not direct knowledge of life, something that we must acquire for ourselves. The most we can do is to compare the knowledge of this individual with our knowledge of how people, in general, act and of what they think, feel, and say.[40] The trouble with this contention is that it assumes that we see and discern just as well as the writer sees and discerns and that our direct or imagined knowledge of life is comparable to the writer's direct or imagined knowledge of life. But the writer's direct knowledge of life is different from our direct knowledge. Life is full of details that we just don't notice. Actions, both our own and those of others, are carried out most of the time in a state of self-forgetfulness. We have goals to reach, problems to resolve, and specific tasks to accomplish. The thoughts, words, and feelings of each present moment are not noticed and examined explicitly. We have no opportunity or desire to ponder our inner life or to get inside people's minds and hearts. Many aspects of our outer life, with their uniqueness and weight, simply fail to attract our attention or are irrevocably forgotten. And to see and remember life in its full richness and diversity, in relation to ourselves and to our fellow human beings, we need some kind of training or tutoring. "This tutoring is dialectical," observes James Wood. "Literature makes us better noticers of life; we get to practice on life itself; which in turn makes us better readers of detail in literature; which in turn makes us better readers of life. And so on and on."[41]

Even if we learn to become attentive to the many details of a real or imagined life, we may still miss what is essential in life, what gives meaning to a life in its totality and in one of its particular instances. Yet many novels or short stories reveal a meaning that people give to their destinies and to all the decisive actions that form these destinies. This meaning is not always expressed explicitly; a direct statement often lacks persuasive force. Rather, it is suggested through actions and dialogues and is often left unsaid. But the implicit meaning of the narrative gradually, or perhaps only after several readings, takes a shape in our mind even if the characters and their world are unfamiliar and even if, sometimes, we don't immediately know how to fit this meaning into our own world.[42] Still, when we read, for instance, the stories of Chekhov or von Kleist, we are often unable to grasp the underlying meaning of events and actions. Rather, we come to face and see before our eyes the ultimate incomprehensibility and strangeness of things and human endeavours. These writers tend to leave us with life's unresolved incongruities and are unable or unwilling to throw light on the deepest motives and characteristics of people. We close their books with the impression that the novelist has no access to the secret thoughts of his characters.[43] Yet, as C.S. Lewis correctly argued, there are many other writers who make possible for us an "enormous extension of our being" and, thanks to their remarkable capacity to bring people closer to us, we are able to place ourselves in the skin of the protagonist of their novels. By reading their stories we come to "see with other eyes," and feel with another heart. We "enlarge" our being; we see, imagine, and feel as others see, imagine, and feel, and we do this without losing ourselves. As Lewis asserts, we acquire this capacity "not only nor chiefly in order to see what they are like but in order to see what they see, to occupy, for a while, their seat in the great theatre, to use their spectacles and be made free of whatever insights, joys, terrors, wonders or merriment those spectacles reveal."[44]

Another English writer, D.H. Lawrence, tells his readers to think of America and American literature in terms of difference and otherness: "There is an unthinkable gulf between us and America, and across the space we see, not our own folk signalling to us, but strangers, incomprehensible beings, simulacra perhaps of ourselves, but *other*, creatures of an otherworld ... It is the genuine American literature which affords the best approach to the knowledge of this othering. Only art-utterance reveals the whole truth of a people. And the American art-speech reveals what the American plain speech almost deliberately conceals."[45] What is this whole truth? The stories of many American writers offer us a glimpse into the strangeness, marvels, and dreariness of ordinary people's everyday lives and thus create the appropriate conditions for a genuine understanding and discovery of what we might call the American reality. At the heart of this reality, beneath all misleading appearances, there is the pervading feeling of solitude, of being always at the edge of the world and of never truly belonging to a place or community. Distracted tourists fail to perceive this uncanny feeling because they are misguided by the apparent gregariousness and smiling chattiness of many American men and women. Yet it is still one of the root conditions in North America, and writers who see through the superficial urbanities of smaller and larger communities, of homes, factories, and offices, dwell upon it with astute and relevant things to say. Many of the protagonists of classic American novels and stories are solitary figures: disconnected from a particular place, distrustful of authorities, yearning for the love, recognition, and understanding of their fellow men and women, for a warmer experience of human contact, which is able to give deeper meaning to their existence.[46]

The idea of creating art-speech leads us to the idea of making things strange, of deliberately defamiliarizing them, of using the technique of *ostrannenie*, which is well known in literary studies. Writers introduce into their works distorting elements (selectivity, partiality, exaggerations, boldness in construction) in order to make the reader more sensitive to the particular places and cultures they are writing about. Their "distorted imagination" creates a "strange, wonderful, terrible, fantastic world."[47] Paradoxically, it is the writer's ability to invent all sorts of people and to place them in all sorts of unusual situations that makes reality accessible and comprehensible. As for readers, their vivid imagination is no less required in understanding those who are far-off from them, their preferences and aversions, and their ways of acting upon them. We might then remember the vivid and early contact with folk tales or the enchanting reading of Voltaire's *Candide*, Saint-Exupéry's *The Little Prince*, or Mark Twain's *Mysterious Stranger*. Fantastic fiction of this kind never loses its relevance and continues to be read and enjoyed by millions of people around the planet. At best, they convey universal and timeless principles about human existence and human conflicts. They create and use a moral world, in which human beings and the springs of their actions, as well as the context provided by the writer, appear in their unmistakable and concrete forms. The realistic is surely the most effective way to portray visible actions and their contexts in all their details; the fantastic, however, can tell us more convincingly and more directly about the characters' inner lives, and the ambiguity of their motives and courses of action, without being distracted by irrelevant information. It helps us focus on what appears to be essential while staying in touch with what is concrete. It allows us to gain a better view of fictional figures because they are not part of our everyday life and we are less involved in their opinions and actions. But the fantastic can do more than just provide vision. As C.S. Lewis aptly remarked, "it can give us experiences we have never had and thus, instead of 'commenting on life,' can add to it."[48]

Even a casual encounter with men and women living in a foreign country may make us aware of some of their views and opinions. We also notice their attitudes towards other people and the judgments they make on the more or less important events occurring in their environment. They support various causes and hold beliefs in order to sustain their decisions. Although we may possess all this information, we still cannot grasp their inner condition, their emotional state. We still do not know why they act in certain ways, what makes them hesitate, why they hold firmly to some opinions and discard others, how they select and interpret facts, and why they engage in inner monologues. We do not know why they are unable to stand up for their convictions and why they reach an unsurpassable limit in their interactions with their friends, spouses, or other members of their families. In order to understand their worldview and the inner springs of their actions, we need to go beyond their everyday speech, the role they play in their society, the characteristics of their work and leisure pursuits, learning more about their inclinations, desires, self-deceptions, and pulses of feelings.

Literature unlocks the realm of emotional responses to human actions and the human actions prompted by emotions, and helps us understand, or at least conjecture, their bearing upon life – ours and other people's. This connection is usually hidden from our view because we are prone to conceal it or to convince ourselves that feelings are blind or muddled and, therefore, play no role in our "impartial" decisions and "rational" actions. The vision of the artist, writes Plessner, "lifts what is invisible in human relations, because it is familiar, into visibility; in this new encounter, understanding is brought into play."[49] The invisible yet familiar in a relation between a man and a woman, a parent and a child, a teacher and a student could be admiration, resentment, fear, self-confidence, trust, or other states of mind. The writer may make familiar human relations strange and significant or relate the common relations to wider contexts or worlds that the readers, to some extent, may share. In both cases, the emotional undertones of the human situation, as well as of the formation of opinions, beliefs, principles, and actions, are made manifest and comprehensible. Whereas, as D.H. Lawrence puts it, a verbal symbol stands for a thought or an idea, the symbols used in literature – art-symbols, art-terms – "stand for a pure experience, emotional and passional, spiritual and perceptual, all at once." In other words, a novel communicates to the reader not only

114 In Vivo

the prevalent habits, mores, and conventions of a historical era and the action that unfolds within the confines of a foreign society but also, and above all, a whole cast of mind or "state of being" of men and women whose greatest challenge is finding a satisfying balance between what they want to be as unique individuals and what they are called to be as ordinary members of a larger society.

EXCURSUS: FOSTERING INTERCULTURAL COMMUNICATION

The most eminent philosophers, engaged in the serious study of human being – Max Scheler, Helmuth Plessner, Michael Landmann, or, more recently, Gerd Haeffner – have repeatedly emphasized the vital role of the diversity of cultural frames of reference, without which humans could not exist. They have acknowledged the value of the plurality of cultural forms and have called for, in the words of Landmann, the "loving contemplation of foreign cultures" and the adoption of ideas, customs, and values generated and cherished by these cultures. Humans do not produce a single culture, but, thanks to their variability and creativity, a large number of cultures. More importantly, the diverse cultures have fundamentally equal rights. According to Landmann, "Everything that has grown organically and with genuine necessity contains an ultimate meaning and stands at the same level."[50] Criticizing the mono-causal interpretation of history – and rejecting the idea of a fixed, singular, and ideal form of culture, understood as the goal of history – Landmann demands the genuine recognition of the variability of philosophies and cultural creations.

In our epoch of globalization, we hear many calls to open ourselves to intercultural perspectives, to the colourful cultural diversity of the world, to a truly international philosophical viewpoint. These appeals tell us that it is time to break with an ingrained habit of thinking within the narrow perspective of a particular cultural tradition and to develop a genuine sensitivity to other cultures. We are told that we may nurture this sensitivity by extensive travel or by reading the literary and scholarly works written by people in these distant lands.

However important these invitations may be, these authors ought to remember that their explicit intercultural orientation is perhaps new, but the implicit viewpoint is certainly not. It is, in fact, the adopted way of doing philosophy by eminent and perhaps still insufficiently studied thinkers of a more or less distant past. In short, the multicultural perspective should not be considered as a recent rectification of a long-entrenched attitude towards the basic problems of human existence or as a new way of philosophizing about the nature of human being. It is an inherent methodological aspect of serious anthropological knowledge, which stretches back in history.[51]

One of these prominent thinkers, Helmuth Plessner, argues that the philosophical study of human being should remain an open inquiry with the purpose of reaching a "universal point of view" that allows one to embrace all cultures and all ages.[52] Plessner is convinced that a singular cultural form cannot represent the whole range of human abilities and creations. Therefore, it is important to recognize the diversity of cultures, become acquainted with their richness, and work out new theories with the help of acquired "multicultural" knowledge. Plessner also speaks in favour of the need to give up the idea of the supremacy of a system of categories and values generated in Europe. He stresses the need of adopting an attitude of receptivity to the diversity of cultures and to their "world aspects."

An intercultural approach to anthropological themes is a dynamic process of observation, questioning, and reflection that requires receptivity to foreign, unfamiliar ways of thinking and living, and an ability to understand, analyze, and value the experiences and conceptual frameworks of different cultures. Engaged in this process, we should avoid the rigid and unfruitful opposition of cultural relativism and trans-cultural universalism. (In fact, culture as a fundamental dimension of being human is both natural and universal.) We, then, come to see that the analysis might focus, first, on a relativistic viewpoint and, later, put forward claims of universal validity, and vice versa, without taking them as exclusive positions and strict alternatives. For example, the inquiry into *ki*-energy, with its use in the areas of meditation, acupuncture, and martial arts, could be carried out from a singular cultural standpoint and, could become a pivotal step in proposing a new and trans-cultural understanding of the body and of our general human makeup.

Or we might single out the basic human experience that is not bound to a specific place or historical age: the aversion to physical pain, for example. This is common to all human life. Then, as we go on to consider the specific ways of dealing with pain, we come to recognize that the various attitudes towards pain – confrontation, submission, or technological neutralization – are, in fact, culturally shaped. Similar relations can be established with regard to the feeling of anxiety in the face of death. Whatever path or direction we take and follow, we should maintain the awareness of the difference between the universal and the singular and the respective validity of both viewpoints.

To be sure, we undertake our anthropological projects from our own particular perspectives, within our own cultural frameworks, and on the basis of our own experiences of being human. We then advance what we consider valid for all other cultures. When, for example, we claim that a universal aspect of our humanity is the ability, through language, to express momentary feelings, represent distant realities, and communicate ideas, we put forward, from our philosophical standpoints, definitions that apply to all human beings. We confidently declare that men and women, wherever they live, are generally endowed with the gift of speech and are also able to communicate at a societal level through various techniques and tools.

There might be a great variation in the manners of covering the body with clothing, regulating the relationship between men and women, playing with objects, or communicating through language. Yet, we can assert that all these experiences are essential features of human life. It would be hard to imagine a normal human life in absence of any one of these functions.

Doubtless, the use of a language presupposes that people have an education provided and supported by the people living in the particular cultural environment. If an appropriate education is in place, this cultural constant is harmonious and fully functioning. The fundamental activities – speaking, playing, and covering the body – remain the same, but the cultural frames vary from society to society, and within a society, from age to age.

We surely have to temper our confidence when we declare, without the slightest hesitation, that the ability to sing in tune in groups is a pivotal aspect of all human communal life. Can we apply this specific musical gift to humans living in distant lands and in dissimilar cultural conditions? How can we verify the validity of our assertions and obtain confirmations from members of a specific human community and musicians belonging to this community? Thus, our claim about group singing may only be true within a particular cultural tradition and may fail to have cross-cultural applicability. We must be careful not to confound universal principles with particular cultural characteristics. When we single out aptitudes and activities, and, without careful study and reflection, make of them common features, we risk advancing a distorted understanding of our humanity.

The growing emphasis on historical and cultural differences may lead someone to reject, or to be suspicious of, the common universal features of human life. The main objection to such an effort evokes the "outdated willingness" to promote the views of the dominant group and the tendency to neglect the ideas and interpretations of less powerful cultural traditions. Here is a representative statement, issued by Gunter Gebauer and Christoph Wulf, who favour a historical and cultural interpretation of human characteristics over the reliance upon essentialist conceptions: "To find out what human beings are, the differences between them are much more important than what they have in common. What is common to mankind is right, especially human rights, which belong in a normative discussion. Anthropology, however, is not a part of morality or any other discipline concerned with what we should be. Instead, it is concerned with empirical human beings, examining the ways they develop diverse differences from given situations, and relating these differences to each other."[53] The rejection of an arrogant philosophy, immune to external influences and insensitive to human variability, is appropriate. Arrogance is often a preemptive self-defence. An eminent African philosopher Kwasi Wiredu called this attitude "parochialistic universalism." As he so aptly put it, the "antidote to parochialistic universalism is not any sort of anti-universalism but rather judicious universalism."[54] The above-mentioned thinkers have not asserted and defended "parochialistic universalism." The most notable ones resisted every sort of unilateral standpoint and adopted complementary approaches to human experiences. As for the different cultural patterns and expressions, we are able to observe them and relate them to each other only if we are able to grasp the underlying universal determinants. We may notice a great number of social gestures, from stiff austerity to polite bowing. However numerous and different these gestures may be, they are all related to a universal feature: our upright posture. The gestures are all variations of one theme: standing on one's feet and meeting others face to face.

Notwithstanding the current openness to different cultural patterns and traditions, we should not turn our backs on the study of the universal features of our human nature. These include, of course, the upright posture, mobility of our hands, play, and humour, and the physical needs of infants during the early years of their lives. We are able to identify these features not by consulting textbooks, but by "intuitive approximation" (Martha Nussbaum).[55]

The call for the study of "empirical human beings" is only half of the work, but it is surely an indispensable part. In this respect, travels and extended stay in foreign countries are valuable springboards for gaining anthropological insights. But our philosophical inquiry cannot, and should not, be carried out according to the methodology adopted by natural and social sciences, even though experimental research also contributes to a better understanding of human behaviour. The purely theoretical analysis, undertaken by scholars of different traditions, is also an indispensable part of the philosophical endeavour. The results of this research set forth conceptual models that constitute the basis of our understanding and modification of the various cultural domains. Educational practices, as well as ethical views, may be shaped according to a more or less explicit, normative theoretical framework. It may also help us to attune ourselves to diversity, to see it with different eyes, and to welcome its unique and transformative impact on our lives.

5

How Can Anything Be So Beautiful?

Music is not a science, but an art; in music an instant of true appreciation and perception is worth an age of learning and lore.

A.L. Bacharach

Marie-Henri Beyle, commonly known by his pen name Stendhal, related, in a letter to his sister, an exquisite and unforgettable sensation that he experienced at the age of seventeen: "The first time I took pleasure in music was at Novara, a few days before the battle of Marengo. I went to the theatre, where they were playing *Il Matrimonio Segreto*. The music delighted me like an expression of love. I think no woman I have ever had gave me so sweet a moment, or at so light a price, as the moment I owe to that newly heard musical phrase. This pleasure came to me without my in any way expecting it: it filled my whole soul."[1]

Those who, later in their lives, become famous composers or brilliant interpreters often recall these kinds of experiences. During his first communion, the young Hector Berlioz heard a chorus of young voices singing an adaptation of Nicolas Dalayrac's aria *Quand le bien-aimé reviendra*. He recalls, "As I took the sacrament a chorus of virginal voices broke into the Eucharistic hymn, and I was filled with a mystic yet passionate unrest which I was powerless to hide from the congregation. I thought I saw heaven open, a heaven of love and chaste delight, a thousand times purer and more beautiful than the one I had so often been told about. Such is the magic power of true expression, the incomparable beauty of a melody that comes from the heart!"[2]

Many people have been carried away and even uplifted by the "magic power" of the sounds while listening to a piano sonata in a concert hall, a haunting folk tune at a festive gathering, or a virtuoso jazz improvisation in a nightclub, the very same way that they have been excited by a thought or a mathematical theory. The exclamation "incomparable beauty of a melody" seems to be universal. The beautiful is not a value that listeners assess, measure, and explain objectively; rather, it involves the apprehension of an all-pervasive and exhilarating quality, which is experienced as an intoxicating delight without the need of justification in terms of clearly articulated aesthetic criteria.

In a lecture given before a recital, the Hungarian composer Zoltán Kodály asked his audience to stop listening to expository talks about music. However thorough and accurate the formal analysis of a piece may be, it would inevitably fail to evoke in listeners what he called the "true understanding" of music. Scholarly articles or lectures may help someone to better appreciate the wondrous beauty of a painting by Rembrandt and even to evoke curiosity for the technical aspects of his art. But, when it comes to music, the conceptual and abstract study of a composition alone can neither create an experience of enchantment nor produce genuine understanding. Kodály illustrated his point with an anecdote derived from personal experience:

> Once I saw a woman, with elementary education, cleaning beside a radio. Suddenly she stopped her work, listened to the music, and, when the piece was over, asked: "How can anything be so beautiful?" I think this is the beginning of all kinds of musical understanding. As long as someone is deprived of this experience of standing still, of wondering, and of crying out "How can anything be so beautiful?," all of the popular literature, specialized books, studies, and programs dealing with music will be read in vain since, in absence of such an experience, he will grasp only the superficial and external aspects of music.[3]

The musical understanding that Kodály wanted to awaken in the lives of men and women is global and intuitive and does not require any extensive theoretical elaboration. All those who possess advanced technical knowledge of music and an analytical ear, but who remain unmoved in the presence of a sublime melody, prove the truth of the claim. There are others, of course, who intuitively and spontaneously understand the beauty of a counterpoint by Bach or a string quartet by Mozart before they come to study and to appreciate the formal aspects of music. Their intuitive understanding *of* music precedes their theoretical understanding *about* music, to use the telling distinction introduced by the music critic Hans Keller. Knowledge *of* music arises out of a direct experience; knowledge *about* music is something obtained by extracting facts from books – facts unattached to a concrete experience. The natural and instinctive relation to music is organic and inexplicit. "Music can be possessed without knowledge," the famous violinist Yehudi Menuhin tells us, "I learned to love music before I learned to say so."[4] Alan Walker wholeheartedly agrees: "Musical appreciation is not the result of rational inquiry … Musical experience is a pre-analytic experience in no way dependent on conceptual notions."[5] Whatever information a technical analysis may offer with regard to the specific temporal and tonal attributes of a fugue or of a theme, it can never cancel out, much less replace, the initial experience. Musicologists and musicians themselves might even enjoy listening to music while in a dreamy and nostalgic frame of mind, without paying attention to the structural build-up of the piece and without trying to translate their purely intuitive appreciation into a conceptual and technical explanation.[6]

In respect to this immediate experience of a reality, Eugène Minkowski proposed a luminous distinction between two ways of looking at stars. One may consider a star as a poet or as a child, seeing in it those expressive and dynamic qualities, which animate it and give life to it. Or one may look at a star with the eyes of a scientist, wanting to identify, with rigour and objectivity, all the observable facts. The scientific investigation does not cancel out the child's discovery of certain expressive qualities; both are right and valid. According to Minkowski, "The child, by looking at the star, discovers a whole world in it. It is in the truth. And we have merely to follow him by trying, however, to translate with words that upon which this discovery rests and that in which this particular movement consists, encompassing into one whole the cosmos, the star, and the soul which contemplates it."[7]

In this chapter, the focus is on the characteristics of the listener's musical experience and not so much on the formal details or meaning of a musical work. It is examined chiefly from the perspective of the philosophy of the human person, though I also turn to the aesthetics of Nicolai Hartmann and others who have discussed issues pertaining to the nature of musical understanding and enjoyment.[8] I propose to write, in the words of the composer Carl Philipp

In Vivo

Emanuel Bach, about the *Liebhaber*'s experience and not that of the *Kenner*. I will examine the response of an enthusiastic music-lover, and not that of a professional musician or musicologist, to a captivating musical piece; this I do as a prelude to a reflection on the significance of uplifting musical experiences for people of all ages. For the former, listening to a musical piece is first a feeling, not a thinking activity. The examples are taken from the domain of classical music, with which I have some familiarity. However, I believe that my reflections are valid for the encounters people may have with any genre of music of high quality and, I dare to think, even with the outstanding creations of other forms of performing art.

THE BEAUTIFUL IN MUSIC

The response to an articulated succession of sounds that I identify as a piece of music is obviously subjective. It is subjective even when I am part of an enthralled audience listening to a symphonic work or a solo recital at a concert hall. Music exists because others play it and I hear it, or I play it and hear it. The way I experience music depends on my mood, attentiveness, taste, the place where I find myself, my previous musical experiences, and, of course, on the artistic characteristics of the piece I am listening to. I may have a thrilling musical experience while attending a concert or singing in a choir or, as the above-mentioned anecdote by Kodály shows, simply standing in a room and listening to a recording. As for the object of my intuitive response, it may cut across all types, styles, lengths, or shades of music. Neither the work nor the performance has to match a critical yardstick or receive recognition from a musicological or aesthetic standpoint. Likewise, the musical examples I am giving here do not require unanimous approval even if, in my opinion, their value is inherent and subject to few or no disputes.

What sort of music do we, musical laypersons, spontaneously qualify as "beautiful" during an exalted moment? It seems to me that, even without knowing much about music's formal intricacies, we tend to display some preferences and describe our experience with a single set of key concepts. Whether we hear a symphony, a sonata, or a song, most of us like to hear tuneful melodies, although we cannot really say what a melody is. (The preference for delightful melodies does not cancel out at all the appreciation of a pleasing sequence of harmonies and rhythmic figures. In fact, it is impossible to organize successive musical tones without rhythm. And the melodic and rhythmic organization of tones has, of course, a harmonic aspect.) If someone were to ask us, we might define the melody as a fine-sounding musical phrase or a singing tune or quite simply as musical music. Melody, with its continuity, inventiveness, repeatability, and completion, makes music significant and enjoyable for most of us: we are able to retain it, identify ourselves with it, and return to it. Sometimes, quite unexpectedly, a melody or part of a melody pops into our head even if we have not heard it for many years. We hear it internally as an uninterrupted sequence of tones moving up and down.

The composer Roger Sessions is correct to say that our relation to music is a healthy one if we first want to find some pleasure in it. The paradoxical statement, evoked also by Sessions, that "the more one loves music, the less music one loves," applies only to expert listeners, those who are often very selective about what they want to hear and whose choices are not necessarily guided by the search for a melodic line and enjoyment.[9] They might look for the complexity of the harmonic construction or the intricacies of the rhythmic elements, regardless of whether the music is tonal or atonal. But those who do not possess expert knowledge of music, its elements and rules, are more likely to enjoy a piece that is melodic in its inspiration. The uninformed music-lover's sensitive ear intuitively knows that a monophonic or a polyphonic melodic line is the basic ingredient of a great number of musical forms. And both are vocally derived. This, of course, may lead to a superficial and exclusive approach to music. If a series of dissonant chords or unusual rhythmic figures meet their ears, their attention may fade away. They may remain on the level of an "atomistic listening" of isolated elements, of a passive and selective approach to music, which has been the object of severe and relentless criticism by Theodor W. Adorno. If, however, a melodic motif truly captures their ears and elicits a response of concentrated listening to an intricate structure, they come to develop a heightened and attentive awareness of music's other elements. They notice, while hearing a complex musical work, not only the vast range of colours and of moods and choices of key-relations, but also the shifts of emphasis from rhythm to harmony and from harmony to melody. Then, the ability to experience music as a composite and balanced construction, with various planes and levels, allows them to identify, without any musical dictionary, the formal density of a composition, its evident and discrete parts, and its deeper meaning.

Composers from the distant and even recent past understood this. Many of their concertos, sonatas, or symphonies are charming and entertaining at first hearing. Indeed, we are able to follow and to enjoy them without much strain of effort. They used a lucid and comprehensible musical language to express their individual ideas and feelings. Why do we find them so appealing? The reason is that these works were composed by a singing mind and heart. Handel, Haydn, and Mozart have written music for "singing instruments" from the "seeds of enduring vocal melodies," to use the expressions of the musicologist and composer Lajos Bárdos. He has demonstrated that a great number of instrumental works evolved from easily singable melodies, such as the one used by Bach in his Passacaglia and Fugue in C minor. According to Bárdos, *an elemental vocal basis* is probably much more significant in the thought processes of composers of instrumental music than is generally realized."[10] His study has important educational significance: it not only prompts us to have a deeper respect for vocal music, but also reminds us that children gain an understanding *of* music primarily through attentive listening or repeated performance of works in which the melody is pre-eminent.

The melodious piece that we find intuitively beautiful makes us forget our usual concerns and introduces a salutary pause into our daily lives. This suspension of ordinary activities and interactions is due to a particular way of perceiving the coming and going of sounds. I suggest that music makes us enter into a distinctive auditory world, in which we experience some of the characteristics of play. We hear a musical piece as a form of play and experience our contact with the sounds as an uplifting ludic experience. Bernhard Welte viewed music as a "model of pure play" because it transcends what he calls the "earnestness of life." "Music offers," he notes, "a perfection that hovers in itself and stands above the habitual and prosaic activities of men and women."[11] Everything that seems pivotal in our existence – joy and pain, strife and reconciliation, cheerfulness and melancholy, chance and order, life and death – comes to the fore symbolically in music. Music, as all other forms of play, obeys strict rules; yet, at the same time, it is freed from the gravity of serious concerns and manifests the "highest and freest vitality."

Beyond the particular emotional content that we often attribute to music, we may listen to a sonata the same way as we watch or play a delightful and captivating game: the tones follow each other in the absence of a previously fixed goal, which would bring them to an abrupt end, or a definite program, which would require the articulation of, and fidelity to, a conception of what the music was supposed to depict. Of course, music, experienced in its peculiar immediacy, reaches a final accord or note, a conclusion, and, as we will see, it may prompt us to identify or to guess a meaning beyond the sounds. However, while we hear it and are taken by it, we are neither concerned with the final resolution of tones nor with the meaning or narrative to which the sounds may refer. Since music enjoys relative freedom from an easily identifiable theme, its central feature is not so much the representation of an experience or an event, but the pure self-representation of play. While listening to a piece, we relish being drawn into the playful sequence of sounds. "Music is *a free play* with the form," says Nicolai Hartmann. "It is a genuine creative activity that takes the place of the representation, a pure play done for its own sake."[12] Hartmann goes so far as to claim that, in music, the "principle of play" reaches a full autonomy and becomes manifest in an unadulterated fashion.

The playful character of music is further emphasized when the musicians take up a light-hearted attitude and truly *play* with the tones. In all play, there must be something with which the player plays; one cannot play alone. Play is a reciprocal relation with something that, in its turn, thanks to its mobility, expressive quality, or dynamic and sensory possibility, plays with the player. The players are relieved of the strain of repeated initiatives to be drawn into the play and ultimately captivated by the playful interaction itself. In the musical performance, the most important partner of play is the tone. The tones press upon the musicians, communicate an impulse value and affective appeal, resonate in them, and induce them to produce other tones. (It is easy to see and hear this strong appeal in the life of children who, at a very young age, start to play with sounds. The sounds become magnets, which, captivatingly, attract other sounds. This play provides a basis for their subsequent musical and verbal expressions.) It is the binding and appealing character of the tones that personally affects the performers and compels them to respond in some way. The tones present a range of dynamic possibilities and these, together with the score and the directives communicated by the conductor or fellow musicians, provide the incentive to create a musical structure with relative freedom and inventiveness. Just like the capricious movements of a ball or a wheel, the lively succession of tones holds the performers in its spell, exerts on them an attraction, generates a playful response, and altogether sustains a spontaneous tendency to play. The atmosphere created by the music itself – especially when it is destined for live performance – further enhances the spontaneous and playful approach to the musical score. The performers, then, perceive the atmospheric quality as an invitation to play with the tones. In short, the atmosphere of *musical play* generates and sustains the performance of *playful music*.[13]

Listeners also respond to both the tones' affective appeal and the playful atmosphere created by the musicians. Because of the deeper resonances created by the coming and going of tones, they are often eager to participate in the unfolding musical play with their whole bodies. If they listen to an enchanting piece at home or while driving their car, they tend to hum the melody or, if they attend a public concert, they accomplish hardly visible movements with their legs or hands. In addition, the listeners' interest in the play of tones is greatly inspired by the fact that music does not represent concrete objects. While some tones are always able to make gripping suggestions, music as a whole has an intrinsic value: it is its own purpose and not a means to represent or imitate something. The vivid variety of tones pleases the ear just as much as a pure geometrical form delights the eye.

However, the sensual pleasure to be derived from this gambol of sounds should not lead us to endorse a strictly formalist position.[14] As Hartmann correctly observes, the "beauty of forms" and the "beauty of appearance" are not irreconcilable realities. They are merely two different aspects of the same reality and, consequently, two different sources of our contentment. At no moment does music's expressive depth disappear. As we will see, even a seemingly neutral composition, signifying neither a concrete reality nor an abstract idea beyond what it is, implicitly reveals something of its creator.

It has been often suggested that music, whether heard in a concert hall or appreciated through the study of the score, transports the listener or the reader into a magical world. Although Theodor W. Adorno worked on the project of a philosophical study of Beethoven for over thirty years, he was unable to combine the wealth of his materials into a completed book. He left behind a great number of preparatory notes, "a diary of his experiences of Beethoven's music," as he put it. In his diary, he tells us that in his youth he experienced *magical power* emanating from the score. His first impressions did not fade away: as an adult he still viewed musical language as something magical and perfect, remote from the objective world, and, at the same time, affirmative, consoling, and true.[15]

The *Benedictus* in Beethoven's *Missa Solemnis* illustrates Adorno's observation. We recognize its magical perfection intuitively when it confronts us. Perfection is a fundamental value that we sense and, if someone happens to inquire about the quality of our experience, we confidently state. We might be asked to provide a careful analysis of the musical material and to explain and perhaps even to justify the value attributed to this piece. It is a reasonable request to which, by consulting the score and a few scholarly texts, we may eagerly respond. What is unreasonable, however, it is to provide an explanation to someone in order to prepare the ground for his or her experience of wonder at the encountered perfection. As I have indicated earlier, the moment of intense musical appreciation does not depend on a structural analysis. If someone remains indifferent to the ethereal violin solo in the *Benedictus*, the knowledge about the initial sonority (G major), the falling thirds and rising sixths and variations of the theme will not help to create an emotional resonance to the music. True, the analysis satisfies our curiosity with respect to the reasons for our aesthetic experience and our value judgment. It also tells us what we have missed during our initial listening and, as we return to the composition, what kind of details and connections we should take note of in a complex musical construction in order to enjoy music's full effect. It may also tell us why the contrapuntal musical lines create in us the effect of deep feelings of tenderness and of serenity, an experience that we can hardly describe in words. (In fact, when we try to put our experience into words, we risk spoiling the magic.) It may, ultimately, also clarify what Beethoven's conception of blessedness was and why, for instance, Aldous Huxley saw in the fine interweaving of melodies of the *Benedictus* an equivalent to the living darkness of the night.[16]

When a musical work is perceived as being perfect, it admits of no attempt to improve upon it. In his famous lecture, Leonard Bernstein has shown, indirectly, why it is not possible to improve upon Beethoven's *Fifth Symphony*.[17] All the ingredients of this composition are built up according to the "principle of inevitability." Thus, thanks to their perfection, masterpieces receive a widespread recognition in the form of frequent performance and repeated listening. In his book *The A-B-C of Aesthetics*, Leo Stein has defined the three chief characteristics of good art: it is *known*, that is, it is acknowledged as a work of art by someone, somewhere; it is *unified*, that is, it is perceived as a complete and coherent form, in music as a piece with some sort of beginning, middle, and end; and it *endures*, that is, it cannot be consumed by use. The third quality is pivotal. No matter how many times we hear a Beethoven symphony, we still feel the need to hear it again. A work lacking the quality of enduring perfection will never retain this kind of hold over us.[18]

The magical perfection that invites us to return to specific compositions may be in the music's charming simplicity and the ease with which we are able to follow the themes, variations, and returns. But the discreet simplicity of, for instance, a Nocturne by Gabriel Fauré or a Mazurka by Fryderyk Chopin has nothing to do with the facility of execution or the plainness of the musical material. We also want to hear a composition again and again because of its purity and authenticity. Authenticity, as we have already seen, has to do with fullness, depth, and vigour, and these are given in a well-ordered manner, without superfluous ornaments. Our unceasing interest in listening to a given piece may be sustained by our ability to recognize the brilliant reintroductions and transformations of themes and passages. Of course, recognizing the subtle and sometimes distorted variation of a theme requires repeated listening, partly because great composers refuse to give a full display of their extraordinary technique of musical construction. Nonetheless, the inventive transformations, as well as the use of litotes, are not characteristics that need to be objectively assessed and measured. We sense them without the need to rely on external criteria or undertake a detailed technical analysis.

Not infrequently, a singular fullness and depth and a sublime climax is experienced in the moment of silence following the last note of a symphony or a mass. "What a moment of silence," writes Bernard Welte, "a moment of fulfilment, of plenitude, of radiant presence."[19] All the tones, chords, themes, all their variations, transpositions, and repetitions are, as it were, condensed into a singular magical moment, into a pure and timeless presence. It often happens that attentive listeners, overcome by one of the majestic symphonic works of Beethoven or of Bruckner, are unable to move or to speak for some time after the orchestra has finished playing the victorious conclusion. They concretely feel music's presence, which is no longer a sonorous reality, yet it is still accessible in the form of silence, because music is, in fact, also a "kind of silence" (Vladimir Jankélévitch). In this precious moment of silence, they encounter a concentration of the whole musical work, its presence above and beyond the temporal succession of tones.[20]

What is this timeless and silent presence? Welte's observation reminds us that we are able to perceive the multiple ingredients of a musical form through two complementary approaches: we either listen to the unfolding of various musical elements or pay attention to the structural coherence of all the elements and, by doing so, we transcend the succession of evanescent tones. If we concentrate on the succession of tones, we notice the musical details and subtleties, which gradually reveal the style of the composer. If we prefer to perceive a complete musical architecture in the moment of its achievement, we grasp an overall impression of a complex structure that may be described as tragic, sarcastic, luminous, sombre, tender, sad, joyful, or nostalgic. We first experience a presence that inevitably becomes an absence and, second, an absence that asserts itself as a presence. Music is heard in the present, as tones yield to other tones and prefigure all the tones that are still to come, or beyond the duration of a musical work, as a living unity of absent tones conveying a singular emotional quality in the moment of conclusion. The paradox of musical listening consists in hearing a melody when the tones are played in the present and when they are irretrievably gone. As Gabriel Marcel has stated, "All musical experience reflects the tragic tension implicit in the struggle against time, the contrast between the musical matter that, through actualized sound, exists only in the present, and its form that can constitute its unity only beyond duration within the immobile and silent judgment."[21] In the moment of dense silence, after the very last chord or tone has been played, we come to fully realize that everything that we hear as music is an elusive and, eventually, an absent reality. Music's sonorous presence escapes us; it eludes our grasp, it recedes always further away into an unattainable distance. A vague feeling of melancholy may seize us: we realize that musical perfection is a transient reality. Nonetheless, as long as there is someone to listen to it, the evanescent melody never moves towards nothingness. In a sense, music is a *présence lointaine* (Vladimir Jankélévitch), fading irrevocably into a mysterious absence that still holds us spellbound as a complete musical form that transcends the sensuous tones. Considered in a phenomenological perspective, silence can be heard. As Gisèle Brelet has reminded us, the final resonant silence is not merely "nothingness" or "privation;" it is a presence and fulfilment. It makes of a musical work both a fading and unfading reality. Brelet adds, "When real sonority fades away, then is born the remembered sonority of thought. Silence gives the act of memory the means to construct form. By withdrawing us from audible and material music, silence compels us to possess it in truth, which is to stay in the mind."[22]

But let us return to our experience of music's sensuous reality. Music's "unspeakable perfection and fineness" creates a magical atmosphere, in which the usual relations and oppositions of our everyday life tend to disappear, and invites us to focus on the succession of tones and chords.[23] We then abandon ourselves to music's captivating presence in a state of effortless absorption and of auditory pleasure. In this atmosphere, the actualized sounds seem to have the mysterious power to captivate, to charm, to lift us to a state of alert receptiveness, and to elicit, as it were independently of the musicians' intentionality, the coming and going of innumerable other sounds. While we are immersed in listening to a recital, we may notice that music's charm, its "magic suggestiveness" (Joseph Conrad), is a fragile thing. As soon as someone or something makes us conscious, directly or indirectly, of our enthrallment and feeling of unity with the sounds, we risk losing it. Music's inherent and imponderable magic exists only for the innocent and unselfconscious ear. Expressly noticing a momentary charming atmosphere contributes to its sudden evaporation. Being aware of something and noticing it are two different acts. I can be aware of a beautiful face, attracted to it, without thinking about its physiognomy and the reason for my attraction. Therefore, submitting listeners to experiments in a laboratory setting and taking physiological measurements while they listen to music yields limited results. These delicate and exquisite moments of being fully taken by a beautiful melody and by its elusive achievement in silence cannot be prepared in advance. Some of the most rewarding and fulfilling human experiences can neither be created by conscious effort nor be subjected to examination and conceptual analysis. A conversation between friends remains an enjoyable experience, a rare gift, as long as its richness and warmth fall outside of the objectifying attention and are merely lived with a lateral awareness. The orientation, ease, humour, and silences of a genuine conversation can be neither predicted nor validated by detached observation. Let us imagine that we are invited to a rehearsal as an orchestra plays Mozart's Sinfonia Concertante for Violin, Viola and Orchestra in E-flat Major. As we give ourselves up to the beautiful dialogue between the instruments in the haunting andante movement, the conductor, with his grating voice, suddenly starts to convey instructions or comments to the soloists and to the orchestra. We then notice the essence that has slipped out of our reach. Similarly, we become aware of the broken magic when the noise of a slamming door or the crackly sound of a candy wrapper intrudes into our experience of the music.

Eminent artists have been viewed as wizards who intentionally seduce their audience and, while they are performing a piece, hold it awestruck. Franz Liszt, considered one of the greatest pianists of all time, was called by his biographer Alan Walker a "magical virtuoso." Because Liszt happened to also be a musician, in the deepest and most complete sense of the word, his play left an unforgettable impression on his listeners. There are brilliant interpreters of the music of Mozart, Chopin, Albéniz, and others who are also widely celebrated today due to the fortunate combination of their artistic sensibility and their remarkable virtuosity. Virtuosity is, of course, not restricted to the piano; all musical instruments, even the most awkward ones, lend themselves to a virtuoso performance. But why does their virtuosity leave such an indelible impact on the listeners?

Let us now consider briefly the virtuoso performance accomplished on a piano. It is chiefly during a live performance that the enthusiastic and admiring audience tends to appreciate pianistic virtuosity. According to Vladimir Jankélévitch, who wrote an entire book on the topic, the listeners are "bewitched" by the "gentle power" of the pianist's charm. The persuasive singing of the human voice seduces and "ensnares in its magic net" through its captivating vocalizations and caressing inflections. "When it comes to the piano," Jankélévitch states, "the bedazzlement lies in the magnetic passes of an agile hand, which caresses the keys, dances on the keys, leaps from one key to another, flies over the whole range of seven octaves."[24] In a concert hall, the virtuoso musician is not only heard but also seen: there, the visible gestures and expressions complement the auditory impressions. The listener sees the pianist's two hands making a multitude of tactile contacts with the piano keyboard and hears the result of these contacts: the music. The piano is seen not only as a source of different tones but also as an object, which makes possible the deployment of the creative resources of the pianist's fingers, hands, arms, and legs, and their flexibility, speed, force, and sensitivity. The white and black keys are seen not merely as an instrument that responds to the motions of the body, but also as a mechanical device that suggests ways of playing and, to a certain extent, influences the intentions of the pianist. Learning and developing note-perfect technical skills is not sufficient to display virtuosity. While remaining faithful to the indications of the score, the pianist has to learn to respond with imagination and poise to the quality of the tones produced by his or her actions. Therefore, virtuosity is more than an act of understanding the composer's ideas and translating them into articulated sonorous expressions; it also consists in an ongoing musical conversation between the hands and the widely varying tones created by the hands. Hence the performance is always precarious and unpredictable. The risk of not being able to keep the proposed tempo, to finish an initiated chord progression flawlessly, to highlight appropriately both harmonic tensions and releases, or to call attention to a note or a lyrical passage is a central part of the art of a virtuoso. This risk is felt intensely by the audience and thus claims its attention. A captivating performance requires the pianist's swift adaptation to all the random aspects of musical diction. It calls for a fine feeling of what should be played and what can be ingeniously modified and what can be creatively introduced into the performance: a subtle gradation of loudness and softness, an unexpected rubato and agogic effect, a shortening of a note, thus allowing the piano to "breathe" like a singer does. (In fact, the pianist Gyorgy Sandor recommended that young pianists imitate "good singers who breathe, phrase and shape music" with flexibility and spontaneity.[25]) Part of the virtuoso performance occurs in an unconcerned state and without conscious control. What matters, above all, is the adoption of an attitude of availability that enables a response to the various impressions that may reach the performer and, above all, the surrender to the expressive and inventive capabilities of the hands. Jankélévitch praises the pianist's tactile sensitivity and inventiveness, his or her *tact*, the ability to guess, in the absence of a previously formulated plan, the propitious moment to play the right notes: "Just as an acrobat bounces and bounces back and lands back on his feet, likewise the moving hand falls with elegance on the right note."[26] The full control of the hands and arms, as well as the thorough understanding of the almost inexhaustible shadings of the musical notations, have to be acquired during the long period of learning. But once the adequate mastery of movements is attained and the musical sensibility is fully developed, the creative performer is able to trust his or her body and allow these abilities to propose subtle changes and embellishments.

In addition to its qualities of being melodic, playful, and magical, we also find a beautiful piece of music meaningful. It is not just a mere pattern of tones; it has some kind of meaning, it tells us something. The sounding meaning of music is neither a conceptual reality nor a perceptual object. Notwithstanding the title of certain compositions with their allusions to moods and actions, music is not the expressive medium for a concrete experience, such as the encounter between two individuals, or for a tangible object, such as the roaring sea. Music's deep emotional content cannot be too specific, easily translatable into words; only a general meaning can become the object of our hearing and understanding. For this reason, many composers are unwilling to provide a verbal explanation of the meaning of their works. However, as Gunther Schuller convincingly argued, these works reveal a specific meaning: they are "informed," above all, by the creative impulse and personality of their authors. Just as much as a folk song tells us something about the people who spontaneously created it, a sonata or a symphony allows the listener to identify, after a short space of time, the unmistakable acoustical fingerprints of their composers, their distinct sound worlds, and even perhaps the characteristics of their social and artistic milieus.[27] These elements are in the music because creative artists cannot completely distance themselves from their own creations. Their individualities, and the particular melodic, harmonic, or rhythmic gifts they possess, are necessarily manifest even in a seemingly abstract and impersonal sonorous form. In his analysis of the structure of the aesthetic object, Hartmann speaks of the possible knowledge of the artist's creative spirit. We come to know this spirit by feeling it, by a sort of sympathetic adaptation to an emotional essence. In Hartmann's words, "The productive spirit – the sculptor, the poet, and the composer – remains always within certain limits, recognizable in it, even when one knows neither his name nor his life. And much stronger than our ability to know of him is our assimilation of him to ourselves: the beholder can be drawn by the power of the work into the way of seeing things as the artist did; it can take him by the hand and teach him new ways to see."[28]

For Mikel Dufrenne, the beautiful in art is the successful combination of a formal perfection and a "meaning in the sensuous." "This meaning is the suggestion of a world," Dufrenne continues, "that can be defined neither in thing-like terms nor in terms of the state of the soul, but is rather the promise of the unity of both. This world can only be given the name of its creator – the world of Mozart, of Cézanne."[29] Although we do not find the appropriate words to describe this "world," the individual musical thought or character is not completely out of our reach. As we are enraptured in some audible perfection, we detect, immediately or after repeated listening to their works, a singular quality, a quality that, together with all the technical subtleties and intricacies, forms a unity. This unity is, for example, the sound world of Joseph Haydn or of Jean Françaix, in which a meaning, marked by lightness and wit, is revealed, a meaning that only music can capture.[30]

THE SENSE OF THE BEAUTIFUL

How do we come to those exalted moments that the beautiful in music gives us? What does such an enchanting experience require from us, the listeners?

As the example presented by Kodály made clear, we have to leave every other sort of occupation behind in order to focus on what we hear. Our attention must be concerned exclusively with the coming and going of the sounds. In this way, we are able not only to establish attentive contact with the music, but also to dwell on each of its elements. Since sounds pursue us, we can undertake many other activities – reading, writing, or exercising – while we superficially hear the music. But when idle, our ears are directed to the sounds, letting the music become the unique object of our otiose perception. Hartmann uses the verb *verweilen* to denote the act of dwelling on a work of art without any reserve, preference, or pragmatic concern.[31] Whereas our habitual perception glides over an object and takes notice of it for the sake of a goal to attain, the aesthetic contemplation considers it, with the outmost attention, for its own sake, recognizes its singular quality, takes pleasure in its fullness, and explores its elements and latent possibilities. Unlike everyday forms of contact, which are there to serve a pragmatic purpose, here perception is autonomous and is able to linger in enjoyment of an appearance of an object and perhaps even in the intensified feeling induced by the object. We perceive the sensible form with its inherent value, detect a qualitative content that the form discloses, and, at the same time, may notice the pleasure evoked by the form.

How is dwelling on music's elements possible? While we listen to music, we are able to hear only a restricted number of sounds. Unless we are concerned with a global structure, the presence of music is fragmentary. Once they have been played and heard, each sound has to make way for other sounds. If all of the audible sounds refused to fade away and persisted in the present, we would hear only an inarticulate noise. The temporal sequence and duration of sounds are defined by the rhythm. As sounds are played from moment to moment, they swell or diminish in intensity, come suddenly or gently to the fore or fade away more or less abruptly. "Hearing is a synthesizing sense," as Erwin W. Straus put it.[32] To be able to hear music, we have to bring into a coherent whole the arising, enduring, and departing sounds. We have to integrate the sounds into the audible *now*, which "endures in flowing and flows while enduring" (Eugène Minkowski).

Whether we are reading a novel or looking at a sculpture, we are drawn to the plot or follow, with our eyes and the gentle movements of our hand, the contours of a three-dimensional figure. Equally, when we pay attention to a musical piece, we go along with the rhythm, harmony, and melody by bringing together present and absent sounds. There is, however, a fundamental difference between seeing a sculpted figure and listening to a song. Whereas the visible object reveals itself at a distance from us, the sounds completely fill and penetrate the space around us; we are unable to hold them at bay. For this reason, we are unable to stand back and contemplate a musical work. When we look at a painting, we may take a few steps backwards and grasp all its elements. We may apprehend a musical work as a whole only in silence in our imagination. Sounds are voluminous, take hold of us, and deliver us to their compelling power. The acoustic sphere entails an element of possessiveness and coercion. "For hearing the striking of a clock differs from looking at it," writes Straus, "in that in seeing the clock we turn actively toward it, whereas sound seizes and compels us ... We say of someone who obeys us that he 'listens to us.' The unusual power of sounds stems from the fact that they can be divorced from their source, and, due to this separation, sounding and hearing occur for us simultaneously."[33] No other sensory element makes its way and soaks into us as does a sound: it provokes resonances at levels deeper than a visible or tactile quality. Not only strident sounds, such as a piercing cry or a loud siren, but also musical works penetrate and reach the depths of our being.

136 In Vivo

While listening to music, we allow ourselves to be carried along to a greater extent by the tones of a musical piece than by the words of a novel or the figures of a painting. Hartmann speaks of a "psychic abduction," of a state of rapture in the presence an acoustical perfection, of an "order of things otherwise not found in one's life."[34] But, when we are deeply moved by beautiful music, this experience of being drawn along, of giving ourselves to a state of floating self-transcendence, is further heightened. We absorb ourselves into the sounds; we become, as it were, one with the music. Our thoughts and feelings resonate with it and, while listening to a musical piece or after it has been played, we take a real pleasure in this particular form of enthrallment. We may even express our contentment at being under the spell of music by dancing to it or singing along with it.[35]

We might, then, be accused by the lurking purist of merely surrendering to the music and of letting ourselves be carried away by the tonal motion. We might be told that we just melt away in the music as if we were lying in a tepid bath, that we fail to consciously adhere to the structural details and subtleties of its construction, and ultimately that we merely find enjoyment mostly in our own feelings, in our own inner states. We might be blamed for "misusing" music: by searching for a gentle intoxication without concern for the intricate structure of the composition, we are merely capitalizing on a musical experience in order to surrender to our emotions.[36]

This misuse of music is surely possible. However, it does not provide an experience of magic and enchantment. When a piece exerts a spell on us, an elementary form of attentive and discriminative listening is indispensable. Without having expert knowledge, we are still able to recognize, for example, a theme, its exposition, repetition, variation, return, and resolution. We can hear, without much concentration and previous learning, the successful combination of overlapping musical phrases, resulting in a coherent and harmonious whole and evoking an exhilarating and gratifying feeling: the fugue. We can also hear, without being a trained musician, how, for example, Joseph Haydn obtains surprising and humorous effects in some of his symphonies. I suggest that we become more attentive to a musical construction when composers use a device similar to the repetitive scheme that children follow when they play. It is a well-known fact that children love to play with objects, which appear, disappear, and return over and over again. In a similar fashion, composers introduce a theme, repeat it, and, by doing so, generate an expectation of its eventual return. But, instead of reintroducing it again, they let the theme undergo all sorts of almost unrecognizable variations, thus arousing and heightening in us an expectative tension. And when, finally, the postponed theme returns, its recognition brings us relief and intense delight. We are more prone to pay attention to the different aspects of the composition because, like children, we find ourselves absorbed by the musical game of hiding, postponing, deceiving, and revealing.[37]

Referring to the danger of establishing superficial contact with music, Helmuth Plessner contended that genuine musical understanding calls for a control over the imperative impulse to allow ourselves to be taken away by the tones. And the control over the tones comes primarily from the control that we have over our own body. For Plessner, "First the detachment from this 'being taken along' makes the sonorous lines understandable."[38] The basic conditions of a conscious and discriminative understanding of music are the refusal to thoughtlessly surrender to the impulsiveness of tones and to arbitrarily select only certain musical elements. As we hear the melody or chords or rhythmic figures, we have to grasp a complex construction in which we identify and recognize relations between motifs, themes, developments, repetitions, transitions, sections, and movements.

In this connection, Gabriel Marcel strongly and astutely disagreed with Henri Bergson who, in his *Time and Free Will: An Essay on the Immediate Data of Consciousness*, used the metaphor of the melody to illustrate his theory of temporality and who understood pure duration as a musical reality.[39] During the musical experience, Bergson tells us, we perceive the notes as a sonorous continuity and our listening is an organized succession and interpenetration of conscious states "melting, so to speak, into one another." While we listen to a melody, we have an impression of continuity and indivisibility. We are merely going along with the melodic progression without apprehending the melody's manifold and distinct elements and without appreciating its complete and unified architecture. If, however, we try to cut up a melody into distinct notes, we think about both a melody and its temporality in terms of space. According to Marcel, to listen to a melody is not insensibly to go from one note to the next as they melt into each other, but, rather, to become conscious of the distinct parts in such a manner that "a certain whole takes shape, a form builds up," and this act requires a "kind of mastery."[40]

How does this form build up? As our ears discriminate between melodic lines, dissonances, consonances, and modulations from one key to another, we perceive a complex sonorous construction in which we identify and recognize relationships between motifs, themes, developments, transitions, sections, or movements. We establish a complex series of orderly relations in a process similar to that which takes place when we relate the words of a sentence to each other and thus, by recognizing their necessary internal connections, apprehend a complex verbal construction and its meaning. Indeed, in order to follow the development of a musical form, we have to exert some control over the progression of individual tones and consciously seize them as a structure. I suggest, however, that genuine musical understanding does not come merely from an attitude of cold detachment, but also from our ability to surrender, to the fullest extent possible, to the playful development of tones. In other words, it is our sympathetic response to musical impressions, and our willingness to go along with the tones, that gives us a purely intuitive experience, without which the detached recognition and precise identification of the ingredients, while accurate and perhaps useful, are too impersonal and abstract. While combining the state of active surrender with the state of discriminative listening, we are open to experiencing a sounding meaning, which, even if it remains global and vague, nonetheless reveals a unity of a style.

It is of some interest to refer to the phenomenological analyses of Moritz Geiger who tried to explore why a work of art is capable of reaching what is the deepest in our existence and why our affective response to art should not be undervalued. There are two different effects produced by a work of art: a surface or vital effect and a depth or artistic effect. To take two examples, in music, the former is reflected in the motion and resolution of the chords or the length, amplitude, and loudness of the sounds, while the later comes forth in the earlier mentioned contradicted expectation. Masterpieces share this quality of unexpectedness: the listener thinks that the melody will move into one direction and the composer contradicts the expectation and, by doing this, keeps the listener's interest alive. The basic model for such a contradiction is the interrupted cadence: the music goes from the dominant chord to the submediant chord, instead of reaching the expected tonic chord. It is, then, the degree and extent of unpredictability, and not that of fulfilment, that provides music with depth, thereby making of the composer an original creator, while providing durable satisfaction to listeners.[41] This very simple model applies in a tremendously sophisticated way to the works of major composers. Good story telling is also based on this same simple principle: a skilled and original writer is able to sustain our interest by contradicting our expectation and by creating in us a salutary tension. The storyline is unpredictable and catches the readers off guard. I would even say that a rich life is filled with interrupted cadences – with moments of happily or unhappily contradicted expectations. This book describes some of life's vital twists and turns.

Vital effects give to music the qualities of fullness, vigour, excitement, and life. Depth effects provide the piece with genuine artistic value and a formal complexity. There are, however, no depth effects in which the vital effects are not "interwoven;" the two sorts of effect are not only added together but permeate, enrich, and intensify each other. "Thus the perfect work of art," writes Geiger, "speaks not only to the spiritual-intellectual person; it speaks to the unity of person and life."[42] Therefore, it is not surprising that the listener first tends to display a vital reaction and later gradually takes delight in music's artistic values.

The intensity of spontaneous and affective responsiveness towards the sequence of tones sets in motion the listener's musicality. From this initial affective experience a rational, detailed, and meaningful assessment of the music's tonal build-up and artistic value emerge. If musicality is the ability to develop and to achieve a heightened appreciation of music, cold detachment and self-control is unlikely to convert anyone to music. Music converts us to itself as long as we approach it with sensibility, sympathy, and elementary discrimination. The same approach holds true for a painting, a poem, or a novel. First they have to keep us spellbound and later, once the emotional bond is formed, to invite us to admire and study the artistic means used by the author. To take a non-musical example, first we have to laugh wholeheartedly at a good joke and only then can we analyze the pattern underlying the story, the logic of humour. Otherwise we don't really know and feel what we are analyzing and describing. The identified pattern means absolutely nothing; it lacks a point of reference. The reverse is not true. To laugh spontaneously, with wet eyes, at a joke, we do not need to clearly identify the elements of the story that makes it humorous and pleasurable and to point out with precision the cause of a particular physiological effect. First we enjoy listening to a joke and only after do we learn about it. Learning in absence of experience is futile and leads nowhere.

ALL IS WELL

Preoccupied with our daily tasks and the means to accomplish them, we are usually ahead of ourselves, not in touch with ourselves. For instance, as we are immersed in the execution of a verbal negotiation or a physical work to be completed sometime in the future, we fail to take notice of our feelings or the subtle bodily sensations and impulses that guide our movements. We need to be affected by a stronger impression or encounter a significant obstacle in order to pay attention to the actual emotional wealth within ourselves.

If a music's presence affects us, resonates in us, it could make us aware of our feelings – an awareness that I tried to highlight in previous chapters. "All authentic musical creation," Marcel tells us, "is a mediation operating within a being incomprehensibly divided and, as it were, torn apart, that is man engaged in time."[43] We may compare this experience of mediation to the encounter with a person we love or to the reception of distressing news. We become aware of a feeling of joy or sadness within us and this awareness provides, in its turn, an occasion to recognize, make peace with, and renew our intimate impulses or desires. Regardless of its tone and quality, music could offer an occasion to revive an inner richness that most of us possess and what we may call the substance of our being.

Assailed by worries and anguish, perhaps even by physical discomforts, we may go to a concert hall or stay at home and listen to a recording. Through this choice we suspend, for a while, the concerns and afflictions of our empirical, everyday world. As we listen, for instance, to the heart-breaking slow movement of Schubert's Piano Sonata in B-flat major, we come to feel that the world is full of harmony and peace and, at least for a short time, find ourselves healed of our ills. A soloist, a chamber-music ensemble, a choir, or an orchestra may produce such a transformation of our way of seeing the world and ourselves. We may realize with satisfaction that, despite its evanescent character, music establishes a temporal order: the musicians bring together the simultaneous and successive sounds into a meaningful and coherent whole. Even if we lack a basic instruction in music theory, we are able to perceive an orderly interrelation between the rise and fall of voices, question and answer of themes, contrast and continuity of phrases, consonance and dissonance of chords, their tension and resolution. Order is sought and found while we bring the various transient elements into a unity and while we contemplate the form beyond the sensory reality of sounds. We not only perceive, in a state of passive listening, a coherent pattern, but also achieve a constructive activity and, as it were, create, together with the musicians, the musical form. Ernest Cassirer is right in stating that when we listen to a fugue of Bach or a concerto of Mozart, we are not in a state of mere passivity. In order to appreciate a musical work we have to take an active part in its creation. "We cannot understand or feel a great work of art without, to a certain degree, repeating and reconstructing the creative process by which it has come into being," writes Cassirer.[44] This creative process is, in a large part, an ordering process that we achieve and of which we become aware even if we hardly know how we do it. In any case, we are just as much delighted to perceive the work's structure, as we are pleased to savour our constructive ordering activity. We are, then, enthralled to know that, despite all the chaotic, arbitrary, incomplete, unpredictable, disorderly, and transient aspects of our everyday life, we are also able to find, and intensely enjoy, order and achievement. As Adorno put it, "the suspension of empirical reality and the forming of a second reality *sui generis* seem to say in advance: all is well."[45] Having this "quality of transfiguration," the presence of music is a source of happiness and consolation because it offers the possibility of reaching a new level of reality – a reality, in which order prevails over chaos, achievement over fragmentation.

Our happiness may stem, as the Canadian scholar Northrop Frye once wrote, from our ability to come to terms with "the panic of time," something that is difficult to attain in our contemporary world. Making time for listening to music or for singing together is "so important as a way of relaxing this sense of panic."[46] We are liable to panic when we live under the impression that the present slips out of our control as we are nervously preoccupied by the multiplicity of tasks to perform. We are unable to keep a salutary distance between present interests and future concerns. The latter intrudes into the former with such haste and such exclusive demand that we are no longer able to be attentive to the present situation as a whole. Relaxing our sense of panic means letting go of all future obligations so that the present experience regains its own value and we become fully and happily aware of whatever this present offers.

How, then, do we experience the presence of music when we have become detached from, and stop worrying about, the disquieting ticking of the clock? To be sure, this presence is sensed as a particular atmosphere, in which past realizations and future concerns fade away and only the unfolding succession of sounds is perceived. This musical present is no longer a stepping stone to the attainment of future objectives; it asserts itself in its gratuitous and purposeless being. But to appreciate music's presence in its full effect, we need to hold our breath, holding at bay non-musical thoughts, images, and concerns, which easily weaken our alert receptivity and distract us from the present. In a witty article, E.M. Forster lists a certain number of obvious and subtle distractions, which unexpectedly pull someone away from attentive listening. He contends that active music-making truly compels us to attend to a piece consistently and steadily and even to grow familiar with the composer's "tricks."[47] Singing or playing an instrument helps us to become absorbed in the present's particular density and extension and to perceive, for instance, how a theme is proposed, transformed, and reintroduced in different keys and why themes stand in *inevitable* relationship to one another.

If we succeed in becoming one with the music, we feel ourselves as fortunate guests who have been invited to take part in an uplifting experience and are filled with gratitude for the blessedness of the *now*. This *now* may be apprehended as a generous gift that we receive as long as we are able to open ourselves to it. Many of us have had the experience of leaving a concert while saying to ourselves that we were privileged to experience an extraordinary encounter and to receive a rare and precious *présent musical*. We have also considered the music as a sign of a deeper meaning that brings enrichment to our lives. Perhaps we find in the *présent musical* a certain response for our yearning for peace, harmony, and a kind of redemption for our shortcomings and pains. I suspect that most of the performers also consider music as a gift and see themselves as transmitting links between the composer and the listener. They feel that they, as individuals, must not get in the way. Their task is to place the essence of the music before the audience by creating a flawless unity of both the act of making something present and the meaning of the presence itself.

People of all ages like to recall that their first encounter with a musical masterpiece evoked in them a passionate interest in music. They had either learned to play an instrument or they had joined a choir or they had become dedicated listeners of recordings or live concerts. They have declared that their lives would have been much poorer in the absence of musical works. Their early musical experiences have been of the highest importance for awakening and reinforcing in their lives a lasting love of music.

The theme of life-altering musical experience brings me to the topic of musical education. Paul Valéry made a classic statement about teaching: "In order to teach something to someone, one must, before anything else, provoke in him the need for this knowledge."[48] How can a teacher trigger this need? Where does this need come from? In the case of music, it certainly does not come from a music teacher or a parent. It is either in the child or not. If it is there, it lays dormant or seeks satisfaction. To teach an unmusical child to understand and to love music is impossible. What is possible is to express sincere enthusiasm for a musical composition and, after hearing it, to draw the child's attention to some of its characteristics. What is also possible is to create profound first-time musical experiences that make the young ones conscious of their latent need and induce them to satisfy it through listening, singing, or playing on an instrument. A teacher is also able to present a broad array of musical pieces that push children to become aware of the difference between simple and complex melodies, of the degree of joy felt in the presence of empty and meaningful pieces or of their trivial and uplifting musical experiences. They are, then, able to react with enthusiasm to compositions, which touch their hearts. A good music teacher inspires and stimulates the children's inner need while encouraging the development of a sense of value; he or she also helps them to develop the ability to communicate and validate their likes and dislikes.[49]

Beyond the refinement of their musical sensibility, children may eventually become active amateur musicians; they may join a choir or play an instrument during their leisure hours. Playing a Mozart sonata or singing a madrigal by Gesualdo helps them to develop a musical ear that consistently discriminates and steadily coordinates musical impressions. It also offers initial instruction about the subtle ingredients of a musical structure and creates a familiarity with what I earlier called the composer's world. It often turns their attention to some aspects of musical performance that professional musicians might have forgotten or ignored. Jacques Barzun pointed out that "the role of the amateur is to keep insisting on the primacy of style, spirit, musicianship, meaning over any technical accomplishment."[50] I would suggest that amateur musicians are also pleased to rediscover the playful character of music. Whether they make music alone or in a smaller ensemble, they *play* the music, in a literal sense of the word. Freed from considerations of flawless and expedient performance, they play for the pleasure of playing. They seem to appreciate what is the primary ingredient of all musical expression: the tones, their impulsiveness and animation, eliciting a creative interplay between the chords, the melody, and the rhythm – a conversation that, under sudden inspiration and by relying on the availability and spontaneity of the voice and the hands, brings into the music subtle ornamentations and slight agogic deviations. If a song is performed with the ease of play, the singers experience temporary relief from their worries, strains, and internal tensions. It is well known by all those who sing in a choir that a singing voice is able to release, in an orderly manner, all sorts of emotions and to bring calmness and relaxation to the body.

THE SPIRIT OF SINGING

In closing this chapter, let us return to Kodály's interest in deeply moving musical experiences. For him, it is chiefly through active singing that music offers, to both young and adult persons, an enriching contact with what we qualified as "beautiful."

But if Kodály forcefully stressed the educational power of vocal music, it was also due to his awareness of the increasing mechanization of human life. These were matters of great concern to him. He was, of course, conscious of the very positive role machines play in our lives. However, he did not fail to notice that once people begin to rely on mechanical devices, they become passive, conformist, and self-absorbed, and they cease to act spontaneously in accordance with their deepest feelings. He warned that by making no demands on and even stultifying "our natural instincts," the widespread use of devices would "mutilate our humanity," and eventually turn us into machines. Hence his striking claim: "Only the spirit of singing can save us from this fate."[51]

In connection with this warning, Kodály aptly brought to our attention the emotional involvement of the singing person: singing, he tells us, unlocks a pathway to "the world of feelings" and provides a framework for its appropriate expression. The French philosopher Paul Ricoeur expressed the same view with greater precision: "Music creates for us feelings that have no names; it expands our emotional space, it opens up in us a region where absolutely original feelings can occur. When we listen to *such* music, we enter into a region of the soul which cannot be explored otherwise than by listening to *this* particular piece. Each work is authentically a modality of the soul, a modulation of the soul."[52] The mainspring of these views is the conviction that as humans we are never mere thought or will, but also a unity of feelings, joy, admiration, fear, sadness, and regret, however muddled these may be. There is an essential connection between sentiment and sense of selfhood; we are able to define ourselves as distinct and relatively autonomous individuals once we become aware of the consistent expansion of our feelings. The expressions "being in touch with myself," "being faithful to myself," and "leading my own life" refer to the emotional experience of our original way of being. Thus, feelings are not only a unifying but also a disjoining factor, so to speak. Accordingly, by putting us in touch with our feelings, singing, or any similar musical activity, enhances a lively sense of our uniqueness, of our individual consciousness.

The prospect of this affective self-awareness seems to be invaluable in an age when some individuals grow up with, and suffer from, the inability to feel, the untimely death of their heart. And this erosion of emotional self-reliance is tied closely to cautious and calculated behaviour. We are able to carry out innovative, transformative, and spontaneous actions if we entrust ourselves to our natural impulses and live in sympathetic contact with our feelings. Conversely, we are able to reshape our deepest feelings if we give up the search for certainty and act without any functional and calculated restraint. The value of this reciprocity and balance manifests itself chiefly when we are hit with adversity or crises at various stages of our lives. If we know ourselves and trust the value of actions that are motivated by feelings, we are able to deal, in a relaxed and serene manner, with such harsh realities.

Still, notwithstanding the serious warnings of eminent thinkers, educationalists, and artists, we persist in focusing our educational efforts almost exclusively on the training of the intellect and tend to structure our social institutions around an instrumental and mechanistic conception of human life. Yet, events of the last century have taught us that a partial or total blindness to vital areas of human experience can be caused by a highly developed and lucid intellect that lacks the appropriate feelings. The sharply intelligent, but cool and unfeeling individual's ear is deaf not only to the aspirations and needs of vulnerable creatures, but also to the demands of life in general. Their thoughts do not involve their nerves. The main problem is, of course, not the intellect, but what has been called the "celibacy of the intellect" (Alfred N. Whitehead); it is the intellect left on its own, detached from other human qualities – namely the capacity to feel and apprehend anything in its completeness – that is so dangerous and portends the most harm for humanity.

Now it seems to be quite clear that the battle against one-sided, heartless intellectualism and the disintegrative effects of a technological civilization cannot be fought without an organic vision of the world – a vision that is acutely aware of the wider angles of life and seeks ways of bringing together the human organism and the environment, thinking and feeling, prose and poetry, the abstract and the concrete, the secular and the sacred. That is what Kodály meant, I believe, by the "spirit of singing" and what he wanted to secure through musical education.

Although Kodály convincingly emphasized the concrete, beneficial effects of serious musical education through singing, he also considered music as a "magical source" of vitality and consolation and suggested that the abiding enjoyment of a song or a piano sonata called for no other justification than itself. When he was asked whence came his enduring interest in the Sekler folk songs, he simply replied: "I would like to make them known wherever I find four or five Hungarians together. And I wish only that people ask not 'why' but rather come to say: 'for nothing and for everything ... for the simple reason that life should be lived in its fullness.'"[53] Indeed, a beautiful song, pouring forth spontaneously and without any purpose in an intimate place, brings to the singers an unparalleled moment of contentment. This does not mean that the experience of the beautiful should be cut off from, or played against, whatever we view as good and useful. "We must always be reminded," notes Carl Friedrich von Weizsäcker, "that the beautiful in itself is not ethical, that the just in itself is not human. And we must return from beauty as presence to the firm ground of the utilitarian. But while we are working for our daily bread, the aching bliss of a melody of Mozart should still remain with us."[54]

6

Actions Like That Make Life Worthwhile

The human, in fact, does not come from us, but we arise out of it.

Eugène Minkowski

Leo Tolstoy's famous short story, "Master and Man," relates the journey of the rich merchant Vasily Andreich Brekhunov. Obsessed with the desire of increasing his wealth, he decides to purchase, before any other competitor, a tract of forest. Despite the threat of a severe snowstorm, he sets out on his journey on a sledge in order to meet the seller. He takes along his servant Nikita. After getting lost in a hostile and stormy environment and after having failed three times to find the correct path, he unties the horse from his sledge, abandons his servant, and continues his journey on the horse alone. But, by following the same ravine into which he and his servant previously plunged, the horse takes him back to the sledge and to his now half-frozen snow-covered servant. Then, suddenly, Brekhunov clears the snow from Nikita's body and covers his servant not only with his fur coat but also with the full length of his body. To his own surprise, he is no longer able to speak, becomes weak and teary-eyed, and experiences a solemn feeling of bliss and a previously unknown joy. He comes to a radical reassessment of what human life is about. He feels free; no material concerns and possessions hold him back. Unconscious of the passage of time, he lies motionless on top his servant and falls asleep. In the morning, Brekhunov is dead and Nikita is alive.[1]

It is tempting to suggest that Brekhunov's sacrifice of his life is a response to a call from God, a sudden and unexpected conversion. Indeed, this could be advanced as one of the possible explanations. It may, however, cause the reader to suspect that the shrewd merchant,

148   In Vivo

realizing that everything is lost, has put all his hope on reaching eternal salvation in compensation for his greed and exploitation of the poor. For the reader not mesmerized by Tolstoy's conception of Christianity and possessing a clear perspective on the two figures, their failure to reach their destination, and the sudden act of covering up a person previously left behind, another interpretation of the story is possible, one which would not require replacement of the Christian interpretation with an atheistic reading. The "person" who calls Brekhunov to perform his salvific act can be someone other than God.

Brekhunov's spontaneous and gratuitous resolution to lie on his servant, giving him warmth and life, is what I call, after Eugène Minkowski, an *ethical action*. Tolstoy describes an exceptional life-saving action carried out in an extraordinary circumstance. Although Brekhunov's initial motive for hastily undertaking the journey is quite plain, the final outcome of his attempt to reach his objective is wholly astonishing. I suggest, however, that an ethical action may be accomplished in a much more prosaic setting and with a much less startling result. Even so, a seemingly mundane occurrence could share some of the features of a deed accomplished in an extraordinary circumstance. The similarity lies precisely in the magnificence and spontaneity of the action.

The French philosopher Gustave Thibon tells us that, walking on a street in Madrid, he was stopped by a shady character who wanted to sell him a supposedly gold watch. After having declined the offer, he asked for directions. "I'll come with you to show you the way," said the other. When, upon arrival, Thibon sought to reward him with a generous tip, he refused to accept it. "Although he was a small time crook," concludes Thibon, "we had established a personal contact; I had asked him a service and one does not accept money for a service rendered. This was the best of the Spanish soul."[2]

Interestingly, Robert Spaemann gives an almost identical example in his introduction to ethical thinking. Reflecting on the characteristics of actions that are "good in an unqualified way," he refers to a young man who, without any moral reflection, stopped doing a task at hand and walked with him to show him the direction and the place he sought to reach. Spaemann asserts, "This was a small incident, hardly worth talking about, but it was a fine thing to do, and that can be said without qualification. Actions like that make life worthwhile."[3] Here again, the young man, prompted by an innate propensity to offer a concrete service to a fellow human being,

Actions Like That Make Life Worthwhile

displays what is the best in him. He accomplishes, discreetly and without any deliberation, an ethical action.

WHAT IS AN ETHICAL ACTION?

In his major work on lived time, Eugène Minkowski presents a subtle phenomenological analysis of the ethical action.[4] He considers it as a constitutive element of human life since every human being is endowed with the potentiality of its realization. Yet, Minkowski tells us, "It is a passing flash, fleeting, exceptional. If we try to situate it in everyday life, it is so rare that one is led to deny its existence."[5] Someone might be raised and educated to be honest, industrious, and kind and, as a result, tries to display all these personal virtues and gifts in his or her daily interactions with fellow human beings. But an ethical action is exempt from an edifying effort and a conscious plan to conform one's behaviour to a set of educational values and moral principles. True, occasionally, it may appear as an exercise of a virtue. But even so, its realization happens unexpectedly, by chance as it were, and regardless of the moral makeup of the person. He or she can be a friend or an enemy, a trustworthy colleague or a suspicious stranger, a model of benevolence or a condemned criminal. We nevertheless look at their unanticipated and surprising behaviour, and the manifestation of what is profoundly human in it, with astonishment and cheerfulness and we keep the image of the action in our memory.

Nothing can be more convincing and expressive, it seems to me, than coming across persuasive and poignant examples. They give us a tangible feel for a barely definable human quality and for the singularity of the moment of action. They do not always highlight admirable and heroic deeds and, in my mind, an ethical action does not always imply the idea of a sacrifice. Unforeseen encounters, taking place in an unremarkable context, could prompt their sudden and discrete realization and bestow upon the persons and their grey circumstances a momentary bright glow. During the First World War, in Zürich, the young Elias Canetti was strolling on a street along with his mother. They met a group of seriously wounded French officers walking with crutches. They were all in Switzerland to convalesce. Suddenly a group of German soldiers appeared as well, also moving slowly, several of them with crutches. Instead of hatred, spite, or anger, the slowly walking soldiers faced their respective enemies with a calm and amiable attitude. As one group approached the other, a French soldier raised his crutch aloft and cried to the Germans: "*Salut.*" A German, who had heard it, turned back, waved with his crutch, and returned the greeting in French: "*Salut.*" Canetti cautiously looked at his mother: she was trembling and weeping.[6] The greeting – just a word, repeated twice – did not end the war and did not involve any political consequence. The unimaginable slaughter of French and German soldiers continued on the battle-fields. Some of the soldiers probably never recovered from their injuries, remaining crippled forever. Some of them perhaps placed little weight on this unusual and perplexing encounter. Yet, the unex-pected greeting and the lifting of the crutches in the air, as well as the hope that these gestures of largesse embodied, did not fade into oblivion and this short moment revealed what is to be most valued in human life: the tendency towards the good. This is what we, the readers of these memoirs, together with the actors and spectators of the event, acknowledge as sublime, greater than ourselves, yet, at the same time, accessible, simple, and immediate. This astounding action remains alive in most of us as a possibility; it is, in the words of Minkowski, "the only action which resists becoming – becoming, whose dark waves threatens to submerge everything in its path."[7]

The relation between the soldiers is direct and lived in the present. Everything that pertains to the past – combats, killings, deaths – becomes, for a short span of time, irrelevant. In the ethical action, the memory of past experiences does not prevail and, if it is still present and effective, its influence does not cancel out the conciliatory and restorative gesture. Nevertheless, the past is not put aside by an act of forgetting, since the present condition of the soldiers manifestly points to the painful experience of being wounded in the recent past. This past is eminently present in the tacit awareness of bodily limita-tions, in the acceptance of "not being able to fight on the battlefield." Every step the soldiers make is tied to this heavy burden brought forward from the past. They are conscious of the street, the onlook-ers, and the approaching adverse group *by means of* their deficient bodies as well as the uniforms covering their bodies. Yet, the act of greeting momentarily blocks the expression of revenge or hatred and thus creates, to everyone's surprise, an atmosphere of peace and relief. This act receives its value not from the disappearance of past hostility and the belligerent feelings defining this past. Its greatness lies in the spontaneous rejection of the negative impulses carried over from the past. In the moment of meeting the enemy, the soldiers are able to forgo these negative impulses in favour of the values of peace and reconciliation which surge in the present. Accordingly, the ethical action does not necessarily transform someone and does not wipe out conflict, hostility, and resentment – those enduring factors of human life. It makes manifest a fundamental human freedom in presence of that which remains alive, at the very core of the person's being, from the past into the present.[8]

The weeping of Canetti's mother may have been induced by her sadness over the crippled condition of the soldiers or by her enjoyment over their unexpected and momentary reconciliation. The solders felt united to each other and mutually recognized their respective dignity and distressing condition. For his part, Tolstoy refers to the tears of Brekhunov as well as to his "joyful condition." Indeed, the ethical action brings with it the feeling of elevation and sensible delight. But these individuals did not accomplish their actions in order to achieve a cozy sense of satisfaction. The feeling of joy has nothing to do with the kind of self-induced state of rapture that one seeks to reach through the machinations of a calculating mind. Minkowski ties the feeling of joy and elation to the awareness of freedom: it accompanies the ability to rise above all hostility, all grudging and petty concerns, all that one finds prosaic and even functional in everyday life, and without any constraint or intermediary. It is a life-defining moment: it helps someone to envision his or her entire life under new light and with other eyes while participating in "what is the greatest and the most precious in the world." Perhaps Thibon is right in saying that "The quality of a being is measured by the rare instants during which he escapes a little from gravity."[9] The wonderful sense of freedom remains outside of any abstract debate between the affirmation of free will and the defence of determinism. It is lived and enjoyed in its unquestionable concreteness through contact with an ideal that human beings potentially carry in themselves. This ideal is what Minkowski calls "being fully human" and acting by rising above "the interests which are constitutive of the materiality of life." The human is not identical with a number of cultural and physical features that philosophical anthropology, together with the other sciences, describes and examines. The human is the unconditional élan to the good, which becomes tangible in the realization of a spontaneous and unexpected action and which induces a feeling of elevation, achievement, and fullness.[10]

An ethical action cannot be placed on the level of a moral problem that we face in a particular situation and that we try to solve by carefully considering motives, circumstances, rules, and possible outcomes and by deciding between what appears to us good and evil. Neither is it a painfully achieved escape from our everyday practical moral world, the realm in which we usually hesitate, calculate, and make compromises. As I have just pointed out, it does not seek consistency between past deed and present decision. When a person, contrary to all advice and expectations, refuses to seize the possibility of taking vengeance upon his fellow human being, an individual who previously wanted to kill him, his conciliatory words "just come out, like an explosion."[11] We risk obliterating the greatness of this act if we attempt to measure its tangible conditions and expected consequences and seek to take pride in its realization. The dubious stranger selling a watch does not try to analyze the grounds of his refusal to accept money. He does not calculate the effect of his response: he does not weigh the value of two possibilities and choose one of them. Without explaining the reasons for his reply, he spontaneously declines the offer and, in his refusal, relies on an unimpaired "inner force" that exceeds his personal capacities. Doubtless this is the reason why Thibon aptly referred to the "Spanish soul," which is larger than any of the individual's characteristics and gifts.

Moral philosophers and sagacious psychoanalysts, hungry for explanations, are probably prone to identify, once the action has been realized, the reasons for acting in a certain way. They distrust an account in which the concept of spontaneity figures centrally; the present moment, with all its novelty and surprising aspects, is, as it were, cut off from past motives and deeds as well as from future gratifications. When they analyze, dismantle, and reassemble an action – that which, to a certain extent, I am doing in these reflections – they inevitably distort it and fail to grasp its chief characteristics and particular nuances. Its full richness and significance is experienced in the pure present as the tangible presence of an exceptional action, accomplished in absence of any calculated or practical intention.

What is this presence? The French writer Antoine de Saint-Exupéry, telling us about his desire to get a cigarette from his guard and his delight at exchanging a smile with him, helps us to better understand it:

Actions Like That Make Life Worthwhile

That smile saved me … It marked the beginning of a new era. Nothing had changed, everything was changed. The table scattered with papers became alive. The oil lamp became alive. The walls were alive. The boredom dripping from every lifeless thing in that cellar grew lighter as if by magic. It seemed that an invisible stream of blood had started flowing again, connecting all things in the same body, and restoring to them their significance. The men had not moved either, but, though a minute earlier they had seemed to be farther away from me than an antediluvian species, now they grew into contemporary life. I had an extraordinary feeling of presence. That is it: of presence. And I was aware of a connection.[12]

In this warmer atmosphere, established by the smile of the guard, the objects are not merely seen with their indifferent material characteristics. They come to life the same way as the swing in the park comes to life when children approach it. As if it was telling them: come sit on me and swing up and down. Similarly, the table, papers, and lamp appear with their animated being, with their immediate and intensive radiance and their almost palpable "self-givenness," their presence. The presence of these objects and of the guard is felt as if they were giving themselves to the perceiving subject; they seem to exist, in this moment, only to the author. While perceiving the individual objects, the author simultaneously notices his own heightened perception. The exchange of a smile creates a singular affective relation between the author and the objects, which are there in an unconstrained and dense present, without the urge of the future and the pressure of the past, but rather in the author's awareness of a remarkable and new way of perceiving the objects.

The guard and the prisoner smile at each other; it is a particular form of communion occurring in the present and referring to the presence of two persons. In this context, the presence of the person is felt as a gift; through the exchange of smiles, the guard gives himself to the writer and, conversely, the writer gives himself to the guard. Such a mutual self-giving presupposes the willingness to open oneself to the other and, for the time being, to accept the other without any restrictive condition. A similar presence may be offered to another person in the form of a genuine conversation, during which the acts of expressing one's thoughts and of searching for clarification, enrichment, and understanding become tangible expressions of disinterested self-giving. The spoken words and the sympathizing ear are the symbols of the people giving themselves to each other and, at the same time, respecting the freedom of the partner to hold on to his or her point. Less conspicuous, an exchange of a few stolen glances with another person may convey a still unavowed feeling of love. As both persons give themselves in the glance and create a unique communion, they freely and consciously determine the degree of intimacy they would like to create. Yet there is something impersonal in these experiences of "discreet miracle." The irradiating expression of sympathy or of love springs from an inner source, without any preparation and practice, regardless of the already achieved moral stance.

In the unexpected contact with this inner source and the subsequent expressive act, we recognize some of the characteristics of spontaneity. Ethical actions are carried out spontaneously, without calculation, artificiality, or utilitarian considerations. They are significant in themselves, in their dynamic and immediate manifestation, and not for some practical reasons. They are accomplished with ease, apparently without any great effort. As I already indicated earlier in this book, there are circumstances, in which we tend to bypass all arguments and justifications and, by drawing on the "dynamic life" of our body, act instantaneously. Our actions provide a direct, prompt, and simple, though not infallible, answer to the requirement of the situation. The meaning and value of the helping hand we spontaneously lend to someone, or the sincere smile we gladly and unaffectedly bring to our face, lies in the origin and purpose of the action: the contact with the impulse towards the good that we, often unconsciously, carry in ourselves and the benevolent caring for, and openness towards, the other persons facing us in their concrete uniqueness.[13]

We speak of ethical action when a person, without any motive or desire of getting a reward or of finding contentment, spontaneously does something astonishing that seems the most appropriate in a situation. But this is not always the case. An ethical action may also be accomplished by not acting and by advancing an ulterior justification for one's passivity: by remaining silent, refusing an undeserved recognition, or by not joining a social movement despite the pressure to do so. In his reminiscences of the Spanish Civil War, George Orwell recounts an incident from when he was fighting on the front line. Seeing a man jumping out of the enemy trench, running half-dressed and holding his trousers with both hands,

Orwell immediately refrained from shooting: "I did not shoot partly because of that detail about the trousers. I had come here to shoot at 'Fascists'; but a man who is holding up his trousers isn't a 'Fascist,' he is visibly a fellow creature, similar to yourself, and you don't feel like shooting at him."[14]

In the above-mentioned contexts of life, the action, as well as the absence of action, are prompted by an inner élan towards the good of fellow human beings. Orwell reacted, as the others have, to someone's word, movement, facial expression, or presence because a deeper layer of his being recognized the necessity and timeliness to act or to refrain from an action. Thanks to this sensibility, people like Orwell are able to assess not only the need to respond but also the appropriate form of response. And if they come up with a fitting response, they do it not by applying some previously learned rules or fixed formulae, transmitted by an education and a culture, and not by imposing on the situation an abstract category, but by relying on their inner sense of what seems to be the right and suitable thing to do. We may call this ability tact, which is the fine sense for the correct form of behaviour: knowing what to do in a unique situation and in the absence of general principles. This particular sensitivity is at work when individuals instantaneously recognize their fellow human beings for what they are and in the absence of the urge to reduce them to a function, title, or role. They are able to recapture a perceptual innocence that, due to built-in prejudices, rigid conceptual schemes, or sheer laziness, many tend to lose. In their eyes, the person is no longer an enemy soldier, a servant, an affluent man walking with a thick wallet, or a Fascist – all those social positions that can easily be considered with a cold and deprecatory frame of mind, with the "spirit of abstraction," vigorously denounced by Gabriel Marcel, or with an attitude of snobbism, described with subtlety by Jean-François Revel. In the moment of accomplishing an ethical action, neither an abstract idea nor a single criterion (wealth, power, and title) is hindering the perception of the persons and the spontaneous gesture towards them.[15]

It might be objected that the momentary return to a perceptual innocence in everyday life is difficult and requires long training. Because our perception of the other takes place in a practical context and is submitted to its possibilities and constraints, it is selective and necessarily tied the to other person's social role: we see the doctor, the patient, the student, or the minister. But, as we have seen, the ethical action does not depend on previously received training or education and cannot be broken down into phases of preparation and execution. There is no survey and selection of modes for perceiving another human being. He or she appears in his or her intrinsic worth and immediate wholeness. We come to see a concrete individuality, in his or her indivisibility, beyond his or her isolated aspects and functions; we consider the other person as *someone like ourselves* (*allos autos*), to use the expression that Aristotle applies for friendship and that we introduce here in order to highlight the correlation between the relation to oneself and to benevolent ethical action.[16]

THE VULNERABLE OTHER

But what exactly is capable of awakening and keeping alive such sensitivity to the integrity of the person? What elicits the "divine spark" (Minkowski) that is greater than us and ignites an unplanned action?

The ethical action, as I have just mentioned, consists of spontaneously responding to another person's presence and action and of adapting this response to what the person tells or signals through his or her bodily expression. What appears and is perceived through the words and gestures of the person is his or her vulnerability. There is no question here of understanding vulnerability in terms of the constituent and defining deficiencies of the human condition that are compensated through cultural and social institutions. At issue here is not the temporary or enduring illness affecting the human body and calling for carefully planned medical assistance or intervention. Neither is it the attribute of the human subject facing another subject and constituting and soliciting an "unexceptionable responsibility" (Emmanuel Lévinas). Finally, it is not the concrete and inevitable exposure of an organism to potential external dangers that one may notice or ignore while carrying out activities in a familiar or a foreign environment.[17]

The vulnerability prompting an ethical action in a human encounter presents itself in the form of a transitory need, absence, or loss of something. The experience of lacking protection, of being disoriented, or of aspiring to a warmer human relationship suddenly announces itself: the existence is menaced; the living body is struck by a weakness, the person's desire to establish human contact meets with resistance. Tied to the present moment, the perception of vulnerability generates a spontaneous response. Bringing help to someone in a state of situational need may have a vital impact or a negligible consequence on the person's condition. Calling for the liberating hand while being trapped in a burning house and seeking a comforting voice after failing an examination are, obviously, two different sorts of need. But, in the moment of acknowledging the need or disturbance and acting for the good of the person, no objective assessment of the gravity of vulnerability is carried out. Perceiving the vulnerability of the person, regardless of its form and extent, is sufficient to generate an ethical action. The action evokes in its author the awareness of the fragility of the person in need. In some instances, however, the vulnerability of an absent person may stir this awareness. Defending vigorously the dignity of those who are either unable or unwilling to stand up for their own rights or needs, even at the cost of committing a seemingly immoral act, is a highly commendable gesture.[18]

True, the thrust towards the good may arise without any sign of vulnerability. Giving to a stranger a cherished possession – a book, a work of art, or an instrument of music – without any hesitation and any expectation of reciprocation, just because these objects have elicited genuine praise or admiration, is an uncommon and generous deed, involving no awareness of vulnerability. The person advancing praise does not seem to request a remedy for a loss or the satisfaction of a need. What the generous donor might perceive, in the moment of extending a gift, is the desire for recognition coming from the person who praised the object and his or her own unsolicited *élan* to satisfy this desire.

While we are conversing with someone, we aspire to be heard, respected for what we affirm and ask, and taken seriously for our knowledge in spite of our possible ignorance. We want to be recognized as an equal partner in the course of an exchange of points of view. Even when we experience a disagreement, a serious clash of opinions, we still entertain a desire for a reciprocal recognition. The philosopher Isaiah Berlin put forward some moving thoughts on the fundamental human search for recognition. These thoughts prove to be true when we apply them to the experience of a confrontation between arguments and counterarguments. We want not to be ignored, taken for a mouthpiece of abstract and irrelevant ideas. As Isaiah Berlin remarked, we seek to avoid "not being treated as an individual, having my uniqueness insufficiently recognized, being classed as a member of some featureless amalgam, a statistical unit without identifiable, specifically human features and purposes of my own."[19] Although the persistent need to be understood is present in all human communications, a sensitive person is able to detect an almost imperceptible but tangible demand for recognition of the partner's sense of being someone and of having something important to say and do.

In this respect, for instance, turning to a lecturer with a question of clarification or further explanation constitutes an appropriate manner of responding to the tacit claim for a sense of relevance and recognition. Or, conversely, when someone, beset by a seemingly insoluble personal problem, unexpectedly asks for our advice, even though he or she knows quite well that no solution can come from us, we, then, feel that our answer meets an attentive ear and our own sense of identity and worth are objects of an indirect act of validation. The same tendency towards the good comes into play when someone offers sincere and unanticipated praise to those who, timid and unsure of their merits, eagerly await approval. Henri Bergson sees in this act a form of politeness: "A well-deserved praise, a kind word, may produce in these delicate souls the effect of a sudden gleam of sunlight on a dreary landscape; like the sunlight, it will make them regain the taste for life and, even more effectively, may sometimes transform into fruits the flowers that, without it, would have dried out."[20] A timely and generous remark addressed to our fellow human beings who find themselves in a tense and distressing situation is comparable to the life-saving rescue brought in a physical danger. It presupposes sensitivity to their inner condition and the capacity to guess the source of their difficulties as well as a capacity to create an atmosphere of trust and broach a subject near to their heart.

This sensitivity in generating an ethical action in the presence of a vulnerable condition is also a form of vulnerability. Because of the constitutive and deeper vulnerability of our bodies, we cannot stand aloof from our fellow human beings and remain unaffected by the impressions we receive from them. We are able to react to the subtlest and most diverse happenings and to distinguish their values and differences. Thanks to our vulnerability, we have a first impression of anyone we encounter and it is up to us to let it sink in, to register it on our deeper sensibilities, or to ignore it. The nature and characteristics of our primary reaction to people, and of our thrust towards the good, depend, to some extent, on this affective attunement of our bodies.

But, as I have already pointed out, the source of the ethical action can neither be located in a particular aspect of our body nor tied to a certain number of psychological characteristics. Without really knowing where it comes from and how it reaches an appropriate mode of expression, it appears in its power and swiftness. What we come to know, however, with greater clarity and intensity is what, in unusual circumstances and sometimes to our own surprise, we are able to do and achieve. We come to know what is the best in us or in our fellow human beings – an ideal of humanity that they or we are able to bring forth in both uncommon and common circumstances.

Not only exceptional or everyday ethical actions, but also discoveries and inventions happen as it were by themselves. Minkowski notes that the sudden emergence of ideas, images, and surprising flashes are the fundamental traits of both ethical spontaneity and a creative life. Indeed, in moments of inspiration, "there is a veritable bursting forth which comes, like lightning, to project its intense and exceptional luminosity on our inner life, without our being able to say whence it comes, and even without that question occurring to us, on the level of immediate data."[21] This emergence of ideas and solutions originates in the "dynamism of life" – a dynamism that carries the person along and asserts itself as one of the fundamental traits of his or her creativity.[22]

TURNING TO THE FUTURE WITH CONFIDENCE

Paul Valéry's statement – "Every person is less than the most beautiful thing he has done" – holds true for the moral character of the person and his or her action.[23] An ethical action does not immediately make someone a morally good or trusted person, and conversely, a morally good and trusted person does not necessarily translate his or her goodness and integrity into ethical action. To be sure, our actions depend to a large extent on the sort of person we are: with good intentions and noble purposes, we usually do good and noble deeds. But these worthy actions may be carried out with indifference or condescendence, sometimes even motivated by a well-disguised sense of self-interest, notwithstanding the fine attributes that we may have. On the other hand, people from whom we expect nothing gracious, generous, or noble may surprise us and act in an admirable fashion. Their action does not seem to originate from their acquired virtues, if they have any, but from what is profoundly human in them and what gives them, for the duration of their action, qualities of sublime greatness and vitality of being.

In this respect, Spaemann refers to the distinction introduced by Friedrich Schiller between "one-sided moral point of view" and "complete anthropological view." The former sees in the act the harmonious realization of the moral character; the later recognizes the difference between the act and the moral plane reached by the person, the discrepancy between the form and the content. On the anthropological level, the quality of actions does not necessarily follow out of being. Here the momentary "living feeling too has a voice."[24] Spaemann adds, "A person can be a well-turned-out human being and still fall to the temptation of breaking promises. Someone can be a weakling or a rogue and yet in the decisive moment prove true and not abandon his companions. Not everyone who behaves morally cuts a good figure the rest of the time."[25] Minkowski's phrase carries the same view: "Civic virtues, in spite of their importance, are not identical with the profound and individual search for ethical action."[26]

In fact, the touching display of ethical tendency in an unexpected situation brings forth the dignity of the person. We take notice of an unplanned and unforced desire to put honour, benevolence, magnanimity, and self-mastery above the search for material advantage, success, and even social recognition. The unprepared distance taken from all petty and selfish concerns lends dignity to the person and to his or her behaviour. The person's dignity is grounded in his or her ability to perceive one's own interest as something relative and secondary and to go beyond this interest by doing what is good and right for the other. The other person is then not considered as a means or as a function, but is respected in his or her own unconditional self-worth. And the potential for showing this kind of esteem for someone's inherent and absolute value is universal, present in every human being.[27]

It seems that, when an action originates in a previously unknown and unsuspected subjective capacity to do things unselfishly, without any wish of reciprocation or reward, the acting person loses his or her individuality. Yet, just as in those moments when an individual comes under the inspiring influence of a model, senses the attraction of a foreign reality, or sees the world from the perspective of a novel, the enlargement of the person's being does not take away the awareness of individuality. C.S. Lewis remarked that in reading great

Actions Like That Make Life Worthwhile

literature, "as in worship, in love, in moral action, and in knowing, I transcend myself; and am never more myself than when I do."[28]

Unexpected, brief, and sometimes even unnoticed, ethical actions nonetheless play an essential role in our lives. Minkowski ties its influence to our relation to the future. In the absence of ethical actions, the future would contract before us and lack the desired openness and wealth of life: "There is only a tendency toward ethical action, which, exceptional as it might be in everyday life, opens the future wide, as wide as possible."[29]

How do we look ahead of us into the open future? There are individuals who, following some painful experiences, understandably relate to future events and encounters with caution and mistrust. They are overwhelmed with an overt fear of a repetition of the past. The future can no longer bring them something new and they can only vouch for past negative experiences. The further they advance in life, the more the accumulated stock of experiences seems identical. There are still others who would like to see a future different from the past but who shy away from the demands and consequences that an innovative and courageous action could entail. They tend to measure the cost and benefit of every undertaking geared to the future. Insecure and losing faith in their own selves, they remain preoccupied with preserving themselves, not wishing anything uncommon and unconventional and not giving themselves away to others. They also lack a basic confidence in their ability to understand and to shape the surrounding world, which frequently appears to them as an impersonal, adverse, and hardly changeable reality. They find some compensation for this loss in the attachment to abstract ideas and causes or in the cherishing of living or lifeless objects. Notwithstanding their failures and deceptions and the futility of some of their actions, some people also turn to the future with fearless confidence and reasonable optimism. Certainly, this attitude is nourished, in part, by the predictability of human actions accomplished within, and guided by a large array of socio-cultural institutions, which have the power to regulate human actions according to predefined patterns.

The confidence in the future also comes from the intermittent perception of pure generosity and of sacrifice of life. The ethical action, as we have seen in Tolstoy's story, cannot be explained by previous accomplishments in terms of either their causes or genesis. It is not rooted in the past, even though it is impossible to ignore previously acquired movements, habits, abilities, and language necessary when accounting for its expression. It is not closely tied to any educational activities that teachers and administrators plan, carry out, measure, and assess in light of possible social benefits. It has its own value and surges from what is profoundly human in every person. It appears as an ideal or a supreme value, for which we yearn and which makes life worthwhile. In the presence of this value, both the recipient and the witness of the ethical action are filled with the belief that the future is worth envisaging with confidence and promise and that "life, in its onward march, entails a dimension of magnificence and elevation, and it is based on it."[30]

Our fellow human beings might be encouraged to give concrete expression to their faith in the future if we display confidence in them and their worth regardless of their attributes or faults. By signalling a sympathetic acceptance of their being, our confidence offers them a new future; a future in which they can act freely, without any restraint and limitation, and accomplish good deeds. If such a propensity for the good is recognized in the person, it might find a fortunate occasion and an appropriate form for its manifestation. It may appear, briefly but eloquently, in the act of showing genuine hospitality to a stranger. It may reach someone in the form of a gift offered without any hidden interest and with pure thoughtfulness. It may come forth in the act of sharing the last loaf of bread in the midst of utter destitution and famine or of coming to someone's rescue in a moment of extreme danger, even at the peril of one's life. But even if we maintain our confidence in the person's disposition to accomplish these actions, this disposition never yields a deep-rooted habit; an ethical action is ultimately unpredictable and always requires spontaneous creation and re-creation.

What we find in these examples is the experience of responsiveness and of openness. The responsive and open communication with human beings and things is primary and present early in the life of the child. Under normal circumstances, children find themselves in a "responsive world" (Erwin W. Straus) and relate to persons and objects with confidence and imagination as partners. An expressive quality is embodied in both living and non-living things: a tree or a piece of stone is seen or touched as alive; it speaks to them and calls for an answer. By the same token, the living presence of an object conveys autonomy and a sense of self-will; it eludes all attempts by the child to bring it under control. The most elementary and immediate objects of the world – a door, a chair, a cloth on the table, a box – exhibit an expressive presence. Through their benevolent touch and imaginative abilities, children tend to identify themselves with a lone tree, a fading flower, or an undernourished animal; they guess their desire and wait for their appeals. But, as they grow older, they inevitably learn modes of contact with a "nonresponsive world" – a world in which people and things gradually become closed, grim, and defensive or oscillate between affable openness and cold indifference.[31] They may eventually turn to poets or painters who are still able to read and hear the language of things and convey their responses to others.

The uninviting and unavailable world, as well as the uncertain and fearful attitude towards this world, are established when people relate to each other with specific interests and each person is reduced to the level of a means envisioned for the attainment of selfish objectives. A responsive world, in which authentic conversations and unselfish co-operations occur, may be regained and enjoyed with confidence if two persons relate to each other with disinterestedness and readily place themselves in the other's shoes. Thanks to the unprompted adoption of this attitude, an inner power of being fully satisfied with the present and fully concerned with the well-being of others becomes, from time to time, manifest in the form of ethical action. Thus, ethical actions entail a radical and unexpected metamorphosis in terms of the ways things and people are related to. They promote the belief that an ineradicable tendency to the good can occasionally find its expression in human interactions and create an affirmative and confident attitude towards others, helping to restore, even if for a short time, a responsive world.

I have repeatedly emphasized the gap between the quality of the action and the sort of person who performs such an action: the ethical action does not necessarily arise out of the goodness that otherwise defines the person's being. There is, however, a human faculty that may play a certain role in the realization of ethical action and sustain the spontaneous impulse towards the good. The various actions and rejections of action – the life-saving help, the conciliatory word or gesture, or the refusal to repay injury with injury – indicate that the person who is doing the good deed is able to imagine the condition and situation of the other person, as well as the possible consequence of his or her own action. Unassumingly giving a hand to someone in need as well as coming up with a life-altering deed are initiated with the help of the imagination. On the other hand, insensitivity to human suffering and disinterested malice is the result of the failure to imagine a condition different from one's own. Quite appropriately, G.K. Chesterton calls this incapacity bigotry. Even if, as I have pointed out, the tendency towards ethical action cannot be reduced to the presence or absence of character traits or capacities, the cultivation of imagination is nonetheless vital, especially if, in our educational endeavours, we try to nurture, beyond the transmission of rules of conduct and moral precepts, "true liberality," which is the capacity to "imagine any other mind."[32]

The possibility of committing evil acts is, obviously, also present in most of us, notwithstanding our inability to imagine and accept the possibility of radical and all-pervading wickedness in humans. The extent and variety of cruelty and atrocity in the forms of deportation, starvation, torture, murder, genocide, and extermination are too great for us to ignore the enduring human propensity for violence and bestiality. And, let us add, the most horrendous crimes were committed, especially in the last century, in the name of a good that was supposed to extirpate evil and misery forever. The incalculably malevolent gestures committed in our own familiar milieu and with regard to everyday, trifling matters may threaten to swiftly destroy the trust we put in our fellow human beings.

Yet a concrete ethical action that we occasionally happen to witness may also energize us and give us the hope, if not the proof, that, despite so much evidence to the contrary, there is a potential for good deeds in the depth of every human person.[33] And even if, day after day, we are unable to detect the "disinterested taste for the good" (Alexis de Tocqueville) in the lives of men and women around us, the intermittent realizations of the ethical tendency will nonetheless be sufficient to keep this hope alive and, at the same time, to help us see with clarity what makes life worth living.

Notes

INTRODUCTION

1 Shakespeare, *As You Like It*, III, 2.

2 See Haeffner, *Philosophische Anthropologie*, 109–13.

3 Guardini, *Die Lebensalter*. Shakespeare's depiction of the stages of human life in *As You Like It* has become proverbial. It is, I would venture, a brilliant and humorous model of reductionism, a parody, so to speak, of all the "this is nothing other than that" views concerning human being, with which we are, I am afraid, all too familiar today. The reader finds a more elaborate division of human life into various ages in Aristotle's *Rhetoric* 2. 12–17. 1388b32–1391b8 and in Arthur Schopenhauer's *Parerga and Paralipomena*, under the heading of *The Ages of Life*.

4 The German historian Joachim Fest lists in his memoirs four fundamental experiences: "first, being overwhelmed by a perfect musical work; then, reading a great book; then, first love; and then, the first irreplaceable loss." Vladimir Nabokov writes beautifully about the "miracle of love's initial moments." John Cowper Powys recalls those singular instances "when, in the midst of our work, we get one of those unaccountable thrills of happiness that seem to arise for no reason at all." These are "moments that make life worth living." For T.S. Eliot, "The experience of a poem is the experience both of a moment and of a lifetime. It is very much like our intenser experiences of other human beings. There is a first, or an early moment which is unique, of shock and surprise, even of terror (*Ego dominus tuus*); a moment which can never be forgotten, but which is never repeated integrally; and yet which would become destitute of significance if it did not survive in a larger whole of experience; which survives

166 Notes to pages 6–21

inside a deeper and a calmer feeling." Fest, *Not I*, 273; Nabokov, *Speak, Memory*, 238; Powys, *The Art of Happiness*, 219; Eliot, "Dante," 216.

5 See Plügge, "Über die Hoffnung," 38–50.

6 Scruton, "Effing the Ineffable," 88.

7 Koestler, *The Act of Creation*, 363; See also his essay "The Truth of Imagination," 103–10.

8 See, for example, Levi, "The Canto of Ulysses," 115–21; Klein, "La littérature européenne et la conscience tragique de l'existence," 57–9. Both authors relate their contact with Dante's *Divine Comedy* under gruesome circumstances.

9 Zweig, *Shooting Stars*.

10 See the stimulating reflections of John Lachs, "Transcendence in Philosophy and in Everyday Life."

11 See Koral Ward's historical approach to the concept in her study *Augenblick*.

12 Kierkegaard, *Stages on Life's Way*, 204–6; Merleau-Ponty, *Phenomenology of Perception*, 281.

13 Scheler, "Phenomenology and the Theory of Cognition," 137–43.

14 I take this quotation from Thomas De Koninck's excellent introduction to philosophy, *À quoi sert la philosophie?*, 10–11. I think that both Nagel and De Koninck would probably have commended this famous line of G.K. Chesterton: "Nothing is poetical if plain daylight is not poetical; and no monster should amaze us if the normal man does not amaze."

CHAPTER ONE

1 Barrett, *Irrational Man*, 167.

2 Daniels, *Conversations with Menuhin*, 179. As it will be shown, Menuhin speaks here of decisions and not merely of choices.

3 Kierkegaard, *Fear and Trembling*, 78.

4 Lübbe, "Zur Theorie der Entscheidung," 13.

5 Plato, *Theaetetus* (trans. Cornford), 189e–90a.

6 Nagel, *The Last Word*, 115–8.

7 In a recent bestseller, the reader finds this misleading statement: "Drawing on some well-established findings in social science, we show that in many cases, individuals make pretty bad decisions – decisions they would not have made if they had paid full attention and possessed complete informa-tion, unlimited cognitive abilities, and complete self-control." Thaler and Sunstein, *Nudge*, 5. If individuals had possessed complete information, unlimited cognitive abilities, and complete self-control, they would *not*

have made a decision at all. They would merely have *followed* the best available option in a state of certainty about the rightness of their action. Strictly speaking, individuals never make bad decisions. Bad is the outcome of a decision. They may qualify, wrongly, their decisions as bad only in retrospect when they become conscious of the unfortunate results of their decisions.

8 Zutt, "Der Lebensweg als Bild der Geschichtlichkeit," 352–7.
9 Morin, "Pour une crisologie," 149–63.
10 Scheler, "Tod und Fortleben," 19–21; Welte, "Meditation über Zeit," 15–27.
11 Straus, "Disorders of Personal Time," 295.
12 See Straus, "The Miser."
13 Kierkegaard, *Either/Or*, 172.
14 Spaemann, "Education as an Introduction to Reality," 114–15.
15 Vizinczey, *The Rules of Chaos*, 95.
16 Price, *Dialogues of Alfred North Whitehead*, 145.
17 Straus, "The Pathology of Compulsion," 315.
18 See Ungar, *Too Safe for Their Own Good.*
19 Gehlen, "Mensch und Institutionen."
20 Nietzsche, "Schopenhauer as Educator," 127–30.
21 Kierkegaard, *Either/Or*, 177.
22 Barrett, *Death of the Soul*, 122–7.
23 Waugh, "General Conversation."
24 Barrett, *Time of Need*, 290–1.
25 Decision is crucial for the "content of the personality." On this central assertion of Kierkegaard's philosophy of existence, see *Either/Or*, 155–79.
26 Ricoeur, *Freedom and Nature*, 174.
27 Spaemann, *Basic Moral Concepts*, 85.
28 Tellenbach, "La réalité, le comique et l'humour," 18.
29 Bettelheim, *The Informed Heart*, 255–65.
30 Hilberg, *Perpetrators, Victims, Bystanders*, 188–90. A concrete confirmation of Hilberg's views can be found in George Klein's description of his daring escape. See his "Confronting the Holocaust," 263–7.

CHAPTER TWO

1 Najder, *Joseph Conrad*, 577.
2 Reitman, "The Good Soldier."
3 Kierkegaard, *The Present Age*, 68.
4 Spaemann, "Human Nature," 19.

168 Notes to pages 39–56

5   On the anthropological concept of world, see Haeffner, *Philosophische Anthropologie*, 50–2.
6   See Straus, "Event and Experience."
7   Minkowski, "L'homme artisan de sa destinée."
8   Scheler, "Ordo Amoris," 100–9.
9   Gmelch, Kemper, and Zenner, eds., *Urban Life*, 282.
10 Kemper, *Migration and Adaptation*, 203.
11 Scheler, "Repentance and Rebirth," 48.
12 Ibid., 47–8.
13 Deeken, *Process and Permanence in Ethics*, 170.
14 Congar, "The Idea of Conversion," 5. See also Hadot, "Conversion," and Ullman, *The Transformed Self*.
15 Plato, *Republic*, 518c.
16 Lajtha's letter was written to his sons on 16 December 1952. See Robert R. Reilly's fine essay on Lajtha's creative independence, "László Lajtha: Music from a Secret Room." In his book on the theme of solitude, published first under the title of *The School of Genius*, Anthony Storr has shown how creative individuals distanced themselves from their social surroundings and retreated into the inner world of fantasy. See *Solitude*, 106–22. See also the reflections of Steiner on solitude inflicted by social and political constraints, in *Grammars of Creation*, 181–200.
17 Peri, *The War Within*, 16.
18 See the numerous examples given by Storr in his *Solitude*, 42–61.
19 Ningkun, *A Single Tear*, 100–1.
20 Moltmann, *Man*, 39–41.
21 Kierkegaard, *The Sickness unto Death*, 37–42.
22 On the experience of boredom in relation to lived time, see Wilhelm Josef Revers, "Die Langweile – Krise and Kriterium des Menschseins." See also Svendsen, *A Philosophy of Boredom*, and the recent partial overview (Pascal is not even mentioned) of the literature on boredom by Kingwell, "In Praise of Boredom."
23 "Condition of Man: Inconstancy, Boredom, Anxiety," Pascal, *Pensées*, fragment 127. The numbering of Brunschvicg is used. For a thorough analysis of Pascal's thoughts on boredom, see Plügge, "Pascals Begriff des 'Ennui' und seine Bedeutung für eine medizinische Anthropologie."
24 Ibid., fr. 131.
25 Ibid., fr. 139.
26 Berger, "Ev'ry Time We Say Goodbye."
27 See Bushway and Paternoster, "Desistance from Crime"; Paternoster and Bushway, "Desistance and the 'Feared Self.'"

Notes to pages 57–68

28 Schapiro, *Impressionism*, 318.
29 Barrett, *Time of Need*, 187.
30 Betteilheim, *A Good Enough Parent*, 177.
31 Hoffer, *The True Believer*, 7–9.
32 Lavelle, *The Dilemma of Narcissus*, 170.
33 Plessner, "Trieb und Leidenschaft," 372.
34 Plessner, "Über den Begriff der Leidenschaft," 73.
35 Ibid.
36 Lavelle, *The Dilemma of Narcissus*, 172.
37 Ibid., 170.
38 Monod, "Le voyage, le déracinement de l'individu hors du milieu natal constituent-ils des éléments déterminants de la conversion religieuse?"
39 See Whitehead, *Religion in the Making*, 37–40.
40 Marquard, "In Defense of the Accidental." See also Bandura, "The Psychology of Chance Encounters and Life Path."
41 Toynbee, *Experiences*, 39.
42 Paquet, *Simon Leys*, 347.
43 Spaemann, *Persons*, 215.
44 Kierkegaard, "Against Cowardliness," 347.
45 Ibid.
46 Ibid., 352.
47 Ibid., 364.
48 Ibid., 356.

CHAPTER THREE

1 Meeting is the act of coming into contact with another person in an objective world. When we encounter someone, we find ourselves in the presence of another person in our subjective environment. A meeting is usually planned; an encounter often happens to us. In an encounter, the modes of contact change, suddenly or gradually, from distance to closeness, from detachment to intimacy. See the fine distinctions between the two terms by Paul Christian, "Begegnen und Antreffen."
2 Walker, *Franz Liszt*, 60.
3 Scheler, *Formalism in Ethics and Non-Formal Ethics of Values*, 572–83 and "Exemplars of Person and Leaders." Scheler wrote this essay between 1911 and 1921. It has been published in the first volume of his posthumous works under the title *Vorbilder und Führer*. I translate the word *Vorbild* by the English *model*.
4 Scheler, *Formalism in Ethics and Non-Formal Ethics of Values*, 574.

Notes to pages 69–81

5   The stoic philosopher Seneca emphasized this point: "Plato, Aristotle, and the whole throng of sages who were destined to go each his different way, derived more benefit from the character than from the words of Socrates." *Moral Letters to Lucillus*, 6, 6.

6   Spaemann, "Education as an Introduction to Reality," 114.

7   Spaemann, *Basic Moral Concepts*, 63.

8   Scheler, "Exemplars of Person and Leaders," 135.

9   Ibid., 139.

10 Scheler, *Formalism in Ethics and Non-Formal Ethics of Values*, 580.

11 Hartmann, *Ethics*, 195.

12 Bergson, *Les deux sources de la morale et de la religion*, 30–1.

13 Scheler, "Exemplars of Person and Leaders," 140.

14 Scheler, "The Forms of Knowledge and Culture," 32.

15 Scheler, *Formalism in Ethics and Non-Formal Ethics of Values*, 579.

16 Rudert, "Die persönliche Atmosphäre," 295.

17 Jaspers, "Die Kraft zu leben," 107.

18 In his *Self-Portrait*, Jaspers further explained why and to what extent Weber served as a model for him. There was an irresolvable tension between Weber's tremendous scientific achievements and his sober reading of the modern world, prompting in him even the urge to commit suicide. Neither the impressive rigour of his scientific work nor his tendency to despair made Weber a model. Weber has become an "absolutely reliable" model inasmuch as his whole life was characterized by the relentless determination to reach the truth. It is Weber's truthfulness (*Wahrhaftigkeit*) and will to truth (*Wahrheitswille*) that left on Jaspers a lasting and pivotal impression. "Ein Selbstportrait," 102–13.

19 Books have their destiny.

20 Greene, "The Lost Childhood," 11.

21 Benjamin, *One-Way Street*, 55.

22. Ryckmans, *The View from the Bridge*, 27–8. See also Goodman, *Ways of Worldmaking*, 102–7.

23 See Spaemann, *Basic Moral Concepts*, 25–7.

24 Steiner, *Lessons of the Masters*.

25 The relevance of Socratic teaching is masterfully highlighted by Thomas De Koninck in his *Philosophie de l'éducation pour l'avenir*, 97–115.

26 Russel, "Some Cambridge Dons of the Nineties," 60.

27 Romilly, *Écrits sur l'enseignement*, 41–8.

28 Koestler, *The Invisible Writing*, 157.

Notes to pages 81–94   171

29   Scheler, "The Forms of Knowledge and Culture," 32–4. On the relevance of Scheler's philosophy of educational models, see Deeken, *Process and Permanence in Ethics*, 213–18.

30   This "moment of grace" is beautifully recounted by Jacqueline de Romilly in Marguerite Léna, ed., *Honneur aux maîtres*, 49–51. This collective work relates several other decisive encounters with admirable teachers.

31   Spaemann, "Education as an Introduction to Reality," 111.

32   "It is not the things you say which children respect; when you say things, they very commonly laugh and do the opposite. It is the things you assume that really sink into them. It is the things you forget even to teach that they learn." Chesterton, "No Such Thing," 96.

33   Farkas, "A Meeting with Jenö Ádám," 39.

34   Mehl, "Structure philosophique de la Notion de Présence," 174.

35   Frankfurt, "The Importance of What We Care About," 83.

36   Frankfurt, "On the Necessity of Ideals."

37   Mitscherlich, *La fin des modèles*, 18. See also Wolf, "Self, Idealization, and Development of Values."

38   Jaspers, *Philosophy and the World*, 43.

39   Whitehead, "The Rhythmic Claims of Freedom and Discipline," 39.

CHAPTER FOUR

1   Borges, "Story of the Warrior and the Captive Maiden," 211.

2   Ryckmans, *The View from the Bridge*, 57.

3   Fink, *Einleitung in die Philosophie*, 95.

4   Tellenbach, *Geschmack und Atmosphäre*, 46–9.

5   Simmel, "The Stranger," 404.

6   Kipling, *Something of Myself and Other Autobiographical Writings*, 78.

7   Lévi-Strauss, "Apprivoiser l'étrangeté."

8   Schutz, "The Stranger," 100–1. Schutz describes the difficulties that an "approaching stranger" has to overcome in order to be accepted by a foreign group. In this chapter, I intend to study the experiences of an "inquisitive stranger or appreciative guest" who is open to being enriched and possibly transformed by a foreign culture.

9   Burgess, "Should We Learn Foreign Languages?," 125.

10   Haeffner, *In der Gegenwart leben*, 136.

11   Storr, *The Dynamics of Creation*, 188–202.

12   Weizsaecker, *Le cycle de la structure*, 211.

13 Schutz, "The Stranger," 100.

14 Segalen, *Essai sur l'exotisme*, 44.

15 Landsberg, *Pierres blanches*, 143.

16 See Haeffner, *Philosophische Anthropologie*, 41; Lévi-Strauss, "Place de la culture japonaise dans le monde."

17 Heller, "The Dismantling of a Marionette Theatre; Or, Psychology and the Misinterpretation of Literature," 207.

18 Santayana, *Persons and Places*, 449.

19 Wittgenstein, *Philosophical Investigations*, 50.

20 Plessner, "With Different Eyes," 30.

21 Marquard, "The Age of Unwordliness?"

22 Augustine, *On Catechising the Uninstructed*, 12, 17.

23 Marcel, "Phenomenological Notes on Being in a Situation," 90.

24 Camus, "Love of Life," 54.

25 Pieper, "Learning How to See Again," 31–2.

26 Lorenz, *The Waning of Humaneness*, 111–15.

27 See the fine analyses of Jean-François de Raymond in his *L'esprit de la diplomatie*, 231–40.

28 Bánffy, *The Phoenix Land*, 365. Conversely, Bánffy's skill at diplomacy was at work when he expressed his ideas obliquely in some of his literary works.

29 See Straus, "Man: A Questioning Being."

30 Haeffner, "Staunen," 15–21.

31 Berg, *A Different Existence*, 39.

32 Sacks, *The Dignity of Difference*, 23.

33 Huxley, *The Art of Seeing*, 77.

34 Linschoten, "Over de Humor," 655.

35 Plessner, "With Different Eyes," 32.

36 Waldenfels, "Das überwältige Leiden."

37 Solzhenitsyn, *Nobel Lecture*, 17.

38 Modiano, *Discours à l'Académie suédoise*, 20.

39 Naipaul, "Conrad's Darkness," 218.

40 T.S. Eliot defends this view in his otherwise remarkable essay "Religion and Literature."

41 Wood, *How Fiction Works*, 65.

42 Patocka, "L'écrivain, son *objet*."

43 Vizinczey, "The Genius Whose Time Has Come."

44 Lewis, *Experiment in Criticism*, 139.

45 Lawrence, "The Spirit of Place," 17–18.

Notes to pages 112–21

46 A remarkable novel of this kind is John Williams's *Stoner*, first published in 1965. On the theme of loneliness, see Thornton Wilder, "The American Loneliness."

47 Frye, *Creation and Recreation*, 10.

48 Lewis, "Sometimes Fairy Stories May Say Best What's to Be Said," 48.

49 Plessner, "With Different Eyes," 31.

50 Landmann, *Philosophical Anthropology*, 223.

51 Haeffner "Die philosophische Anthropologie und der interkulturelle Dialog."

52 Plessner, "Macht und menschliche Natur."

53 Gebauer and Wulf, "After the 'Death of Man,'" 182.

54 Wiredu, "Can Philosophy Be Intercultural?," 154.

55 Nussbaum, "Human Functioning and Social Justice," 216.

CHAPTER FIVE

1 Stendhal, *To the Happy Few*, 109.

2 Berlioz, *The Memoirs of Hector Berlioz*, 6.

3 Kodály, "Ki az igazi zeneértö?" (Who is the True Music Expert?), 299–300. The composer, conductor, and writer Antony Hopkins was also sceptical about the value of programme notes. In his book, written for the common music-lover rather than for the learned musician, he related a few "special moments" or "turning-points" in his youth when his analytical knowledge of music was minimal. *Understanding Music*, 228–33.

4 Menuhin, *Unfinished Journey*, 88.

5 Walker, *A Study in Musical Analysis*, 15.

6 The French conductor Pierre Monteux was asked how he arrives at a judgment about a new work: "I listen to it with closed eyes – one should never begin with an analysis. If I am bored, I consider the score without value; if I am moved, or at least interested, then I read it and analyse it and can believe in its importance." Landowski, *La musique n'adoucit pas les moeurs*, 50.

7 Minkowski, "Prose and Poetry (Astronomy and Cosmology)," 246. C.S. Lewis expressed a similar view when he deplored the habit of first approaching a literary work with a critical mind: "We thus fail of that inner silence, that emptying out of ourselves, by which we ought to make room for the total reception of the work." *An Experiment in Criticism*, 92–3.

174 Notes to pages 121–6

8   In our times, conventional students of musical aesthetics like to refer, in their contributions, to the ideas of the greatest figures in the field (Hegel, Schopenhauer, Hanslick, and Nietzsche) and to the writings of a number of well-respected and competent colleagues (Peter Kivy, Stephen Davies, and Jerrold Levinson to name the most prolific ones). These scholars seem to consult books and papers written and published in English. Accordingly, they tend to take little or no notice of other philosophers who have written their texts in one of the foreign languages and who have proposed imaginative insights into the chief characteristics of our musical experience. Even recent translations fail to spark their interest. (A happy exception is the recent doctoral dissertation of Benjamin M. McBrayer, "Mapping Mystery: Brelet, Jankélévitch, and Phenomenologies of Music in Post-World War II France," Kenneth P. Dietrich School of Arts and Sciences, University of Pittsburgh, 2017.) Some of these ignored or neglected thinkers have had intimate practical knowledge of musical compositions. Their accounts of the nature and significance of music is not only original but, I believe, also relevant for all who seek to understand why music exerts such a powerful effect on people and why it plays a central role in our culture. Their insights throw additional light on the complexity of our relationships to music and thus happily complement the conclusions of the philosophical approaches of current authors. My own thinking about the human responses to musical forms has been influenced by the lesser-studied but equally stimulating writings of Nicolai Hartmann, Gabriel Marcel, Vladimir Jankélévitch, Helmuth Plessner, and Anthony Storr.

9   Sessions, *The Musical Experience of Composer, Performer, Listener*, 93.

10   Bárdos, "Singing Instruments," 20.

11   Welte, "Dasein im Symbol des Spiels," 107.

12   Hartmann, *Aesthetics*, 114.

13   I discussed in more detail the playful dimension of music in my article "Musical Performance as Play."

14   Eduard Hanslick famously defended the self-containedness of music. However, he was careful to point out that the absence of content does not mean "music lacks *substance*." The composer's ideas and emotions provide music with its substance. "Clearly 'spiritual substance' is what those people have in mind who fight with sectarian ardour for the 'content' of music ... Music is play (*Spiel*) but not frivolity (*Spielerei*). Thoughts and feelings run like blood in the arteries of the harmonious body of beautiful sounds. They are not that body; they are not perceptible, but they animate it." *On the Musically Beautiful*, 82. Elsewhere, Hanslick made a

distinction between "inspired form and empty form." An inspired form surely must contain something. *Music Criticism: 1846–99*, 26–7. The reader finds a lucid presentation of the dispute between formalists and expressionists in Anthony Storr's *Music and the Mind*, 65–88. See also Plessner, "Anthropologie der Sinne," 27–40.

15 Adorno, *Beethoven*, 1–9.

16 Huxley, "Music at Night." See also Scruton, *The Aesthetics of Music*, 433–7 and Adorno, *Beethoven*, 141–53.

17 Bernstein, "Beethoven's Fifth Symphony."

18 Stein, *The A-B-C of Aesthetics*, 46. I owe this reference to Alan Walker. See his article "Schopenhauer and Music," 42.

19 Welte, "Meditation über Zeit," 23. In Germany, the audience holds a pause before starting to applaud. Together with the pause before the first note is played, it encloses the music in silence.

20 Jankélévitch, "Music and Silence."

21 Marcel, "Music According to Saint Augustine," 118. With respect to the temporal aspect of our musical experience, it is customary to refer to Edmund Husserl's phenomenological discussion of the perception of a melody. Husserl had no explicit intention to propose a detailed analysis of the human encounter with music, which would consider all constituents of the phenomenon and explore various connections with adjacent phenomena. He merely used the example of melody to develop his own thinking about the phenomenology of subjective time-consciousness or of the lived experience of "immanent time." This sentence makes his intention clear: "Let us take a particular melody or cohesive part of a melody as an example" (*The Phenomenology of Internal Time-Consciousness*, 43). Rather than repeating what, in a way, many contributions more or less thoroughly present, I have chosen, in this chapter, to turn to the observations of Gabriel Marcel, Vladimir Jankélévitch, and Gisèle Brelet. Their ideas are of specific relevance to the theme of the moment as it is lived not only while listening to a musical piece, but also right after the last note has been played. Silence, which marks both the beginning and end of a movement or of the entire composition, is an integral part of our musical experience. Understandably, Husserl is not interested in the description of the listener's experience of silence.

22 Brelet, "Music and Silence," 118. See also her *Esthétique et création musicale*, 111–6.

23 Marcel, "Music and the Marvelous," 128.

24 Jankélévitch, *Liszt et la rhapsodie*, 53.

25 Sandor, *On Piano Playing*, 211.

176 Notes to pages 132–6

26 Jankélévitch, *Liszt et la rhapsodie*, 84, 91. See also my observations on Vladimir Jankélévitch's views on musical virtuosity and improvisation. "La musique et le corps."

27 Schuller, "Form, Content, and Symbol," 281. In his already mentioned essay, Robert R. Reilly confirms Schuller's views: "Lajtha's sound world is identifiably distinct. After immersing myself in his music, I could easily identify a piece of his I had never heard before within a few measures." "László Lajtha," 187. The composer Béla Bartók made a somehow similar statement: "Even the most abstract works, as for instance my string quartets ... reveal a certain indescribable, unexplainable spirit – a certain *je ne sais pas quoi* – which will give to anyone who listens, and who knows the rural backgrounds, the feeling: 'This could not have been written by any but an Eastern European musician.'" "Hungarian Music," 396.

28 Hartmann, *Aesthetics*, 122.

29 Dufrenne, "The Beautiful," 83.

30 This meaning is more clearly manifest in the chosen mood and theme of an opera. Marcel Landowski asserted that a composer must be "consumed" by a theme in order to "lend force to it through the music." "For this reason I believe that the meaning I confer upon my existence can be found in my music, and in the libretto of my operas. But the same is true for my symphonic music." Livio, *Conversations avec Marcel Landowski*, 89–90.

31 Hartmann, *Aesthetics*, 61–4.

32 Straus, *The Primary World of Senses*, 377.

33 Ibid., 378.

34 Hartmann, *Aesthetics*, 217.

35 Notwithstanding Kodály's shrewd recommendation about the proper way of listening to music, I tend to agree with Éric Rohmer who believes that we truly appreciate an abstruse dance music, and feel it in its depth, when we dance to it. We have to dance with our whole body and not merely in our imagination. *De Mozart en Beethoven*, 15. Roger Scruton's comment on this particular point illustrates the not surprising fact that music, its nature, meaning, and experience elicit profound and never-ending disagreements among those who think and write about this art. "And it has been true since ancient times and in all cultures the peculiar power of music is most noticeable *not* when we are dancing to it or singing along, but precisely when the pure tone arrests us and when we stand to listen." *The Soul of the World*, 154.

36 In a prophetic lecture, delivered in January 1937 at the Ferenc Liszt Academy of Music of Budapest, Béla Bartók had noticed that, for many

Notes to pages 137–42

people, listening to music on the radio had become "nothing more than a caress of a kind of tepid bath, a kind of coffee-house music, a droning in the background so that one can perform other tasks with less boredom and with hardly any attention to music." "Mechanical Music," 296. Many years before Bartók presented his thoughts on recorded music, Eduard Hanslick made some provocative statements about the average listener's musical experience: "The aesthetical criterion of intellectual pleasure is lost to them; for all they would know, a fine cigar or a piquant delicacy or a warm bath produces the same effect as a symphony. Some sit there mindlessly at ease, others in extravagant rapture, but for all the principle is one and the same: pleasure in the elemental in music." *On the Musically Beautiful*, 59.

37 Storr, *The Dynamics of Creation*, 117. In this connection, Storr refers to the fifth movement of Beethoven's String Quartet in C-sharp minor, Op. 131, which was analyzed by Leonard B. Meyer in his *Emotion and Meaning in Music*, 199–204.

38 Plessner, "Zur Anthropologie der Musik," 198.

39 Bergson, *Time and Free Will*, 99–103.

40 Marcel, "Bergson and Music," 89–90. See also the discussion of musical time by Susanne K. Langer, *Feeling and Form*, 115–7, and the perceptive distinction between the sounds of nature and of music by Erwin W. Straus in his *The Primary World of Senses*, 323–4.

41 Keller, "Towards a Theory of Music." See also Storr, *Music and the Mind*, 84–7.

42 Geiger, *The Significance of Art*, 56.

43 Marcel, "Music and the Reign of the Spirit," 114.

44 Cassirer, "The Educational Value of Art (1943)," 212.

45 Adorno, *Beethoven*, 6–7. In his lectures on aesthetics, Adorno further emphasized the liberating and uplifting character of our experience of art. When the pulse and rhythm of our lives are intensely united with the "life of the work of art," we come to living "moments of breakthrough." The notion of breakthrough refers to the immediate experience of transcending our everyday existence, all its concerns and activities that distract us from the present. In addition, an artistic work may captivate us to such an extent that we feel the most intense enjoyment. These "supreme moments of happiness" (*obersten Glückaugenblicken*) have the same power over us as the "highest real moments" (*höchsten realen Augenblicke*) that we experience in other areas of our lives. Ästhetik (1958/59), 195–7.

46 Frye, "Criticism as Education," 148–9.

47 Forster, "Not Listening to Music."

48 Valéry, *Cahiers II*, 1556.

49 See Alan Walker's persuasive article, "Music and Education."

50 Barzun, "The Indispensable Amateur," 34.

51 Kodály, "A zenei nevelés Magyarországon (Music Education in Hungary)," 152.

52 Ricoeur, *La critique et la conviction*, 261.

53 Kodály, "Mit akarok a régi székely dalokkal? (What Do I Want to Do with the Old Sekler Songs?)," 29.

54 Weizsäcker, *The Ambivalence of Progress*, 102.

CHAPTER SIX

1 Tolstoy, "Master and Man."

2 Barthelet, *Entretiens avec Gustave Thibon*, 173.

3 Spaemann, *Basic Moral Concepts*, 76.

4 Minkowski, *Lived Time*, 111–21.

5 Ibid., 113.

6 Canetti, *The Tongue Set Free*, 165.

7 Minkowski, *Lived Time*, 116.

8 See the still relevant observations of Max Scheler, *Ressentiment*, 83–113.

9 Barthelet, *Entretiens avec Gustave Thibon*, 237.

10 See Minkowski, "L'homme et ce qu'il y a d'humain en lui (Biologie et anthropologie)," 149–50.

11 Kleinman, *What Really Matters*, 103.

12 Saint-Exupéry, *A Letter to a Hostage*, 44.

13 Minkowski, "Spontaneity."

14 Orwell, "Looking Back on the Spanish War," 254.

15 Marcel, "The Spirit of Abstraction, as a Factor Making for War"; Revel, *Sur Proust*, 77–96.

16 Aristotle, *Nicomachean Ethics* 9.4, 1166a29–32

17 See Have, "Respect for Human Vulnerability."

18 See the example given by Dietrich Bonhoeffer in his *Ethics*, 362–3.

19 Berlin, "Two Concepts of Liberty," 155.

20 Bergson, "La politesse," 53.

21 Minkowski, "Spontaneity," 176.

22 Ibid.

23 Valéry, "Analecta," 714.

24 Schiller, "Letters on the Aesthetic Education of Man," 93.

25 Spaemann, "What Does It Mean to Be Cultured? (1955)," 123.

26 Minkowski, *Lived Time*, 120.

Notes to pages 160–4

27 Spaemann, "Human Dignity," 55; Spaemann, *Basic Moral Concepts*, 59.

28 Lewis, *An Experiment in Criticism*, 141.

29 Minkowski, *Lived Time*, 112.

30 Minkowski, "Le problème du temps vécu," 78.

31 See the observation of Erwin W. Straus following his lecture on the human sensory experience, "Embodiment and Excarnation," 250. See also the reflections of Hendrik M. Ruitenbeek, "Mechanization versus Spontaneity: Which Will Survive?"

32 Chesterton, "The Bigot," 151–3. As writers and philosophers such as Hannah Arendt have repeatedly pointed out, one of the biggest shortcomings of mass murderers is the total lack of imaginative ability. The killing of millions of men and women was made possible by "thinking nothing of it" (Vizinczey), by people's "matter-of-fact unimaginativeness" (Koestler). The neglect of imagination in our societies can produce disastrous results.

33 See Jacques Lecomte's heartening book *La bonté humaine*, and Jean-Marc Rouvière's fine essay *L'homme surpris*.

Bibliography

Adorno, Theodor W. Ästhetik (1958/59). Edited by Eberhard Ortland. Frankfurt am Main: Suhrkamp Verlag, 2009.

– *Beethoven: The Philosophy of Music*. Edited by Rolf Tiedemann and translated by Edmund Jephcott. Stanford: Stanford University Press, 1998.

Bandura, Albert. "The Psychology of Chance Encounters and Life Path." *American Psychologist* 37 (1982): 747–55.

Bárdos, Lajos. "Singing Instruments." In *Selected Writings on Music*, translated by Alexander Farkas and Kata Ittzés, 7–20. Budapest: Editio Musica, 1984.

Barrett, Willam. *Death of the Soul: From Descartes to the Computer*. Garden City, NY: Anchor Books, 1987.

– *Irrational Man: A Study in Existential Philosophy*. New York: Anchor Books, 1990.

– *Time of Need: Forms of Imagination in the Twentieth Century*. New York: Harper and Row, 1972.

Barthelet, Philippe. *Entretiens avec Gustave Thibon*. Monaco: Éditions du Rocher, 2001.

Bartók, Béla. "Hungarian Music." In *Essays*, selected and edited by Benjamin Suchoff, 393–6. Lincoln: University of Nebraska Press, 1976.

– "Mechanical Music." In *Essays*, selected and edited by Benjamin Suchoff, 289–92. Lincoln: University of Nebraska Press, 1976.

Barzun, Jacques. "The Indispensable Amateur." In *Critical Questions: On Music and Letters, Culture and Biography, 1940–1980*, selected, edited, and introduced by Bea Friedland, 30–8. Chicago: The University of Chicago Press, 1982.

Benjamin, Walter. *One-Way Street.* Translated by Edmund Jephcott. Cambridge, MA: Belknap Press of Harvard University Press, 2016.

Berg, Jan Hendrik van den. *A Different Existence: Principles of Phenomenological Psychopathology.* Pittsburgh: Duquesne University Press, 1995.

Berger, John. "Ev'ry Time We Say Goodbye." In *Keeping a Rendezvous,* 10–24. New York: Pantheon Books, 1991.

Bergson, Henri. *Les deux sources de la morale et de la religion.* Paris: Presses Universitaires de France, 2000.

– "La politesse." In *Écrits philosophiques,* 47–58. Paris: Presses Universitaires de France, 2011.

– *Time and Free Will: An Essay on the Immediate Data of Consciousness.* Translated by F.L. Pogson. New York: Cosimo Books, 2008.

Berlin, Isaiah. "Two Concepts of Liberty." In *Four Essays on Liberty,* 118–72. Oxford: Oxford University Press, 1989.

Berlioz, Hector. *The Memoirs of Hector Berlioz.* Translated by David Cairns. New York: Alfred A. Knopf, 2002.

Bernstein, Leonard. "Beethoven's Fifth Symphony." In *The Joy of Music,* 73–83. Pompton Plains, NJ: Amadeus Press, 2004.

Bettelheim, Bruno. *A Good Enough Parent: A Book on Child-Rearing.* New York: Vintage Books, 1988.

– *The Informed Heart: The Human Condition in Modern Mass Society.* London: Thames and Hudson, 1961.

Bonhoeffer, Dietrich. *Ethics.* Edited by Eberhard Bethge. Translated by Neville Horton Smith. New York: Simon and Schuster, 1995.

Borges, Jorge Luis. "Story of the Warrior and the Captive Maiden." In *Collected Fictions,* translated by Andrew Hurley, 208–11. London: Penguin Books, 1998.

Brelet, Gisèle. *Esthétique et création musicale.* Paris: Presses Universitaires de France, 1947.

– "Music and Silence." In *Reflections on Art: A Source Book of Writings by Artists, Critics and Philosophers,* edited by Suzanne K. Langer, 103–21. Oxford: Oxford University Press, 1958.

Burgess, Anthony. "Should We Learn Foreign Languages?" In *A Mouhtful of Air: Language and Languages, Especially English,* 119–29. Toronto: Stoddart Publishing, 1993.

Bushway, Shawn D., and Raymond Paternoster. "Desistance from Crime: A Review and Ideas for Moving Forward." In *Handbook of Life-Course Criminology: Emerging Trends and Directions for Future Research,* edited by C.L. Gibson and M.D. Krohn, 213–31. New York: Springer Science+Business, 2013.

Camus, Albert. "Love of Life." In *Lyrical and Critical Essays*, edited by Philip Thody, translated by Ellen Conroy Kennedy, 52–7. New York: Alfred A. Knopf, 1969.

Canetti, Elias. *The Tongue Set Free: Remembrance of a European Childhood*. Translated by Joachim Neugroschel. London: Granta Books, 2011.

Cassirer, Ernst. "The Educational Value of Art (1943)." In *Symbol, Myth, and Culture: Essays and Lectures*, edited by Donald Phillip Verene, 196–215. New Haven: Yale University Press, 1979.

Chesterton, G.K. "The Bigot." In *Lunacy and Letters*, edited by Dorothy Collins, 151–3. London: Sheed and Ward, 1958.

– "No Such Thing." In *The Man Who Was Orthodox: A Selection from the Uncollected Writings*, arranged and introduced by A.L. Maycock, 94–6. London: Dennis Dobson, 1963.

Christian, Paul. "Begegnen und Antreffen: Zur Problematik einer 'anthropologisher' Psychologie." In *Begegnung: Ein anthropologisch-pädagogisches Grundereignis*, edited by Berthold Gerner, 79–93. Darmstadt: Wissenschaftliche Buchgesellschaft, 1969.

Congar, Yves. "The Idea of Conversion." *Thought* 33 (1958): 5–20.

Csepregi, Gabor. "Musical Performance as Play." *Nordic Journal of Aesthetics* 46 (2013): 96–114.

– "La musique et le corps: Vladimir Jankélévitch sur l'art du piano." In *Sagesse du corps*, edited by Gabor Csepregi, 103–14. Aylmer: Édition du Scribe, 2001.

Daniels, Robin. *Conversations with Menuhin*. London: Futura, 1980.

Deeken, Alfons. *Process and Permanence in Ethics: Max Scheler's Moral Philosophy*. New York: Paulist Press, 1974.

De Koninck, Thomas. *Philosophie de l'éducation pour l'avenir*. Quebec: Les Presses de l'Université Laval, 2010.

– *À quoi sert la philosophie?* Quebec: Les Presses de l'Université Laval, 2015.

Dufrenne, Mikel. "The Beautiful." *In the Presence of the Sensuous: Essays in Aesthetics*, translated and edited Mark S. Roberts and Dennis Gallagher, 75–84. Atlantic Highlands, NJ: Humanities Press, 1987.

Eliot, T.S. "Dante." In *Selected Prose of T.S. Eliot*, edited by Frank Kermode, 205–30. London: Faber and Faber, 1975.

– "Religion and Literature." In *Selected Prose of T.S. Eliot*, edited by Frank Kermode, 97–106. London: Faber and Faber, 1975.

Bibliography

Farkas, Alexander. "A Meeting with Jenö Ádám." *Bulletin of the International Kodály Society* 21.2 (1996): 38–9.

Fest, Joachim. *Not I: Memoirs of a German Childhood*. Translated by Martin Chalmers. New York: Other Press, 2013.

Fink, Eugen. *Einleitung in die Philosophie*. Edited by Franz-A. Schwarz. Würzburg: Königshausen + Neumann, 1985.

Forster, E.M. "Not Listening to Music." In *Two Cheers for Democracy*, 127–30. New York: Harcourt, Brace, and Company, 1951.

Frankfurt, Harry G. "The Importance of What We Care About." In *The Importance of What We Care About: Philosophical Essays*, 80–94. Cambridge: Cambridge University Press, 1988.

– "On the Necessity of Ideals." In *The Moral Self*, edited by Gil G. Noam and Thomas E. Wren, 16–27. Cambridge, MA: MIT Press, 1993.

Frye, Northrop. *Creation and Recreation*. Toronto: University of Toronto Press, 1980.

– "Criticism as Education." In *On Education*, 138–52. Markham: Fitzhenry and Whiteside, 1988.

Gebauer, Gunter, and Christoph Wulf. "After the 'Death of Man': From Philosophical Anthropology to Historical Anthropology." *Iris: European Journal of Philosophy and Public Debate* 1 (2009): 171–86.

Gehlen, Arnold. "Mensch und Institutionen." In *Anthropologische und sozialpsychologische Untersuchungen*, 69–77. Reinbek bei Hamburg: Rowohlt Verlag, 1993.

Geiger, Moritz. *The Significance of Art: A Phenomenological Approach to Aesthetics*. Edited and translated by Klaus Berger. Lanham, MD: Center for Advanced Research in Phenomenology and University Press of America, 1986.

Gmelch, George, Robert V. Kemper, and Walter P. Zenner, eds. *Urban Life: Readings in the Anthropology of the City*. 5th ed. Long Grove, IL: Waveland Press, 2010.

Goodman, Nelson. *Ways of Worldmaking*. Indianapolis: Hackett, 1978.

Greene, Graham. "The Lost Childhood." In *The Lost Childhood and Other Essays*, 11–6. Harmondsworth: Penguin Books, 1966.

Guardini, Romano. *Die Lebensalter: Ihre ethische und pädagogische Bedeutung*. 13th ed. Tevelaer: Topos Plus, 2010.

Hadot, Pierre. "Conversion." In *Exercices spirituels et philosophie antique*, 223–35. Paris: Éditions Albin Michel, 2002.

Haeffner, Gerd. *In der Gegenwart leben: Auf der Spur eines Urphänomens*. Stuttgart: Verlag W. Kohlhammer, 1996.

Bibliography

– Philosophische Anthropologie. 4th ed. Stuttgart: Verlag W. Kohlhammer, 2005.

– "Die philosophische Anthropologie und der interkulturelle Dialog." In *Wege in die Freiheit: Philosophische Meditationen über das Menschsein*, 53–68. Stuttgart: Verlag W. Kohlhammer, 2006.

– "Präsenz." In *Wege in die Freiheit: Philosophische Meditationen über das Menschsein*, 121–38. Stuttgart: Verlag W. Kohlhammer, 2006.

– "Staunen." In *Wege in die Freiheit: Philosophische Meditationen über das Menschsein*, 11–25. Stuttgart: Verlag W. Kohlhammer, 2006.

Hanslick, Eduard. *Music Criticism: 1846–99.* Translated and edited by Henry Pleasants. New York: Dover, 1988.

– On the Musically Beautiful: A Contribution Towards the Revision of the Aesthetics of Music. Translated and edited by Geoffrey Payzant. Indianapolis, IN: Hackett, 1986.

Hartmann, Nicolai. *Aesthetics.* Translated by Eugene Kelly. Berlin/Boston: Walter de Gruyter GmbH, 2014.

– Ethics. Vol. 1: Moral Phenomena. Translated by Stanton Coit. London: George Allen and Unwin, 1932.

Have, Henk ten. "Respect for Human Vulnerability: The Emergence of a New Principle in Bioethics." *Journal of Bioethical Inquiry* 12 (2015): 395–408.

Heller, Erich. "The Dismantling of a Marionette Theatre; or, Psychology and the Misinterpretation of Literature." In *In the Age of Prose: Literary and Philosophical Essays*, 193–213. Cambridge: Cambridge University Press, 1984.

Hilberg, Raul. *Perpetrators, Victims, Bystanders: The Jewish Catastrophe, 1933–1945.* New York: HarperCollins, 1992.

Hoffer, Eric. *The True Believer: Thoughts on the Nature of Mass Movements.* New York: Harper Perennial Modern Classics, 2010.

Hopkins, Antony. *Understanding Music.* London: J.M. Dent and Sons, 1979.

Husserl, Edmund. *The Phenomenology of Internal Time-Consciousness.* Edited by Martin Heidegger, translated by James S. Churchill. Bloomington: Indiana University Press, 1964.

Huxley, Aldous. *The Art of Seeing.* London: Flamingo Modern Classic, 1994.

– "Music at Night." In *Music at Night and Other Essays*, 28–34. London: Flamingo Modern Classic, 1994.

Jankélévitch, Vladimir. *Liszt et la rhapsodie: Essai sur la virtuosité.* Paris: Plon, 1989.

- "Music and Silence." In *Music and the Ineffable*, translated by Carolyne Abbate, 130–55. Princeton: Princeton University Press, 2003.
Jaspers, Karl. "Die Kraft zu leben." In *Die Kraft zu leben: Bekenntnisse unserer Zeit*, edited by H. Walter Bähr, 102–14. Gütersloh: C. Bertelsmann Verlag, 1964.
- "Ein Selbstportrait." In *Das Selbstportrait: Grosse Künstler and Denker unserer Zeit erzählen von ihrem Leben und Werk*, edited by Hannes Reinhardt, 77–108. Hamburg: Christian Wegner Verlag, 1967.
- *Philosophy and the World: Selected Essays*. Translated by E.B. Ashton. Washington, DC: Gateway Edition, 1989.
Keller, Hans. "Towards a Theory of Music." In *Essays on Music*, edited by Christopher Wintle with Bayan Northcott and Irene Samuel, 121–5. Cambridge: Cambridge University Press, 1994.
Kemper, Robert V. *Migration and Adaptation: Tzintzuntzan Peasants in Mexico City*. Beverly Hills, CA: Sage, 1977.
Kierkegaard, Søren. "Against Cowardliness." In *Eighteen Upbuilding Discourses*, edited and translated by Howard V. Hong and Edna H. Hong, 347–75. Princeton: Princeton University Press, 1990.
- *Either/Or. Part II*. Edited and translated by Howard V. Hong and Edna H. Hong. Princeton: Princeton University Press, 1987.
- *Fear and Trembling: Repetition*. Edited and translated by Howard V. Hong and Edna H. Hong. Princeton: Princeton University Press, 1983.
- *The Sickness unto Death: A Christian Psychological Exposition for Upbuilding and Awakening*. Edited and translated by Howard V. Hong and Edna H. Hong. Princeton: Princeton University Press, 1983.
- *Stages on Life's Way: Studies by Various Persons*. Edited and translated Howard V. Hong and Edna H. Hong. Princeton: Princeton University Press, 1988.
Kingwell, Mark. "In Praise of Boredom: The Modern Life of a Timeless Condition." *Literary Review of Canada* 25.5 (2017): 5–7.
Kipling, Rudyard. *Something of Myself and Other Autobiographical Writings*. Edited by Thomas Pinney. Cambridge: Cambridge University Press, 2013.
Klein, George. "Confronting the Holocaust: An Eyewitness Account." In *The Auschwitz Reports and the Holocaust in Hungary*, edited by Randolph L. Braham and William J. vanden Heuvel, 255–83. New York: Columbia University Press, 2011.
- "La littérature européenne et la conscience tragique de l'existence." Translated by Anne Wilhelmi. *Les Temps Modernes* 640 (2006): 37–59.

Bibliography

Kleinman, Arthur. *What Really Matters: Living Moral Life amidst Uncertainty and Danger.* Oxford: Oxford University Press, 2006.

Kodály, Zoltán. "Ki az igazi zeneértö? (Who Is the True Music Expert?)" In *Visszatekintés (Looking Back)*, vol. 1, edited by Ferenc Bónis, 299–301. Budapest: Editio Musica, 1989.

– "Mit akarok a régi székely dalokkal? (What Do I Want with the Old Sekler Songs?)" In *Visszatekintés (Looking Back)*, vol. 1, edited by Ferenc Bónis, 29–30. Budapest: Editio Musica, 1989.

– "A zenei nevelés Magyarországon: Elöszó (Music Education in Hungary: Preface)." In *Visszatekintés (Looking Back)*, vol. 3, edited by Ferenc Bónis, 152. Budapest: Editio Musica, 1989.

Koestler, Arthur. *The Act of Creation.* London: Penguin Books, 1990.

– *The Invisible Writing.* New York: Macmillan, 1954.

– "The Truth of Imagination." *Diogenes* 25.100 (1977): 103–10.

Lachs, John. "Transcendence in Philosophy and in Everyday Life." *The Journal of Speculative Philosophy* 11 (1997): 247–55.

Landmann, Michael. *Philosophical Anthropology.* Translated by David J. Parent. Philadelphia: Westminster Press, 1974.

Landowski, Marcel. *La musique n'adoucit pas les moeurs.* Paris: Pierre Belfond, 1990.

Landsberg, Paul-Louis. *Pierres blanches: Problèmes du personnalisme.* Paris: Le Félin Poche, 2007.

Lavelle, Louis. *The Dilemma of Narcissus.* Translated by W.T. Gairdner. London: Allen and Unwin, 1973.

Lawrence, D.H. "The Spirit of Place." In *The Symbolic Meaning: The Uncollected Versions of Studies in Classic American Literature*, edited by Armin Arnold, 15–31. London: Centaur Press, 1962.

Lecomte, Jacques. *La bonté humaine: Altruisme, empathie, générosité.* Paris: Odile Jacob, 2014.

Léna, Marguerite, ed. *Honneur aux maîtres.* Paris: Criterion, 1991.

Levi, Primo. "The Canto of Ulysses." In *If This Is a Man*, translated by Stuart Woolf, 115–21. London: Abacus, 1987.

Lévi-Strauss, Claude. "Apprivoiser l'étrangeté." In *L'Autre Face de la lune: Écrits sur le Japon*, 127–32. Paris: Éditions du Seuil, 2011.

– "Place de la culture japonaise dans le monde." In *L'Autre Face de la lune: Écrits sur le Japon*, 13–55. Paris: Éditions du Seuil, 2011.

Lewis, C.S. *Experiment in Criticism.* Cambridge: Cambridge University Press, 2012.

– "Sometimes Fairy Stories May Say Best What's to Be Said." In *On Stories and Other Essays on Literature*, 45–8. Orlando: Harvest, 1982.

Bibliography

Linschoten, Jan. "Over de Humor." *Tijdschrift voor Philosophie* 13 (1951): 603–66.

Livio, Antoine. *Conversations avec Marcel Landowski*. Paris: Éditions Denoël, 1998.

Lorenz, Konrad. *The Waning of Humaneness*. Translated by Robert Warren Kickert. Boston: Little, Brown, 1987.

Lübbe, Hermann. "Zur Theorie der Entscheidung." In *Theorie und Entscheidung: Studien zum Primat der praktischen Vernunft*, 7–31. Freiburg: Verlag Rombach, 1965.

Marcel, Gabriel. "Music according to Saint Augustine." In *Music and Philosophy*, translated by Stephen Maddux and Robert E. Wood, 117–24. Milwaukee: Marquette University Press, 2005.

– "Music and the Marvelous." In *Music and Philosophy*, translated by Stephen Maddux and Robert E. Wood, 127–8. Milwaukee: Marquette University Press, 2005.

– "Phenomenological Notes on Being in a Situation." In *Creative* Fidelity, translated by Robert Rosthal, 82–103. New York: Fordham University Press, 2002.

– "The Spirit of Abstraction, As a Factor Making for War." In *Man Against Mass Society*, translated by G.S. Fraser, 153–62. South Bend, IN: St Augustine's Press, 2008.

Marquard, Odo. "The Age of Unwordliness? A Contribution to the Analysis of the Present." In *In Defense of the Accidental: Philosophical Studies*, translated by Robert M. Wallace, 71–90. New York: Oxford University Press, 1991.

– "In Defense of the Accidental: Philosophical Reflections on Man." In *In Defense of the Accidental: Philosophical Studies*, translated by Robert M. Wallace, 109–29. New York: Oxford University Press, 1991.

Mehl, Roger. "Structure philosophique de la Notion de Présence." *Revue d'Histoire et de Philosophie Religieuse* 38 (1958): 171–6.

Menuhin, Yehudi. *Unfinished Journey*. New York: Alfred A. Knopf, 1977.

Merleau-Ponty, Maurice. *Phenomenology of Perception*. Translated by Colin Smith. London: Routledge and Kegan Paul, 1962.

Meyer, Leonard B. *Emotion and Meaning in Music*. Chicago: University of Chicago Press, 1956.

Minkowski, Eugène. "L'homme artisan de sa destinée." *Tijdschrift voor Philosophie* 20 (1958): 443–58.

– "L'homme et ce qu'il y a d'humain en lui (Biologie et anthropologie)." In *Vers une cosmologie. Fragments philosophiques*, 142–53. Paris: Aubier-Montaigne, 1967.

Bibliography

- *Lived Time: Phenomenological and Psychopathological Studies.* Translated by Nancy Metzel. Evanston: Northwestern University Press, 1970.
- "Le problème du temps vécu." *Recherches Philosophiques* 5 (1935–6): 65–99.
- "Prose and Poetry (Astronomy and Cosmology)." In *Phenomenology and the Natural Sciences*, edited by Joseph J. Kockelmans and Theodore J. Kiesel, 239–47. Evanston: Northwestern University Press, 1970.
- "Spontaneity (… Spontaneous Movement Like This!)." In *Readings in Existential Phenomenology*, edited by Nathaniel Lawrence and Daniel O'Connor, 168–77. Englewood Cliffs, NJ: Prentice-Hall, 1967.

Mitscherlich, Margaret. *La fin des modèles: Fonctions et méfaits de l'idéalisation.* Translated by Robert S. Ponsard. Paris: Des femmes, 1983.

Modiano, Patrick. *Discours à l'Académie suédoise.* Paris: Éditions Gallimard, 2015.

Moltmann, Jürgen. *Man: Christian Anthropology in the Conflicts of the Present.* Translated by John Sturdy. Philadelphia: Fortress Press, 1974.

Monod, Victor. "Le voyage, le déracinement de l'individu hors du milieu natal constituent-ils des éléments déterminants de la conversion religieuse?" *Revue d'Histoire et de Philosophie Religieuse* 305 (1936): 385–99.

Morin, Edgar. "Pour une crisologie." *Communications* 25 (1976): 149–63.

Nabokov, Vladimir. *Speak, Memory: An Autobiography Revisited.* New York: Vintage, 1989.

Nagel, Thomas. *The Last Word.* New York: Oxford University Press, 1997.

Naipaul, V.S. "Conrad's Darkness." In *The Return of Eva Peron: With the Killings in Trinidad*, 197–218. Harmondsworth: Penguin Books, 1981.

Najder, Zdzislaw. *Joseph Conrad: A Life.* Translated by Halina Najder. Rochester, NY: Camden House, 2007.

Nietzsche, Friedrich. "Schopenhauer as Educator." In *Untimely Meditations*, translated by R.J. Hollingdale, 127–94. Cambridge: Cambridge University Press, 1983.

Ningkun, Wu. *A Single Tear: A Family's Persecution, Love, and Endurance in Communist China.* Boston: Little, Brown, and Company, 1993.

Nussbaum, Martha C. "Human Functioning and Social Justice: In Defense of Aristotelian Essentialism." *Political Theory* 20.2 (1992): 202–46.

Orwell, George. "Looking Back on the Spanish War." In *My Country Right or Left: The Collected Essays, Journalism and Letters of George*

Orwell, vol. 2, edited by Sonia Orwell and Ian Angus, 249–67. New York: Harcourt, Brace, and World, 1968.

Paquet, Philippe. *Simon Leys: Navigateur entre les mondes*. Paris: Éditions Gallimard, 2016.

Paternoster, Ray, and Shaw Bushway. "Desistance and the 'Feared Self': Toward a Identity Theory of Criminal Desistance." *The Journal of Criminal Law and Criminology* 99 (2009): 1103–56.

Patocka, Jan. "L'écrivain, son 'objet.'" In *L'écrivain, son 'objet': Contribution à la philosophie de la literature*, translated by Erika Abrams, 78–100. Paris: P.O.L. éditeur, 1990.

Peri, Alexis. *The War Within: Diaries from the Siege of Leningrad*. Cambridge, MA: Harvard University Press, 2017.

Pieper, Josef. "Learning How to See Again." In *Only the Lover Sings: Art and Contemplation*. Translated by Lothar Krauth, 31–2. San Francisco: Ignatius Press, 1990.

Plessner, Helmuth. "Anthropologie der Sinne." In *Philosophische Anthropologie. Zweiter Teil*, edited by Hans-Georg Gadamer and Paul Vogler, 3–63. Stuttgart: Georg Thieme Verlag, 1974.

– "Macht und menschliche Natur: Ein Versuch zur Anthropologie der geschichtlichen Weltansicht." In *Macht und menschliche Natur: Gesammelte Schriften*, vol. 5, 135–234. Frankfurt am Main: Suhrkamp Verlag, 1981.

– "Trieb und Leidenschaft." In *Conditio humana: Gesammelte Schriften*, vol. 8, 367–79. Frankfurt am Main: Suhrkamp Verlag, 1983.

– "Über den Begriff der Leidenschaft." In *Conditio humana: Gesammelte Schriften*, vol. 8, 866–76. Frankfurt am Main: Suhrkamp Verlag, 1983.

– "With Different Eyes." In *Phenomenology and Sociology: Selected Readings*, edited by Thomas Luckmann and translated by A.L. Hammond, 25–41. New York: Penguin Books, 1978.

– "Zur Anthropologie der Musik." In *Ausdruck und menschliche Natur: Gesammelte* Schriften, vol. 7, 184–201. Frankfurt am Main: Suhrkamp Verlag, 1982.

Plügge, Herbert. "Pascals Begriff des 'Ennui' und seine Bedeutung für eine medizinische Anthropologie." In *Wohbefinden und Missbefinden: Beiträge zu einer medizinischen Anthropologie*, 1–16. Tübingen: Max Niemeyer Verlag, 1962.

– "Über die Hoffnung." In *Wohbefinden und Missbefinden: Beiträge zu einer medizinischen Anthropologie*, 38–50. Tübingen: Max Niemeyer Verlag, 1962.

Bibliography

Powys, John Cowper. *The Art of Happiness*. London: Faber and Faber, 2011.

Price, Lucien. *Dialogues of Alfred North Whitehead*. Boston: Little, Brown, and Company, 1954.

Raymond, Jean-François de. *L'esprit de la diplomatie: Du particulier à l'universel*. Paris: Les Belles Lettres, 2015.

Reilly, Robert R. with Jens F. Laurson, "László Lajtha: Music from a Secret Room." In *Surprised by Beauty: A Listener's Guide to the Recovery of Modern Music*, 185–91. San Francisco: Ignatius Press, 2016.

Reitman, Janet. "The Good Soldier: Why a Suicidal Officer Had to Go AWOL to Save His Life." *Rolling Stone*, 24 September 2015.

Revel, Jean-François. *Sur Proust: Remarques sur "À la recherche du temps perdu."* Paris: Éditions Grasset et Fasquelle, 1987.

Revers, Wilhelm Josef. "Die Langweile – Krise and Kriterium des Menschseins." *Jahrbuch für Psychologie, Psychotherapie und Medizinische Anthropologie* 4 (1956): 157–62.

Ricoeur, Paul. *La critique et la conviction: Entretien avec François Azouvi and Marc de Launay*. Paris: Fayard/Pluriel, 2010.

– *Freedom and Nature: The Voluntary and the Involuntary*. Translated by Erazim V. Kohák. Evanston: Northwestern University Press, 1966.

Rohmer, Eric. *De Mozart en Beethoven: Essai sur la notion de profondeur en musique*. Arles: Actes Sud, 1998.

Romilly, Jacqueline de. *Écrits sur l'enseignement*. Paris: Éditions de Fallois, 1991.

Rouvière, Jean-Marc. *L'homme surpris: Vers une phénoménologie de la morale*. Paris: L'Harmattan, 2013.

Ruitenbeek, Hendrik M. "Mechanization versus Spontaneity: Which Will Survive?" *Humanitas* 2 (1966): 261–9.

Russell, Bertrand. "Some Cambridge Dons of the Nineties." In *Portraits from Memory and Other Essays*, 60–6. New York: Simon and Schuster, 1963.

Ryckmans, Pierre. *The View from the Bridge: Aspects of Culture*. Sydney: ABC Books, 1996.

Sacks, Jonathan. *The Dignity of Difference: How to Avoid the Clash of Civilizations*. London: Bloomsbury, 2003.

Saint-Exupéry, Antoine. *A Letter to a Hostage*. Translated by Jacqueline Gerst. London: Pushkin Press, 2008.

Sandor, Gyorgy. *On Piano Playing: Motion, Sound and Expression*. New York: Schirmer Books, 1981.

Santayana, George. *Persons and Places: Fragments of Autobiography. The Works of George Santayana*, vol. 1, edited by William G. Holzberger and Herman J. Saatkamp, Jr. Cambridge, MA: MIT Press, 1987.

Schapiro, Meyer. *Impressionism: Reflections and Perceptions.* New York: George Brazillier, 1997.

Scheler, Max. "Exemplars of Person and Leaders." In *Person and Self-Value: Three Essays*, translated by Manfred S. Frings, 127–98. Dordrecht: Martinus Nijhoff, 1987.

– *Formalism in Ethics and Non-Formal Ethics of Values: A New Attempt toward the Foundation of an Ethical Personalism.* Translated by Manfred S. Frings and Roger L. Funk. Evanston: Northwestern University Press, 1973.

– "The Forms of Knowledge and Culture." In *Philosophical Perspectives*, translated by Oscar A. Haac, 13–49. Boston: Beacon Press, 1958.

– "Ordo Amoris." In *Selected Philosophical Essays*, translated by David R. Lachterman, 98–135. Evanston: Northwestern University Press, 1973.

– "Phenomenology and the Theory of Cognition." In *Selected Philosophical Essays*, translated by David R. Lachterman, 136–201. Evanston: Northwestern University Press, 1973.

– "Repentance and Rebirth." In *On the Eternal in Man*, translated by Bernard Noble, 13–65. New York: Harper and Brothers, 1960.

– *Ressentiment.* Translated by William W. Holdheim. New York: The Free Press of Glencoe, 1961.

– "Tod und Fortleben." In *Zur Ethik und Erkenntnislehre: Schriften aus dem Nachlass*, vol. 1, 4th ed., 9–64. Bern: Francke Verlag, 2000.

– *"Vorbilder und Führer."* In *Zur Ethik und Erkenntnislehre: Schriften aus dem Nachlass*, vol. 1, 4th ed., 255–318. Bern: Francke Verlag, 2000.

Schiller, Friedrich. "Letters on the Aesthetic Education of Man." In *Essays*, edited by Walter Hinderer and Daniel O. Dahlstrom, translated by Elizabeth M. Wilkinson and L.A. Willoughby, 86–178. New York: Continuum, 1993.

Schuller, Gunther. "Form, Content, and Symbol." In *Musings: The Musical World of Gunther Schuller*, 272–86. New York: Oxford University Press, 1986.

Schutz, Alfred. "The Stranger. An Essay in Social Psychology." In *Studies in Social Theory: Collected Papers*, vol. 2, edited by Arvid Brodersen, 91–105. The Hague: Martinus Nijhoff, 1964.

Scruton, Roger. *The Aesthetics of Music.* Oxford: Clarendon Press, 1997.

– "Effing the Ineffable." In *Confessions of a Heretic: Selected Essays*, 86–9. Devon: Notting Hill Editions, 2016.

– *The Soul of the World*. Princeton: Princeton University Press, 2014.

Segalen, Victor. *Essai sur l'exotisme: Une esthétique du divers*. Saint-Clément-de-Rivière: Fata Morgana, 1978.

Sessions, Roger. *The Musical Experience of Composer, Performer, Listener*. Princeton: Princeton University Press, 1974.

Simmel, Georg. "The Stranger." In *The Sociology of Georg Simmel*, translated and edited by Kurt H. Wolff, 402–8. New York: The Free Press, 1967.

Solzhenitsyn, Alexander. *Nobel Lecture*. Translated by F.D. Reeve. New York: Farrar, Straus, and Giroux, 1972.

Spaemann, Robert. *Basic Moral Concepts*. Translated by T.J. Armstrong. London: Routledge, 1989.

– "Education as an Introduction to Reality: A Speech Commemorating the Anniversary of Children's Home (1988)." In *A Robert Spaemann Reader: Philosophical Essays on Nature of God, and the Human Person*, edited and translated by D.C. Schindler and Jeanne Heffernan Schindler, 111–20. Oxford: Oxford University Press, 2015.

– "Human Dignity." In *Essays in Anthropology: Variations on a Theme*, translated by Guido de Graaf and James Mumford, 49–72. Eugene, OR: Cascade Books, 2010.

– "Human Nature." In *Essays in Anthropology: Variations on a Theme*, translated by Guido de Graaf and James Mumford, 1–24. Eugene, OR: Cascade Books, 2010.

– *Persons: The Difference between 'Someone' and 'Something.'* Translated by Oliver O'Donovan. Oxford: Oxford University Press, 2006.

– "What Does It Mean to Be Cultured? (1995)." In *A Robert Spaemann Reader: Philosophical Essays on Nature of God, and the Human Person*, edited and translated by D.C. Schindler and Jeanne Heffernan Schindler, 121–4. Oxford: Oxford University Press, 2015.

Stein, Leo. *The A-B-C of Aesthetics*. New York: Boni and Liveright, 1927.

Steiner, George. *Grammars of Creation: Originating in the Gifford Lectures for 1990*. London: Faber and Faber, 2001.

– *Lessons of the Masters*. Cambridge, MA: Harvard University Press, 2003.

Stendhal. *To the Happy Few: Selected Letters of Stendhal*. Translated by Norman Cameron. London: John Lehmann, 1952.

Storr, Anthony. *The Dynamics of Creation*. London: Secker and Warburg, 1972.

– *Music and the Mind*. New York: The Free Press, 1992.

– *Solitude*. London: Flamingo, 1989.

Bibliography

Straus, Erwin W. "Disorders of Personal Time." In *Phenomenological Psychology*, 290–5. New York: Garland, 1980.

– "Embodiment and Excarnation." In *Toward a Unity of Knowledge*, edited by Marjorie Grene, 217–50. New York: International University Press, 1969.

– "Event and Experience." In *Man, Time, and World: Two Contributions to Anthropological Psychology*, translated by Donald Moss, 1–139. Pittsburgh: Duquesne University Press, 1982.

– "Man: A Questioning Being." In *Phenomenological Psychology*, 166–87. New York: Garland, 1980.

– "The Miser." In *Patterns of the Life-World*, edited by James M. Edie, Francis H. Parker, and Calvin O. Schrag, 157–79. Evanston: Northwestern University Press, 1970.

– "The Pathology of Compulsion." In *Phenomenological Psychology*, 296–329. New York: Garland, 1980.

– *The Primary World of Senses: A Vindication of Sensory Experience*. Translated by Jacob Needleman. New York: The Free Press of Glencoe, 1963.

Svendsen, Lars. *A Philosophy of Boredom*. Translated by John Irons. London: Reaktion Books, 2005.

Tellenbach, Hubertus. *Geschmack und Atmosphäre: Medien menschlichen Elementarkontaktes*. Salzburg: Otto Müller Verlag, 1968.

– "La réalité, le comique et l'humour." In *La réalité, le comique et l'humour, suivi des actes du colloque réunis par Yves Pelicier: Autour de la pensée de Tellenbach*, translated by Philippe Forget, 7–18. Paris: Economica, 1981.

Thaler, Richard H., and Cass R. Sunstein. *Nudge: Improving Decisions about Health, Wealth, and Happiness*. New York: Penguin Books, 2009.

Tolstoy, Leo. "Master and Man." In *Master and Man and Other Stories*, translated by Ronald Wilks and Paul Foote, 230–81. London: Penguin Books, 2005.

Toynbee, Arnold. *Experiences*. New York: Oxford University Press, 1969.

Ullman, Chana. *The Transformed Self: The Psychology of Religious Conversion*. New York: Plenum Press, 1989.

Ungar, Michael. *Too Safe for Their Own Good: How Risk and Responsibility Help Teens Thrive*. Toronto: McClelland and Stewart, 2007.

Valéry, Paul. "Analecta." In *Oeuvres II*, edited and annotated by Jean Hytier, 700–49. Paris: Éditions Gallimard, Bibliothèque de la Pléiade, 1960.

Bibliography

– *Cahiers II*. Edited, presented, and annotated by Judith Robinson. Paris: Éditions Gallimard, Bibliothèque de la Pléiade, 1974.

Vizinczey, Stephen. "The Genius Whose Time Has Come." In *Truth and Lies in Literature: Essays and Reviews*, 150–79. Chicago: The University of Chicago Press, 1988.

– *The Rules of Chaos: or, Why Tomorrow Doesn't Work*. New York: McCall, 1970.

Waldenfels, Bernhard. "Das überwältige Leiden." In *Der Stachel des Fremden*, 120–34. Frankfurt am Main: Suhrkamp Verlag, 1991.

Walker, Alan. *Franz Liszt: The Virtuoso Years, 1811–1947*. New York: Alfred A. Knopf, 1983.

– "Music and Education." *The Piano Quarterly*, no. 148 (1989): 25–7.

– "Schopenhauer and Music." *The Piano Quarterly*, no. 144 (1988): 38–46.

– *A Study in Musical Analysis*. London: Barrie and Rockliff, 1962.

Ward, Koral. *Augenblick: The Concept of the 'Decisive Moment' in 19th- and 20th-Century Western Philosophy*. Hampshire: Ashgate, 2008.

Waugh, Evelyn. "General Conversation: Myself ..." In *The Essays, Articles and Reviews of Evelyn Waugh*, edited by Donat Gallagher, 190–2. Boston: Little, Brown and Company, 1984.

Weizsäcker, Carl Friedrich von. *The Ambivalence of Progress: Essays on Historical Anthropology*. New York: Paragon House, 1988.

Weizsaecker, Viktor von. *Le cycle de la structure (Der Gestaltkreis)*. Translated by Michel Foucault and Daniel Rocher. Paris: Desclée de Brouwer, 1958.

Welte, Bernhard. "Dasein im Symbol des Spiels." In *Zwischen Zeit und Ewigkeit: Abhandlungen und Versuche*, 96–108. Freiburg im Breisgau: Verlag Herder, 1982.

– "Meditation über Zeit." In *Zeit und Geheimnis: Philosophische Abhandlungen zur Sache Gottes in der Zeit der Welt*, 15–27. Freiburg im Breisgau: Verlag Herder, 1975.

Whitehead, Alfred N. *Religion in the Making*. New York: New American Library, 1974.

– "The Rhythmic Claims of Freedom and Discipline." In *The Aims of Education and Other Essays*, 29–41. New York: The Free Press, 1967.

Wilder, Thornton. "The American Loneliness." In *The Riddle of America: Essays Exploring North America's 'Native Expression-Spirit'*, edited by John Wulsin Jr, 207–16. Chatham, NY: The Association of Waldorf Schools of North America, 2012.

Bibliography

Wiredu, Kwasi. "Can Philosophy Be Intercultural? An African Viewpoint." *Diogenes* 46, no. 184 (1998): 147–67.

Wittgenstein, Ludwig. *Philosophical Investigations*. Edited by Rush Rhees and G.E.M. Anscombe, translated by G.E.M. Anscombe. Oxford: Blackwell, 2001.

Wolf, Ernest S. "Self, Idealization, and Development of Values." In *The Moral Self*, edited by Gil G. Noam and Thomas E. Wren, 56–77. Cambridge, MA: MIT Press, 1983.

Wood, James. *How Fiction Works*. New York: Picador, 2008.

Zutt, Jurg. "Der Lebensweg als Bild der Geschichtlichkeit: Über Krisen auf dem Lebensweg." In *Auf dem Wege zu einer anthropologischen Psychiatrie*, 352–7. Berlin: Springer-Verlag, 1963.

Zweig, Stefan. *Shooting Stars: Twelve Historical Miniatures*. Translated by Anthea Bell. London: Pushkin Press, 2015.

Index

Adorno, Theodor Wiesengrund, 123, 141; Beethoven, 126–7; moments of breakthrough, 177n45

adventure, 14, 25, 51, 60, 77, 89; sense of, 33

Aristotle, 156, 165n3

art of living, 4, 86

artist, 9, 11, 27, 67, 72, 76, 97, 131, 133, 145; foreign, 102; living under totalitarian regime, 48–50; vision of, 113

atmosphere: around persons, 48, 73–5; children's response to, 74; of the conversation, 106; created by music, 126, 130; established by the smile, 153; of foreignness, 90–1

Augustine of Hippo, 61, 99

authenticity, 75, 80, 128

Bach, Carl Philipp Emanuel, 121–2

Bach, Johann Sebastian, 71, 120; Passacaglia and Fugue in C minor, 124

Bánffy, Miklós, 103

Bárdos, Lajos, 124

Barrett, William, 13; children and their parents, 58; misunderstanding of emotions, 29–30

Bartók, Béla, 176n27, 176–7n35

Barzun, Jacques, 143–4

Beethoven, Ludwig van, 128; as Franz Liszt's model, 67; *Missa Solemnis*, 127, Symphony no. 5 in C minor, 127–8

Benjamin, Walter, 76

Berg, Jan Hendrik van den, 106

Berger, John, 55

Bergson, Henri: form of politeness, 158; models, 72; musical experience, 137

Berlin, Isaiah, 157

Berlioz, Hector, 119

Bernstein, Leonard, 127

Bettelheim, Bruno: absence of leisure, 59; decision, 34

body: abilities of, 133; attitudes and actions of, 70; control of, 137; covering, 116; dynamic life of, 154; facing another, 106–7; healthy, 5; involved in speaking, 92; of listeners, 126; reaching height, depth, and speed, 54;

Index

relaxation of, 144; silently transcended, 15; transcultural understanding of, 115; vulnerability of, 156

boredom, 52–6; experience of time in, 52–3; positive distractions from, 54–5; and quiet time alone, 55–6

Borges, Jorge Luis, 3, 88

breaking away: act of, 37–42; through arts, 48–50, 55; and lived time, 37–8; motives and conditions of, 51–63; to a new destination, 42–3; occurs by accident, 62; from parents, 57–8; restraining factors in, 36–7; through translation and transcription, 49; ways of, 42–51

Brelet, Gisèle, 129–30, 175n21

Bruckner, Josef Anton, 128

Buenos Aires, 88

Burgess, Anthony, 92

Camus, Albert, 88, 100

Canetti, Elias, 149

caring, 84

Cassirer, Ernst, 141

cautious behaviour, 24, 145, 161

Cézanne, Paul, 134

Chesterton, Gilbert Keith: bigotry, 164; education, 82, 171n32

children: emotional maturity of, 25; exposed to values and norms, 69; free decision of, 24; play of, 69; reading in the lives of, 76–7; risks taken by, 25

choice, 19–21, 32

Christian, Paul, 169n1

commitment: absence of, 24

Congar, Yves, 45

Conrad, Joseph, 35, 109, 130

conversation, 106–8, 130, 153–4, 157–8, 163

conversion: appeal of a community in, 56–7; of the fanatical person, 44–8; moral, 45–7; religious, 45, 47, 61–2; while travelling, 61–2

courageous: action, 36, 161; decision, 31; inner conviction, 27; leap into the unknown, 18; to overcome fear, 62; resolution, 40

creativity, 85; characteristics of, 93–4, 159; conditions of, 94; crisis generates, 22; of a model, 72; produces cultures, 114

crisis, 4, 21–2, 27–8, 47, 145

cultures: distance from, 98–101, 103–4; diversity of, 114–15, 117–18; familiar, 93, 95–8

death, 4, 6, 8, 38, 48, 54, 56, 90, 116, 124; of the heart, 145

decision: burden of, 13–14, 20–1, 25–6; and choice, 19–20; and contact with the self, 17; and determination of motives, 18; difficulty of, 16, 22–30; in extreme situations, 34; freedom of, 17–18; learning to make, 31–4; maturation of, 20; motives of, 17; and personal convictions, 29–31; in the presence of possibilities, 7, 15–17, 19–20, 22–3; and risk of failure, 19, 32; solitude of, 14–22, 27–8; temporality of, 19–20, 22–3; and uncertainty, 18, 21, 24, 26; urgency of, 21

decision-making faculty, 29, 31; and renunciation, 31; training of, 31

Index

desistance, 56
destiny, 41, 46
dignity, human, 160
diplomacy, 102–3
discomfort: benefits of, 95, 108
distress, 5–6, 30, 60, 99, 108, 158
diversity, 53, 95–6, 110; of cultures, 114–15, 118
Dufrenne, Mikel, 133–4

education, 72, 74, 155, 164; central aims of, 58–9; corrective, 50; in a cultural environment, 101, 116; of feelings, 145–6; formal, 31; models in, 82–4; moral, 69, 149; musical, 143–6; outside the traditional context, 6, 31, 58, 82; revolutionary, 81
educational institutions, 59; and academic conformity, 27; and transformative experiences, 82
Eliot, Thomas Stearns, 165–6n4
encounter: with beauty, 69; captivating, 53; casual, 113; chance, 56, 62; chief characteristics of, 106; decisive, 10; with the foreign, 91–3, 95; meeting and, 169n1; with a model, 71–8, 102; with music, 142–3; striking, 6–7, 83–4; unexpected, 5, 7, 83, 151; with the unfamiliar, 98; unpredictable, 33, 149–50
equanimity, 23, 32–4
ethical action, 149–64
event, 39
exotic knowledge, 95–6
experience, 39; personal, 10; of time, 3–4; vital, 4–5; of a work of art, 138–9

failure, 24, 33
fanatical person, 30, 79
Farkas, Alexander, 82–3
fate, 41, 62
fear, 25; of making mistakes, 27
feeling: acting upon, 36; advice of, 31; of alienation, 99; and authenticity, 80; confidence in, 30; of dissatisfaction, 51; escape from, 54; fear of, 29; of joy, 151; neglect of, 113, 140, 144; resonate with music, 136, 144–5; and selfhood, 145; and spontaneity, 6; wealth of, 94; and wondering, 105
Fest, Joachim, 165n4
Fink, Eugen, 90, 92
foreign cultures: adaptation to, 92–3; atmospheric participation in, 91; encounter with, 89–97; immersion into, 90; superficial contact with, 89–90
foreign realities, 61, 99, 101, 102; integration of, 94; receptivity to, 115
foreigners: definition of, 90; as guests, 99; facing obstacles, 94–5; and their search for the familiar, 100; sense of unfamiliarity, 99; understanding of, 94; verbal communications with, 91–2
Forster, Edward Morgan, 29; attentive listening, 142
Frankfurt, Harry G., 84–5
Franks, Lawrence J., Jr, 35–6
freedom: awareness of, 17, 151; and decision, 17–18; inner, 50–1; self-determining, 57; sense of, 151

Index

friendship, 33, 37–8, 65, 78, 156
Frye, Northrop, 141
fulfilment, 5–6, 57, 60, 128–9, 138

Gauguin, Paul, 56
Gebauer, Gunter, 117
Gehlen, Arnold, 27
Geiger, Moritz, 138–9
generosity, 9–10, 26, 77, 79, 85, 161
Ginzburg, Lidiia, 49–50
good: acknowledging the, 35; acting for the, 157, 160; deeds, 162–4; essential, 50; and evil, 152; insight into the, 68; knowing the, 69, 146; propensity for the, 162; tendency towards the, 150–1, 154–5, 157–8, 162–3
good life, 68, 81
Greene, Graham, 76

habits, 16
Haeffner, Gerd, 114
hand: mobility of, 11, 117; movements of, 75; pianist's, 131–3; in verbal communication, 92, 107
Hanslick, Eduard, 174n8, 174–5n14
Hartmann, Nicolai, 121, 134, 136, 174n8; aesthetic contemplation, 134; artist's creative spirit, 133; choice of models, 72, 78; music, 125–6
Haydn, Franz Joseph, 124, 134
Heller, Erich, 97
Hilberg, Raoul, 34
history, 4, 10, 32, 84, 115; of humankind, 30; interpretation of, 114; of a person, 83; world, 9

Hoffer, Eric, 59
Hopkins, Antony, 173n3
Horváth, József G., 71
hostility, 24, 150–1
human behaviour: habitualization of, 16
human life: essential features of, 116–18; progress of, 21; stages of, 4; temporality of, 4
humour: in conversation, 107–8; equanimity and, 33–4; and playful attitude, 34
Husserl, Edmund: perception of a melody, 175n21
Huxley, Aldous, 127

ideal, 36; attachment to, 85; contact with, 151; educational, 86; of humanity, 159; influence of, 45–7; which makes life worthwhile, 162
identity, 67; change in, 56; new, 36; sense of, 31, 158
illness, 5–6, 15, 61
imagination: cultivation of, 164; lacking, 47, 53; listener's, 135; objects trigger, 54, 82, 105; pianist's, 132; in play, 69, 162; reader's, 109, 112
inner richness, 93, 140
inner world, 49–50, 57, 168n16

Jankélévitch, Vladimir, 128–9, 174n8, 175n21; the pianist's virtuosity, 131–3
Jaspers, Karl, 9; education, 86; and Max Weber, 75, 170n18

Keller, Hans, 121
Kemper, Robert V., 44

Index

Kierkegaard, Søren, 9, 10, 24, 35; the act of decision, 13–14; cowardice, 64–5; decision about oneself, 13, 28; despair, 51–2; failure of resolution, 63–5; temporality of human existence, 52

Kipling, Rudyard, 91

Klein, George, 167n30

Kleist, Heinrich von, 32, 110

Kodály, Zoltán, 122, 134, 176n35; spirit of singing, 144–6; understanding of music, 120

Koestler, Arthur, 8, 14, 80–1, 179n32

Lajtha, László, 49, 176n27; letter to his sons, 168n16

Landmann, Michael, 114

Landowski, Marcel, 176n27

Lavelle, Louis, 59–60

Lawrence, David Herbert, 111, 113

leaders, 69–70

Leningrad, 49–50

Lévinas, Emmanuel, 156

Lewis, Clive Staples, 111, 160, 173n7

Linschoten, Jan, 107

Liszt, Franz, 67, 75; virtuosity of, 131

literature, 10–11, 76–8, 108–14; fantastic, 112; helps us to see, 109–11; models in, 76–8; reveals the inner springs of actions, 113–14; reveals American reality, 111–12

Lorenz, Konrad, 101

love: alteration of, 33; being in, 8, 74, 161, 143; expressing, 90; falling in, 9; finding, 38; first, 165n4; hoping for, 65; of music,

71, 121, 123; genuine, 96; unavowed feeling of, 154; yearning for, 112

Lübbe, Hermann, 16, 19

Marcel, Gabriel, 174n8, 175n21; critic of Bergson's analysis, 137; spirit of abstraction, 155

Marquard, Odo: accidents deciding one's fate, 62–3; appreciation of the usual, 98

maturity, 4, 25, 30–1

Maugham, Somerset, 89, 93

mechanical devices, 25–7

Menuhin, Yehudi, 14, 29, 121

Merleau-Ponty, Maurice, 10

Meyer, Leonard B., 177n37

migration, 43–4

Minkowski, Eugène, 73, 147, 156; destiny and fate, 41; ethical action, 148–9, 160; two ways of looking at stars, 121

miser, 23

mistakes, 25–6

misunderstanding, 24, 58; of the emotions, 29

Mitscherlich, Margarete, 85–6

models: atmospheric impression of, 73–4; attachment to, 72–3; authenticity of, 80; choice of, 72; civic virtues of, 80–1; encounter with, 68, 71–81; influence of, 45, 67–73, 81–7; irradiating presence of, 76; and leadership styles, 86; manifest values and norms, 68–9, 78; positive, 86; promote ideals, 85–6; qualities and flaws of, 71–2; teachers as, 78–80; in totalitarian states, 80–1; and values, 67–70

Modiano, Patrick, 109
modification: of beliefs and convictions, 48; of diplomats' views, 102; of ways of interacting with people, 43
Moltmann, Jürgen, 50
moment: of action, 65, 149; altering our lives, 7; of breaking away, 40, 43, 46–7; of conclusion, 129; of contentment, 146; of decision, 14, 19, 24–5, 34, 37–8, 52, 86; decisive, 8, 21, 33, 46; definition of, 9–10; ennobling, 28; favourable, 3; historical, 9; significant, 83; of silence, 128–9; of understanding, 97; of wondering, 105
Monod, Victor, 61
Monteux, Pierre, 173n6
moral: actions, 45, 161; character, 159–60; excellence, 70; interpretations, 100; outlook, 48, 68; principles, 68, 149; problem, 152; rectitude, 80; stance, 50, 154; traditions, 97; values, 69, 72–4; world, 112, 152
Mozart, Wolfgang Amadeus, 120, 143; Sinfonia Concertante for Violin, Viola and Orchestra in E-flat Major, 130–1
music: affective response to, 138–40; atmosphere created by, 130–1; beautiful in, 122–34; as complete architecture, 129; and enjoyment of a melody, 122–4; experience of order in, 140–1; familiar and foreign, 101–2; intuitive understanding of, 120–1; listening to, 123, 134–8; magical power of, 126–31; meaning

of, 126, 133–4; perceived as perfect, 127–8; as play, 124–6; and silence, 128–30; as source of consolation, 141; as succession of tones, 129; vital and artistic effects of, 138–9; vocal, 123–4, 144
musicality, 139

Nabokov, Vladimir, 165n4
Nagel, Thomas, 12
Naipaul, Vidiadhar Surajparad, 109
Najder, Zdzislaw, 35
Nietzsche, Friedrich, 27, 174n8
norms, 16
Nussbaum, Martha, 118

Orwell, George, 154–5
order: perceived in music, 140–1

Pascal, Blaise: boredom, 53–5
passion: absence of, 23; blind, 29; and breaking away, 59–61; definition of, 59–60
peace, 151
perceptual innocence, 155–6
Petrov, Stanislav Yevgrafovich, 20–1
phenomenology, 11–12, 68, 129, 139, 149
philosophical anthropology, 5, 114–18, 121, 151
Pieper, Josef, 100
Plato, 17, 47
play: relief from boredom, 54; inclination for fairness in, 69; music as, 124–6, 143–4
Plessner, Helmuth, 114, 137, 174n8; passion, 60; perceiving the unfamiliar, 97–8

Index

Powys, John Cowper, 165n4
presence: of cultures, 115; expressive, 162–3; imaginative, 75; of living and lifeless realities, 104–5, 153, 162–3; of music, 129–30, 141–3; of an older person, 75, 83–4; of persons, 74–5, 153–4

questioning, 103–5

recognition: desire for, 157–8
reconciliation, 5, 124, 151
regret, 23
Reilly, Robert R., 168n16, 176n27
repentance, 45
resolution, 7, 37, 40, 43–4, 51, 58, 63–5
Revel, Jean-François, 155
Ricoeur, Paul, 19; feelings created by music, 144; risk of decision, 32
risk, 8; of breaking away, 42–3, 51, 54; of a decision, 24–5, 27, 31–2, 34, 37; of failure, 65; and passion, 60–1; of the virtuoso, 132
Rohmer, Éric, 176n3
Romilly, Jacqueline de, 82, 171n30
Russell, Bertrand, 79
Ryckmans, Pierre (Simon Leys), 62; reading novels, 77; extended stay in a foreign country, 88–9

Sacks, Jonathan, 106
Saint-Exupéry, Antoine, 112, 152–3
Sandor, Gyorgy, 131
Santayana, George, 97
Scheler, Max, 11, 66, 114; destiny and fate, 41–2; definition of a model, 68–70; human time, 45;

influence of models, 81–2; rebirth, 44–5; repentance, 45
Schiller, Friedrich, 160
Schopenhauer, Arthur, 165n3, 174n8
Schubert, Franz: String Quintet in C major, 48; Piano Sonata in B-flat major, 140
Schuller, Gunther, 133, 176n27
Schutz, Alfred, 92, 94, 171n8
Scruton, Roger, 6, 176n35
Segalen, Victor, 95–6
self: conventional and criminal, 56; flight from the, 28, 96; inner, 47; performing, 28
self-awareness, 61, 69, 145
service: ideal of, 84–5
Sessions, Roger, 123
Shakespeare, William, 3, 50, 165n3
singing, 144–6
social institutions, 25–7, 145, 156; offer a relief from decision, 26; weakening of, 26–7
solitude: and conversion, 61; of creative people, 59; and decision, 14–22, 27–8; enforced, 53–4
Solzhenitsyn, Alexander, 108–9
Spaemann, Robert: characteristics of good actions, 148–9, 160; conversion, 63; disclosure of the world, 38; education, 82; equanimity, 32–3; moral education of children, 69
spontaneity, 6, 34; of the action, 148; characteristics of, 154; ethical, 159; of voice and hands, 144; youth's, 30
spontaneous: acts, 62, 144–5, 148, 150–2; creativity, 133; feelings,

204 Index

29; play, 54, 126; resolution, 148; response, 37, 139
stability: desire for, 56
Stein, Leo, 127–8
Steiner, George, 78, 168n16
Stendhal (Marie-Henri Beyle), 119; *The Red and the Black*, 36, 77
Storr, Anthony, 174n8, 177n37; creative persons, 93–4, 168n16
Straus, Erwin W.: hearing music, 135; responsive communication, 162–3; unconstrained attitude, 25
Sunstein, Cass R., 166–7n7

tact, 132, 155
teachers: admiration of, 79–80; music, 143
teaching, 78–9
Teilhard de Chardin, Pierre, 88
Tellenbach, Hubertus, 33
temporality. *See* time
Thaler, Richard H., 166–7n7
Thibon, Gustave, 148, 152
thinking: conversion and, 44; critical, 47; everyday, 109; and feeling, 122, 146; habits of, 27, 114; leisurely, 59; metamorphosis of, 68, 97; models affect our, 70, 73; process of, 17; unfamiliar ways of, 115; without, 16, 130
time, 3–4; ally of cowardice, 65; Bergson's theory of, 137; control of, 23; of human existence, 52; lived, 15–16, 22–3, 150–1; living in the present, 9, 38, 74, 83, 142, 150, 153, 163; panic of, 141; turning to the future, 161–2; returning to the past, 22, 45

Tocqueville, Alexis de, 164
Tolstoy, Leo, 151; *War and Peace*, 36; *Anna Karenina*, 77; *Master and Man*, 147
transformation: through contact with foreign cultures, 88, 90, 94, 97–103; by means of conversation, 82–3; through conversion, 44–5; calls for striking encounters, 83; generated by passion, 60–1; of habits and mentalities, 70; obstacle to, 96; of one's life, 48; possibility of, 7; through reading, 76; refusal of, 8, 89; of social relations, 56; of the world, 40–1
travelling, 33, 44, 52, 55, 61, 89–90, 95, 97
trust, 65

uncertainty, 50, 55–56. *See also* decision
understanding, 11, 94–5, 97; of the composer's ideas, 132; in conversation, 154–5; of foreign realities, 100–5, 107–15, 117–18; of music, 120–1, 124, 133, 137–8
unexpected: action, 151, 161; chord progression, 138; encounter, 5, 76, 79; experiences, 7; illumination, 46; metamorphosis, 163; occurrence, 105; orientation, 83; possibilities, 26; reconciliation, 151; situation, 62, 160
uniformity: of behaviour, 51, 55, 63; eliminates self-knowledge, 96; sustained by tourism, 95

Index

Valéry, Paul, 143, 159
values: adoption of new, 39–41, 44–6, 61; children develop a hierarchy of, 78; children are able to see, 69; educational, 149; inner standard of, 93; migration is influenced by, 43–4; models embody, 72–6, 86; motivating, 40; parental, 14; reassessment of, 5; rejected, 46–7; sense of, 79; spiritual, 47; system of, 89, 92; transformative power of, 69
violence, 26, 30
virtuosity, 131–3
vital experiences, 5–9
voice: seduces, 131; tone of, 74–5; vibrations of the, 73
vulnerability, 145, 156–9

Walker, Alan, 67, 121, 131
Waugh, Evelyn, 29

Weber, Max, 75
Weizsäcker, Carl Friedrich von, 146
Weizsaecker, Viktor von, 94
well-being, 15
Welte, Bernhard, 124; silence in music, 128–9
Whitehead, Alfred North, 7, 25, 55, 146; education, 86
Wiredu, Kwasi, 117
Wittgenstein, Ludwig, 98
wondering, 104–5
Wood, James, 110
world: anthropological concept of, 38–40; inner, 49–51; in the state of boredom, 53; and sub-worlds, 39; uninviting and unavailable, 163; and values, 40
Wu, Ningkun, 50
Wulf, Christoph, 117

Zweig, Stefan, 9